THE PSYCHOLOGY OF
NETAHOLICS

THE PSYCHOLOGY OF NETAHOLICS

CARLA G. SURATT

Novinka Books
An imprint of Nova Science Publishers, Inc.
New York

NOTICE TO THE READER

Library of Congress Cataloging-in-Publication Data:

Available upon request

ISBN 1-59454-743-2

Published by Nova Science Publishers, Inc. ✦ New York

For Matt

CONTENTS

Chapter 1

INTRODUCTION

The year 1998 witnessed the birth of a new disorder–Internet Addiction Disorder. As the number of linkage points, host computers, connected networks and individual users plugged in to the Internet have continued to increase exponentially, some have begun to question the Net's impact on our psychological well-being. And among the issues under debate is the question of whether or not Internet use is addictive. Though many regular Internet participants scoff at such an idea, and create satirical Web sites, IRC chat rooms and Usenet newsgroups to make their point, a growing number of professionals in the field of psychology disagree. They argue that Internet participation is addictive, and that in many ways, its symptoms, diagnosis and treatment parallel that of other addictions, such as compulsive gambling, shopping and even drug and alcohol abuse.

What are we to make of this new disorder? What, precisely, does 'addiction' mean, and does the social label of 'addict' provide a satisfactory explanation of the human behavior patterns to which it is commonly attached? Can individuals really become addicted to the Internet? Is there an alternative explanation as to why people choose to spend time, in some cases very large amounts of time, online? This book examines these questions from a sociological perspective. In the pages that follow, the reader is invited to explore the evolution of the concept of addiction and the apprehension that has historically surrounded systems of mediated communications, and to examine how the intersection of these trends lends itself first to 'computer addiction', and later to 'Internet Addiction Disorder'.

In a sense, the 'discovery' of Internet Addiction Disorder (IAD) comes as no surprise; it has surfaced within the discipline of psychology as interactive computer technologies such as the World Wide Web, Usenet,

Internet Relay Chat, and Multi-User Dungeons have become increasingly sophisticated. But its discovery was by no means instantaneous. Nor was it an accident, borne of chance research or sudden insight. Behind the birth of IAD lay nearly 150 years of research into, theorizing about, and labeling of so-called addictive behaviors. A brief glimpse into such research will serve to illustrate this point.

According to Norman Miller [1995], the formal concept of addiction was first applied by a French physician in 1849 to the case of heavy drinking, and the condition we now call alcoholism was born. But even before this formalized theory of addiction was developed, the general idea of 'drunkenness as an uncontrollable disease' was introduced to colonial America (during the late 1700s) by Benjamin Rush, a prominent physician and signer of the Declaration of Independence [Peele 1985]. Since that time, the concept of addiction has simultaneously become increasingly formalized and increasingly generalized, a combination which has allowed the term to be used, not only by professionals, but by members of the general public, as an explanation of an ever-broadening range of human behaviors. This trend is best illustrated by the explosive growth of the 'bible' of mental disorders-- the Diagnostic and Statistical Manual of Mental Disorders (DSM). First published by the American Psychiatric Association in 1952 and subsequently revised four times by 1994, the DSM has expanded from 132 to 886 pages. And during that time, 'addiction' shifted from a 'personality disturbance or disorder' encompassing alcoholism and drug abuse to 'substance-related' and 'impulse control' disorders, encompassing eleven categories of drug or alcohol substances as well as behavioral patterns such as pathological gambling, stealing (kleptomania), and so forth.

How can we account for these ever-expanding and changing definitions of 'addiction', a concept which is purported to rest on the commonly accepted medical model of scientific research? Quite simply, definitions change as the socio-political context of the research informing those definitions changes. Since the 'discovery' of alcoholism, professionals in the fields of psychology, psychiatry, social work and sociology have attempted to explain this, and other, so-called addictive behaviors in a variety of ways. But, rather than basing these changing explanations on new insights gleaned from objective, scientific research, individuals involved in the field of mental health and illness have constructed theories and definitions of addiction that proved functional within the evolving political culture of American society.

UNDERSTANDING ADDICTION: AN OVERVIEW

According to Dennis Thombs [1994], alcohol and drug addiction has been defined alternatively as 'sin', 'disease' or 'maladaptive behavior patterns'. In the sin framework, which was historically the first means people used to explain excessive use of drugs or alcohol, the individual in question was defined as refusing to abide by the common moral code. In this way, drug or alcohol abuse was seen as a freely chosen behavior; individuals have free will. Accordingly, the only appropriate 'treatment' for problems caused by excessive substance use was punishment, and no further discussion of the issue was required.

With the rise in social status of the medical profession in the late 1800s, a rise due largely to the relative success of the 'germ theory of disease' (a topic which will be discussed in Chapter Two), came the creation of the 'disease' model of addiction. Within this framework, addiction is viewed as the result of an 'underlying disease process', usually brought about by early childhood psychological damage, genetic predisposition, or a combination of both. Such factors render the individual susceptible to addiction. This susceptibility, in combination with environmental stress and exposure to drugs and alcohol, leads first to addiction and ultimately to the problems commonly associated with such a state – criminal behavior, family breakdown, depression, aggression, and so forth. [Alexander 1988] In other words, a core disease within the individual *causes* the compulsive act of drinking or drugging excessively, rather than vice versa. This disease renders the abuser helpless; his or her actions are not freely chosen. As a result, the individual requires treatment, specifically medical treatment, rather than punishment

While practitioners and researchers within the mental health professions may emphasize the importance of various biological, psychological and spiritual factors to differing degrees, those who subscribe to this disease model of addiction generally accept five core concepts which have traditionally represented the model: addiction as a primary disease; loss of control; addiction as a progressive disease; addiction as a chronic disease; and denial. [Thombs 1994] While all of these concepts have been disputed and often disconfirmed by empirical research, it is important to understand the underlying structure of the disease framework. Only then can we understand its appeal as a functional, socially useful argument, and its perseverance and growth even in the face of significant evidence to the contrary.

First, within this framework, addiction is a 'primary' disease. As such, alcoholism (for example) is not *caused by* heavy drinking; it is the *cause of* heavy drinking. Therefore, those who lack a genetic susceptibility to alcohol cannot become alcoholics, no matter how much they drink. Second, as noted above, addicts have no control over their behaviors. They are compelled, by a strong physiological need for the substance, to procure and use the substance, often going to extreme measures in order to do so. Further, addiction is both a progressive and chronic disease. The addict will, without intervention and treatment, deteriorate progressively as he or she builds up a tolerance for the substance and requires ever increasing amounts to satisfy the physiological need. Even with treatment, the disease of addiction is chronic; it never 'disappears'. In other words, one cannot be a 'cured' alcoholic, only a continuously 'recovering' alcoholic. Finally, the individual who refuses to accept that he is in the grip of this disease is said to be 'in denial'. He is "perceptually incapacitated" and thus incapable of perceiving an unacceptable reality; a reality that is so apparent to those around him.

In contrast to the disease model, the 'maladaptive behavior' model of addiction suggests that, because all human behavior is learned, the behavior of addiction is learned as well. Rather than being a victim of an underlying disease process, the individual is the victim of "destructive learning conditions" found in the surrounding cultural, social and family environment. Environmental stress, faulty upbringing and 'genetic unfitness' contribute to the individual's inability to fully mature. As a result, the individual experiences depression, family breakdown, aggressive tendencies, and so forth that lead him or her to seek out alternative solutions to such life problems. If drugs or alcohol are readily available, the individual may utilize such alternatives to provide meaning and an organizing structure to life. Thus, addictions to drugs, alcohol and even gambling, food and sex are 'substitute adaptations'. That is, they are alternate means of adapting to life circumstances that, while not as satisfying as full integration, are better than other perceived alternatives. [Alexander 1988]

Again, addictive behaviors are not entirely freely chosen. Rather, they are learned behavioral responses that represent an attempt (a maladaptive attempt) to cope with an unpleasant environment. While the addicted individual is not 'sick' in the same respect he is conceived to be through the disease model, he does suffer from a combination of poor environmental conditions and dysfunctional family life. Addiction to drugs or alcohol is the *result* of attempting to adapt to such problems, rather than the *cause* of such problems. Consequently, the addict is in need of 'training' in new, more productive behavioral patterns, rather than medical treatment.

Within this general framework, there are several more specific theories with corresponding treatment approaches, including: psychoanalytic theory; conditioning theory; social learning theory; family systems theory; and multiple sociocultural theories. The first four of these approaches focus on the interaction between the individual and her immediate environment, while the sociocultural theories focus on broad cultural norms, values and beliefs and how they shape our very definitions of and beliefs about the concept of addiction. As with the disease model, a brief overview of these maladaptive behavior models will provide insight into many of the fundamental issues underlying the changing nature of addiction.

What all of these models have in common is an emphasis on the role that the social environment, rather than biological factors, plays in creating addictive behaviors. For example, in the psychoanalytic perspective, behavior is thought to result from the interaction of the three personality subsystems (id ego and superego). The id is said to consist largely of instinctual drives, commonly called wishes or cravings. Such cravings, particularly when stimulated by environmental stimuli (such as advertisements for alcohol), motivate the individual to seek out the substance that will satisfy that craving. [Thombs, 1994]

Conditioning theory, which has its roots in the psychoanalytic perspective, suggests that addiction is simply another learned behavior. The individual does not choose to become addicted, but instead becomes conditioned to the use of drugs or alcohol because she has no other, more constructive, behaviors reinforced by the external environment. Interestingly, this behaviorist perspective argues that physical dependence on a substance is neither necessary nor sufficient for developing the condition of addiction.

Similarly, the social learning theory is a behaviorist approach to human learning that focuses on stimuli and reinforcers in the external environment. However, rather than arguing a deterministic approach to human behavior as does conditioning theory, social learning theory argues that learning involves 'cognitive mediating variables'. In other words, a certain amount of self-direction and choice is possible, within the limits of the external environment, because rather than responding in rote fashion to external stimuli, people think about the complete range of responses available to them and select that which they believe best suits their goals. People do not automatically choose to consume alcohol in ever increasing amounts simply because they are trapped in an unpleasant environment. Instead, they evaluate their environment and the range of options available to them, and make decisions based upon their *perceived* alternatives. Sometimes, the consumption of large quantities of alcohol is functional for them at that place and time.

Family systems theory is similar to social learning theory in that it allows for cognition and choice on the part of the individual. However, rather than looking at the addict in isolation, this perspective is primarily a treatment approach that attempts to examine the entire family as a social system. Mental health professionals utilizing this approach examine the ongoing rules of interaction and levels of intimacy and individuality within the family unit, and approach addiction as a group problem within the family unit.

Finally, there are several sociocultural perspectives on addiction, all of which focus on the macro, or system level, environment in which the addict finds himself. What all of these approaches have in common is a focus on broad cultural beliefs and values, and how those systems of beliefs change over time. Regarding addiction then, sociocultural perspectives examine large scale historical shifts in cultural, political and technological systems and how those shifts enable and sometimes demand redefinitions of 'socially acceptable' behaviors. Labeling theory is perhaps the most instructive of all of these perspectives, particularly when it comes to explaining the ever changing field of mental health, and will be discussed in detail in Chapter Three.

THE BIRTH OF INTERNET ADDICTION DISORDER

How did we get from theorizing about the biological, psychological and sociological natures of physically ingested substance addictions to debating the existence and extent of addiction to computers? After all, ingestion of substances that have a scientifically documented impact on the central nervous system of human beings would appear to be a far cry from typing on a keyboard or even 'clicking' with a mouse, much as some may enjoy those activities. While the details of this evolution are reserved for Chapters Two and Three, a brief overview here of the current body of knowledge regarding Internet Addiction Disorder will serve to outline the factors that this disorder purportedly has in common with the more commonly accepted substance related disorders. Once these points are clarified, the reader is invited to decide for herself about the nature of addiction, Internet-related or otherwise.

Internet Addiction Disorder (IAD) made its first significant appearance on the journalistic radar screen in a March, 1995 article in the New York Times entitled, "The Lure and Addiction of Life On Line". [O'Neill] The article, while it did not cite any specific scientific research that had been conducted, made the argument that increasing numbers of individuals were spending a great deal of time online–so much time, in fact, that the Internet was interfering with other aspects of their lives. Quoting addictions specialists and computer industry professionals, the article likened such Internet use to compulsive shopping, exercise and gambling.

While sporadic reports of this emerging social problem appeared in less well known media during that time frame, the concept did not reappear in the popular press in a significant way until the spring of 1996, when it re-emerged in publications such as the Seattle Times, Computer Currents Magazine, ComputerWorld, and, by the end of that same year, in the New York Times again. Since that time, the fervor has continued; the years 1997 and 1998 saw a steady stream of articles devoted to analyzing the meaning and extent of this latest mental disorder. What caused this renewed interest in Internet addiction? It was due in large part to the work of Kim Young, a psychologist and faculty member of the University of Pittsburgh at Bradford, and perhaps the most ardent supporter of the concept of Internet Addiction Disorder. [1]

Young began studying Internet addiction in 1994, after her interest in the concept was kindled by personal experiences with friends and clients and by anecdotal reports (like those above) which claimed that some on-line users were becoming addicted to the Internet ". . .in much the same way that others become addicted to drugs or alcohol. . ." [Young, 1996, p. 1] And in August, 1996, at the annual meeting of the American Psychological Association, she presented the results of her research in a paper entitled, "Internet Addiction: The Emergence of a New Clinical Disorder."[2]

In this research, Young asked volunteers from a number of sources to respond to a survey consisting of eight questions about amount of time spent online, preoccupation with Internet use, feelings about that Internet use, its impact on other significant relationships, and so forth. Respondents who answered 'yes' to five or more of those eight criteria were classified as

---

[1] While a detailed discussion of this interaction between academics and journalists is reserved for Chapter Three, it is interesting to note that this perceived social problem, like many others, is rooted in the symbiotic nature of the relationship between these two disciplines. That is, the 'discovery' of new social problems, particularly those that involve elements of social pathology or the 'dark side' of human nature, is mutually

[2] Young's research, including the significant aspects of both her methodology and results, will be discussed in detail in Chapter Three. Young's research, including the significant aspects of both her methodology and results, will be discussed in detail in Chapter Three.

addicted Internet users, and those who responded 'yes' to fewer than five were classified as normal Internet users. Based upon the results, Young reached several conclusions. First, addicts had, in general, less computer experience and expertise and had been online for a shorter amount of time (usually less than one year) than normal users. Second, addicts spent a significantly greater number of hours per week online than normal users, and had built up this high usage habit over time. Third, the more interactive the application, the more addictive it is. For example, participating in chat rooms and newsgroups is more addictive than surfing the Web or working with more traditional information protocols (e.g. gopher and ftp). And finally, while normal users reported few or no adverse consequences of Internet use, addicts reported academic, relationship, financial and occupational problems similar to those reported by pathological gamblers, alcoholics, and people suffering from eating disorders.

Young is not the only researcher who has become interested in Internet addiction. Other academics, following her lead, have theorized about or conducted their own studies of IAD in order to contribute to the body of knowledge surrounding this new disorder. In the spring of 1996, Oliver Egger, a researcher in Switzerland, conducted an online study that asked questions similar to those asked by Young. For example, he asked respondents about the specific Internet applications used and their reasons for doing so; duration of and changes in Internet usage; feelings regarding that usage; and experiences while online (e.g., staying on longer than intended, losing track of time, and so forth). Not surprisingly, he reaches many of the same conclusions that Young reached. Those respondents who self-described as "addicts" reported: negative consequences of Internet use; feelings of anticipation about and guilt over Internet use; complaints from friends or colleagues about the amount of time spent online; and increased participation in online self help groups. [King, 1996]

Viktor Brenner, a Ph.D. Candidate at Marquette University, also conducted a study in early 1996 in order to "address issues of Internet use, abuse, and its potential for a behavioral addiction". [Brenner, 1997]. Again, the survey was administered online and asked questions in a true/false format, each of which was designed to assess the extent to which Internet users' experiences paralleled those of other substance-related and impulse control disorders already accepted in the most recent version of the Diagnostic and Statistical Manual of Mental Disorders. [1994] According to Brenner, the results (which he states should be interpreted cautiously) indicate that ". . .the skewed distribution and base rate of endorsement of more severe interference is consistent with the existence of a deviant subgroup who experience more severe problems due to Internet use. This is also preliminary evidence of phenomenon that can be interpreted as tolerance, withdrawal, and craving." [1997, p. 881].

The discussion among academics about the existence and attributes of Internet Addiction Disorder continued during the 1997 annual meeting of the American Psychological Association, and the number of participants continued to grow. British psychologist Mark Griffiths presented a paper on case studies that he argued could be explained under the rubric of "technological addictions"; they exemplified non-chemical, behavioral addictions which involve human-machine interactions. Viktor Brenner, whose work is outlined above, had continued his study of normal versus excessive online usage, and reported updated findings. And, interestingly, Kathleen Scherer of the University of Texas at Austin presented a separate study on online usage for 'addicted' and 'normal' users which claimed far fewer hours per week were required to declare an individual addicted than did Brenner's study; results which were supported by a third study which classified respondents as pathological, limited symptom or no symptom users. [Morahan-Martin and Schumaker, 1997]

While all of these studies cite differing requirements for 'addicted' versus 'normal' levels of usage and differing degrees of external negative consequences of that usage, they are all based upon three interrelated underlying assumptions. First, they assume that mental disorders, specifically the disorder of addiction, exist and that they can be understood, diagnosed and treated through the disease (or medical) model outlined at the outset of this chapter. Second, they assume that, within this medical framework, people may theoretically become addicted to a process or behavior in the same way that they become addicted to a substance. Third, they assume that, given the diagnostic categories and criteria made available in official manuals and casebooks (in this instance, those for pathological gambling have been utilized), they can construct an objective, scientific survey that will accurately assess the extent and specific etiology of another, newly discovered disorder. An examination of whether these assumptions are warranted is left for Chapters Two and Three.

Despite the research cited above, there do exist a few voices of, if not opposition, at least apprehension about leaping into the creation of a new clinical disorder, complete with etiology, symptomology and treatment recommendations. And while they do not question the existence of mental disorders per se, or even that of addiction within the disease framework, they do raise some important questions about the extent to which a process may be likened to an ingested substance. One such voice is that of John Grohol, director of the Mental Health Net, an online source of information regarding psychological health. As Grohol suggests, and as the surveys outlined above indicate, one of the key problems in labeling an individual as 'addicted' to the Internet is that it implies an objective definition of 'normal' use. Because definitions of 'normal' are in constant flux, there is simply no way to determine what an appropriate level of Internet usage is. ". . .How can one talk of 'overuse' when the data which exists today is very preliminary in terms of 'normal' Internet use? Who , exactly, is defining 'excessive' use?. . . This complexity has not yet been adequately addressed in any research to date. Therefore, no causal statements, such as 'People are addicted to the Internet' can be made with any scientific certainty or validity." [Grohol, 1997]

A few others agree with Grohol. Kenneth Gergen, professor and psychologist at Swarthmore College says, "It's too easy to say that what's going on is an addiction. I'd hate to give it a label as if it's a sickness, as if it's got to have a cure, and as if it's got to have doctors to do it." Steve Jones, chair of the Communications Department at the University of Tulsa agrees, stating that no mass medium, including movies, television, radio and even books, has achieved widespread use without making people fearful that it will become 'addictive'. [Hamilton and Kalb, 1995] Even Maressa Hecht Orzack, director of the computer addiction clinic at McLean Hospital in Boston, states that Internet Addiction Disorder is not an addiction. Rather, it is better suited to the category of 'impulse control' disorders, such as compulsive shopping or gambling.

Where do we stand? Can people become addicted to the Internet in the same way as they evidently can to alcohol and drugs? Or, is excessive Internet use closer to the family of impulse control disorders such as pathological gambling and kleptomania? Or, as psychologist Ivan Goldberg stated, is it ". . .all bullshit. . .There is no such thing as Internet addiction."? And if there really is no such thing, then how, Dr. Young queries, can we explain all of those people out there who feel addicted, who claim they are addicted, and who spend inordinate amounts of time online, often to the detriment of their other relationships and life goals? It is this author's argument that there *is* another explanation, one which can account not only for the ever changing definition of addiction, but also for the 'discovery' of Internet addiction in particular, and for the fact that people feel and claim to be addicted to the Internet. And it is to this explanation that the following chapters are dedicated.

Chapter Two discusses the historical context, or framework, of the concept of addiction. It offers the reader some early definitions from the time of its discovery by social scientists and discusses how those definitions changed over time, as the social, political, and economic environments in which people found themselves evolved. The chapter examines the ideas of biological and psychological addiction, and discusses the rise of 'process' addiction within the co-dependency movement.

With this information as background, Chapter Three discusses in detail the chronology of the discovery of Internet Addiction Disorder. Using the social psychological framework of symbolic interaction, the chapter outlines how intellectuals, journalists and online participants worked in concert to create this new label and to define it as 'real'. Chapters Three and Four utilize a content analysis of popular press and academic journal articles and the ongoing discussion in online groups devoted to Internet addiction, respectively, to explain how individuals self label as 'addicts' and the functions that such a label serve for them. And Chapter Four argues that such labeling is possible only within a culture which places a high value on the 'medicalization' of human behavior, particularly behavior that involves interaction with or through technologically sophisticated 'mass' media formats.

Chapter Five offers an alternative perspective as to why people choose to spend time, in some cases very large amounts of time, online. From a symbolic interactionist perspective, it argues against the underlying, commonly held beliefs critics of online interaction have about the nature of that interaction; that it is meaningless, identity-less, and essentially, not at all 'real'. The chapter argues that people can and do create meaningful identities and communities online, and that such activity is just as 'real' as any other. Thus, claiming that people are 'addicted' to the Internet is essentially a claim that they are 'addicted' to human interaction and companionship.

Finally, Chapter Six revisits the key questions this book addresses within the historical context of the meaning of addiction. It discusses the specific social circumstances that make online interaction such an easy target of critics and summarizes a more fruitful way of understanding why life online is so attractive to so many people. The chapter concludes by arguing that the basic concept of addiction is untenable, and as a result, that the idea of people being addicted to the Internet is simply not plausible.

Chapter 2

FROM ADDICTION TO DEPENDENCE: CHANGING DEFINITIONS OF HUMAN BEHAVIOR

"Although descriptions of madness and its subtypes have been around since the ancient Greeks, until the last half of the 20th century a handful of unofficial, broad categories appeared to be sufficient for the task. By the 1990s, however, the count had grown to about three hundred and appears to be rising rapidly. Moreover, categories of disorders are all now carefully encrusted in a nationally approved classification system. How, in brief, did this evolve?" [Kirk and Kutchins, 1992]

With respect to addiction, it is precisely this question that this chapter seeks to answer. Since the time of its discovery, addiction has been cast as a mental disorder of one form or another. Alternately described as a 'sociopathic personality disturbance', a 'personality disorder', a 'substance use' disorder, a 'substance-induced' disorder or a 'substance-related' disorder, addiction has been the domain of *mental* health professionals. And while 'common sense' dictates that this connection is justified and self-evidently correct at the end of the 20th century, the disease, or medical, model upon which this common sense is based does not support such a connection.

Thus, in order to understand the intellectual leap that has allowed professionals in the field of mental health to liken extensive participation in Internet interaction to drug and alcohol addiction, one must first understand the basic history of mental health and 'mental disorders' within the American cultural framework. For, as we shall see, it is this framework, and not scientific evidence, which validates the concept of mental disorder in general, and addiction as a mental disorder in particular.

A BRIEF HISTORY OF ADDICTION
AS MENTAL DIS-ORDER

The birth of addiction as a mental disorder, and indeed of the very concept of 'mental disorder', is rooted in the intersection of two key social forces of the 1800s: the rise in status of the medical profession that resulted from the relative success of the 'germ theory' of disease, and the social construction of drinking and drugging as self-evidently serious social problems. Taken together, these forces would yield a society committed to the belief that behaviors are diseases and that certain behaviors, namely those labeled as 'addictions', are out of the control of the individual engaging in them.

According to Peele [1989], there are three generations of diseases: physical ailments, mental disorders and addictions. Physical ailments are the first generation, and include disorders that are defined by 'measurable physical effects'. In other words, malaria, for example, is known to be caused by a specific microbe in the environment and is known to result in specific physical damage to the human body. This germ theory of disease, this discovery that one could, in a laboratory setting, isolate specific agents in the external biological environment that caused physical ailments, ushered in the era of modern medicine as we know it, and paved the way for the two generations of disease that were to follow.

But the relative success of this medical model in defining cause-effect relationships for physical ailments also set in motion a social force. According to Kirk and Kutchins [1992] the science of epidemiology 'spawned a variety of methods of counting and sorting people who were at risk of having some disease'; it furthered the Enlightenment belief in science and rationality by assuming that people can be placed into *only one* of two possible groups: those who have a given disease, and those who do not. We will return to this point momentarily.

The second generation of diseases are those classified as mental illnesses or emotional disorders. However, unlike the first generation diseases, which are apparent to the observer because he or she can measure them in the body and observe the physical damage that results, second generation diseases ". . .are apparent to us. . . because of the feelings, thoughts and behaviors that they produce in people, *which we can only know from what the sufferers say and do.*" [Peele 1989, emphasis mine] It is this reliance on the say-so of the sufferer which renders a diagnosis of mental illness that is qualitatively different from a diagnosis of physical illness. As will be argued in detail in the chapters that follow, one cannot simultaneously claim adherence to the medical or disease model for diagnosing mental disorder, which by definition implies an objectively identifiable biological cause of an ailment, and rely on the subjective accounts of the sufferer to construct that diagnosis.

However, that is precisely the intellectual leap that has been made time and again, particularly by individuals involved in the addiction industry, to the point that the disease model of addiction has been rendered 'common sense'.[3] As noted above, the science of epidemiology had been used for first generation diseases to devise various methods of categorizing people as either diseased or not-diseased. When such a framework is applied to the second generation of diseases, however, the logical end result is that people are categorized not for medical reasons, but for social ones--for the purpose of declaring who is 'normal' and who is not.[4]

This is particularly true in the case of addictions, the third generation of illness. In this generation, the logical connection between biological cause and measurable physiological effect that was the hallmark of the original disease model continues to disintegrate, though the reliance on and assumed relevance of that model itself does not. Whereas mental disorders become apparent through the feelings, thoughts and behaviors they produce, either as

[3] A Gallup poll conducted in 1987 revealed that almost 90 percent of Americans believe that alcoholism is a disease, up from: 80 percent in 1982, 65 percent in the early 1960s, and 20 percent in the late 1940s. [Peele 1985, 1989]
[4] Initially, these methods of counting and sorting were used by the federal government for the U.S. census and allowed for the creation of multiple classification categories which would eventually be used by various 'moral entrepreneurs' [Pfuhl and Henry, 1993] for this very purpose. For example, the 1840 census included only one category, 'idiocy', which included insanity. In 1850, the mentally ill were placed into a separate class, distinct from idiocy, and by the 1880 census, this mentally ill class, then called the 'defective, dependent and delinquent classes' consisted of seven categories of insanity. Interest on the part of census officials in standardizing the classification of mentally ill individuals continued to grow, and by 1918, at their request, the American Medico-Psychological Association (forerunner to the American Psychiatric Association) created the first standardized classification of mental disorders, the Statistical Manual for the Use of Institutions for the Insane. Biological in orientation, the publication eventually went through ten editions, was incorporated into the American Medical Association's Standard Classified Nomenclature of Disease, and would be the forerunner of the modern Diagnostic and Statistical Manual of Mental Disorders (DSM).

described by the sufferer or interpreted by the observer, *addictions are nothing more and nothing less than the behaviors they describe*: "How do we know a given individual is addicted? No biological indicators can give us this information. We decide the person is addicted when he *acts* addicted. . . . we believe a person is addicted *when he says that he is.*" [Peele 1985, 18 emphasis mine] That is, addiction cannot be said to exist in the absence of the ongoing behavior that the specific addiction label describes; behaviors themselves, an ever-expanding list of behaviors, are the disease.

Evidence of this expansion of the concept of disease to include the second and third generations, mental disorders and addictions, is perhaps most clearly visible in the construction and re-construction of the diagnostic 'bible' for mental illness, the American Psychiatric Association's (APA) Diagnostic and Statistical Manual of Mental Disorders. As noted briefly in Chapter One, the year 1952 witnessed the publication of the first edition of the (DSM). Couched in the then-newly-adopted psychoanalytic perspective, this first version emphasized the role of environmental factors, rather than biological ones, in the development of mental disorders within the individual, and divided mental disorders into two major groups: 1) disorders caused by or associated with impairment of brain tissue function; and 2) disorders of psychogenic origin or *without clearly defined physical cause* or structural change in the brain. It is this second category of mental disorder with which we are concerned here.

Within this second category, addiction is discussed as a personality disorder; specifically, it is categorized as one form of 'sociopathic personality disturbance', along with antisocial reaction, dyssocial reaction and sexual deviation. Reliance on the newly popularized psychoanalytic theory of mental disorder is evident in the descriptions of these sub-categories. For example, personality disorders in general are defined as "those cases in which the personality, in its struggle for adjustment to internal and external stresses, utilizes primarily a pattern of action or behavior. . .These disorders are characterized by developmental defects or pathological trends in the personality structure. . .manifested by a lifelong pattern of action or behavior, rather than by mental or emotional symptoms." [p. 13, 34] Clearly implied in such a description is the psychoanalytic framework of id, ego, and superego, as the personality of the individual struggles (unsuccessfully) to simultaneously maintain its individuality while integrating itself with the norms of society as a whole.

The sub-category of 'sociopathic personality disturbance', to which the conditions of alcoholism and drug addiction are claimed to belong, indicates that:

"Individuals to be placed in this category are ill primarily in terms of society and of conformity with the prevailing cultural milieu, and not only in terms of personal discomfort and relations with other individuals. However, sociopathic reactions are very often symptomatic of severe underlying personality disorder, neurosis, or psychosis. . .strict attention must be paid to the possibility of the presence of a more primary personality disturbance. . ."

Though the amount of space dedicated to the discussion of addictions themselves in this first edition is limited to ten lines of text, their mere inclusion in the category of sociopathic personality disturbance as defined above would allow for, and in fact demand, the social construction of what would come to be known as 'process addiction' and the creation of an enormous self-help recovery industry that was built up around that construction some 30 years later. While a more detailed discussion of the birth of process addiction is reserved for later in this chapter, a brief examination of the definition above will serve to make this point.

Consider first the point that individuals in this category are 'ill in terms of . . . conformity'. While this statement was originally meant to argue that individuals who do not to conform to society's values and norms to a sufficient degree may be justifiably 'treated' and even institutionalized by those who do, that idea would be turned upside down by the addiction movement of the 1980s. As we will see shortly, the process addiction, or co-dependency movement, of the 1980s would argue that the problem lay not with the individual, but with society itself.

Now consider the second point—that sociopathic reactions, addiction being one of those, are often symptomatic of other, underlying 'root cause' personality disorders. Such a statement clearly implies the acceptance of the disease model of addiction, but with a twist; environmental factors, and not biological ones, are responsible for addiction. Taken together, these two statements lay the groundwork for what would become the battle cry of the process addiction movement; all behaviors are addictive, and addictions are caused by repressive socialization practices that are grounded in and characteristic of American culture as a whole. [Rice 1996] Anyone may potentially become addicted to any activity, and if they do, it is the fault of a repressive and fundamentally 'ill' society.

In 1968, the second edition of the DSM was published. And while there was no appreciable increase in length between it and the first version, both the coverage and definition of 'addiction' were expanded and altered significantly. In DSM II, drug and alcohol use are referred to in two sections; Section Two, titled Organic Brain Syndromes; and Section Five, titled

Personality Disorders and Certain Other Non-Psychotic Mental Disorders. Section Two in DSM II covers issues similar to those covered by DSM I in the discussion of 'impairment of brain tissue function'. But it is Section Five, Personality Disorders, in which the treatment of addiction becomes interesting. While the first edition of DSM encouraged the classification of drug and alcohol addictions as 'secondary diagnoses', attributable to some underlying disease process, the second edition encourages the classification of drug and alcohol addiction as the main, or primary, diagnosis, attributable to environmental conditions.

This shift was accomplished in two ways. First, the subcategory of 'sociopathic personality disturbance', under which drug and alcohol addiction were listed in DSM I, was removed. As a result, drug and alcohol addiction were no longer classified as subsets of 'personality disorders'; they were elevated to the same status as personality disorders within the diagnostic hierarchy, and categorized simply as 'Certain Other Non-Psychotic Mental Disorders'.

Second, and perhaps more importantly, the very word 'addiction' was removed from standardized usage, and replaced with 'dependence'. This change was intended to reflect the APA's conformity to the new diagnostic standards set forth in the World Health Organization's (WHO) latest edition of the *International Classification of Diseases*. WHO claimed that such a change was the result of recent research indicating that addiction was not the 'biochemical invariant' response to substance ingestion it had previously been thought to be. Accordingly, "In DSM I, a diagnosis of drug addiction could be made only while the individual was actually addicted. DSM II provides a more comprehensive diagnosis, drug dependence, which does not require the presence of physiological addiction but *merely evidence of habitual use or a clear sense of need for the drug*." [1968 p. 132]

What was wrong with diagnosing an individual as addicted only while the individual was 'actually' addicted? By 1968 it had become increasingly clear, as the WHO comment alludes to, that there was little scientific evidence to support the theory of physiological addiction to any ingested substance, raising the question, 'what does "actually addicted" actually mean?' (We will return to this point in the second section of this chapter.) Focusing on 'evidence of habitual use' and 'clear sense of need' removed any remaining thread of logic that once tied this third generation of disease to its progenitor, physical ailments. And, according to Peele [1985], such efforts ". . . were impelled by . . . the desire to highlight the harmful use of substances popularly employed by young people in the 1960s and thereafter that were not generally regarded as addictive–including marijuana, amphetamines, and hallucinogenic drugs. These drugs could now be labeled as dangerous because they were reputed to cause psychic dependence." [p. 21] Thus, with clear and convincing evidence of *physiological* addiction eliminated as a diagnostic requirement, truth about 'addiction' rested on the notion of *psychological* addiction; a concept dependent upon the subjective interpretation of the observer and bounded by prevailing social norms of behavior. What is habitual use, and what evidence is required to support such a claim? How clear is this clear sense of need for the drug? Addiction was in the eye of the beholder–but not for long. These questions would be answered in 1980, in a surprising way, with the creation of DSM III.

In that 1980 edition of the DSM, two significant changes occurred with regard to mental disorder in general. First, mental disorder was re-conceptualized as:

". . .a clinically significant behavioral or psychological syndrome or pattern that occurs in an individual and that is typically associated with either a painful symptom (distress) or impairment in one or more important areas of functioning (disability). In addition, there is an inference that there is a behavioral, psychological, or biological dysfunction, and that the disturbance is not only in the relationship between the individual and society. When the disturbance is limited to a conflict between an individual and society, this may represent social deviance, which may or may not be commendable, but is not by itself a mental disorder." [p. 6]

In other words, mental disorder was no longer a matter of 'illness with regard to conformity'; it was a scientific 'fact' resulting in objectively identifiable ailments (distress and disability). According to Kirk and Kutchins [1992] DSM III revolved around the replacement of *psychoanalytic* psychiatry, within which truth is based upon the authority of the individual doing the defining, with *scientific* psychiatry, within which truth is based upon scientific experimentation. In DSM II, truth equaled theory plus authority. In DSM III, truth equaled scientific fact. [p. 7] This transformation occurred not as a result of a newer, more scientific, explanation of mental illness or even as a result of the discovery of new disorders and treatments. Rather, the authors argue, DSM III was psychiatry's response to challenges raised by sociologists regarding the very existence of mental disorder. Though a more detailed explanation of the symbolic interactionist approach to mental disorder as a form of deviant behavior is reserved for the next chapter, a brief discussion here will serve to illustrate the dilemma faced by the APA as they attempted to formulate this latest version of the DSM.

Any discipline that claims to be a science has two concerns; reliability and validity. With regard to psychiatry, reliability is the extent to which clinical practitioners can agree on the diagnosis of individual patients. Validity, on the other hand, has two meanings. On a superficial level, validity is the extent to which a model actually measures what it purports to measure. On a deeper level, however, validity is the extent to which the mental constructs underlying that measurement are accurate. Throughout the 1960s and 1970s, symbolic interactionists within the field of sociology challenged the validity of mental illness at this deeper level. They challenged the very nature of this constructed reality, arguing that the nosology (classification system of diseases) presented in DSM I and II were based entirely on 'symptomology', and not on a biologically-based etiology. As such, there was no logical basis for the distinction the mental health field had attempted to create between mental disorder as a medical problem and simple social deviance. The interactionists argued, in essence, that mental illness itself was merely a label for deviant behaviors that had been placed within a medical frame for the purpose of classifying individuals as either 'normal' or 'sick'.

Of those two problems, the task force in charge of revising the DSM found it easier to confront the issue of reliability; creating a system for improved diagnostic reliability was scientifically a more manageable task than confronting the nature of reality itself. Thus we have the second major distinction between DSM II and DSM III. Though this manual had purported all along to be a tool–the tool–for diagnosing mental disorders, this is the first version which provided specific diagnostic criteria as guidelines for each disorder. Prior to that, each clinical practitioner was on his or her own in defining both the content and the boundaries of such diagnostic criteria. For example, in DSM II, 'unsocialized aggressive reaction of childhood' is given one paragraph of coverage highlighting that this disorder is generally marked by disobedience, aggressiveness and destructiveness and includes temper tantrums, stealing and lying. In DSM III, however, this categorization is one form of 'conduct disorder', coverage of which includes five pages of 'facts' regarding: associated features, age at onset, course, impairment, complications, predisposing factors, prevalence, sex ratio, familial pattern, and extensive (though not necessarily specific) diagnostic criteria. By decreasing the diagnostic discretion of individual clinical practitioners, the APA sought to improve diagnostic reliability, and thereby imply the validity of mental illness as a legitimate, objectively observable classification.

With regard to the third generation of disease, addiction, such changes would prove to be significant indeed. The argument that mental disorder involved distress and disability, coupled with official criteria to be utilized in identifying that distress and disability, elevated addiction to new heights within the diagnostic hierarchy; rather than subsuming addiction within the framework of 'personality disorders', DSM III devoted a completely separate category to the discussion of 'Substance Use Disorders'. In this way, drugs became 'substances', and regular use of a substance presumably resulted in certain physiological effects upon the central nervous system (read distress and disability), namely craving, tolerance and withdrawal. Thus, despite the fact that reliance on physiological addiction as proof of 'actual addiction' had been removed from DSM II in favor of 'habitual use and clear sense of need' (psychological addiction), DSM III attempted to resurrect the link between the first and third generations of disease simply by declaring craving, tolerance and withdrawal to be objectively observable, official evidence of physiological addiction. Psychoanalytic psychiatry was supplanted by scientific psychiatry.

Substance Use Disorders were further sub-categorized as substance abuse and substance dependence, where dependence is worse than abuse and requires evidence of tolerance or withdrawal. So, for example, alcoholism could now be classified as either alcohol abuse, which involves a pattern of pathological use, impairment in social or occupational functioning, and a minimal duration of disturbance of at least one month, or as alcohol dependence, which, in addition to these three criteria, also requires evidence of "dependence syndrome", the symptoms of which are tolerance and withdrawal.

Equally important to the birth of Internet Addiction Disorder, DSM III also included an entirely new section entitled 'Disorders of Impulse Control'. Defined as a 'residual diagnostic class for disorders of impulse control that are not classified in other categories, for example, substance use disorders', this category includes: pathological gambling, kleptomania, pyromania, intermittent explosive disorder, isolated explosive disorder, and a 'residual' class labeled atypical impulse control disorder. Essential features include:

> ". . . failure to resist an impulse, drive or temptation to perform some act that is harmful to the individual or others. There may or may not be conscious resistance to the impulse. . . An increasing sense of tension before committing the act. An experience of either pleasure, gratification, or release at the time of committing the act. . .Immediately following the act there may or may not be genuine regret, self-reproach, or guilt." [p. 291]

This new category is of particular interest because, quite simply, it describes behaviors as mental disorders, as diseases. As the definition above indicates, disorders in this category are clearly utilizing the framework of substance use disorders. As if driven by tolerance and withdrawal, individuals suffering from impulse control disorders *cannot* resist doing something that is harmful. They experience an ever-increasing sense of tension (craving), experience pleasure while committing the act (intoxication), and feel guilty afterwards and promise to stop—until they experience withdrawal and must seek out the experience again. Thus, even with the term 'addiction' long gone, the underlying premise is alive and well.

Nowhere is this more clear than in the diagnostic criteria for pathological gambling, according to which, "the individual is chronically and progressively unable to resist impulses to gamble". The pathological gambler is diagnosed as one who cannot help himself. He has lost control (is unable to resist the impulse), will continue to deteriorate (as his disease is progressive) and can never fully recover (since his disease is also chronic). Those are the precise hallmarks used to define addiction to alcohol in the mid 1800s, and they continue to be used today in programs such as Alcoholics Anonymous. Interestingly, it is this model of gambling as an addiction, revised in the next version of the DSM, that would become Young's [1996] model for Internet Addiction Disorder.

The DSM III was revised in 1987 and became the DSM III-R. While it is unnecessary to detail the relatively minor changes made with regard to mental disorder as a whole in this revision, it is important to point out that, once again, the diagnostic process for substance use disorders takes a 180 degree turn. In a nutshell, in order to make a diagnosis of 'dependence', clinical practitioners were no longer required to rely on clear evidence of tolerance or withdrawal. The task force in charge of writing the manual had determined that,

> "There are many problems with the DSM III distinction between substance abuse and dependence: problems using social and occupational consequences to define abuse, inadequacy of tolerance or withdrawal as a required criterion for dependence, and inconsistencies in the relationship of abuse to dependence for various substances. In DSM III-R the definition of dependence is broadened to define a syndrome of clinically significant behaviors, cognitions, and other symptoms that indicate loss of control of substance use and continued use of the substance despite adverse consequences. Most cases of DSM III abuse will be subsumed under the DSM III-R category of dependence." [p. 417]

Thus, the objectively observable, scientific facts of tolerance and withdrawal, defined in DSM III as the true gauges for a diagnosis of substance dependence, are apparently insignificant seven years later. Yet the underlying disease model, in which the user has lost control of his actions and is in the grips of a chronic, progressive disease, lives on. Whether there is any sort of biological or environmental 'root cause' is no longer at issue; behavior as disease had taken on a life of its own, as the following newly defined diagnostic criteria illustrate [APA 1987, p. 167-168]:

1. Substance taken in larger amounts or over a longer period than intended
2. Persistent desire or one or more unsuccessful efforts to cut down or control use
3. A great deal of time spent in procuring and using the substance and in recovering from that use
4. Frequent intoxication or withdrawal symptoms when expected to fulfill major role obligations
5. Important social, occupational, or recreational activities given up or reduced because of substance use
6. Continued substance use despite knowledge of having a persistent or recurrent social, psychological or physical problem that is caused or exacerbated by use of the substance
7. Marked tolerance: need for markedly increased amounts of the substance in order to achieve desired effect (i.e. at least 50%)
8. Characteristic withdrawal symptoms
9. Substance often taken to relieve or avoid withdrawal symptoms

Exactly how one might use such criteria (of which a minimum of three are required) to distinguish between 'behavioral or psychological dysfunction' and mere 'social deviance' is unclear, as all of these criteria locate dysfunction in relation to socially approved behaviors.[5] Taken together, these criteria are nothing more and nothing less than a list of behaviors, each of which violates a social norm, and each of which requires subjective interpretation on the part of both the user and the observer. As we shall see in the following section, and as Peele [1985] has more than adequately argued, even symptoms such as craving, intoxication, tolerance and withdrawal, presumed to be biological in nature, are actually ". . .social constructs delineated entirely by how addicts are observed to act and what they say about their states of being". [p. 19]

---

[5] The reader will recall that one of the stated objectives in DSM III-R was to avoid having to rely on social or occupational consequences in diagnoses of substance abuse. However, it is precisely those consequences that are emphasized in the revised diagnostic criteria.

This notion of behavior as disease is again most apparent in the example of 'pathological gambling', the diagnostic criteria for which had been altered significantly in DSM III-R to reflect this newfound truth and to "emphasize the similarity to the essential features of substance dependence"; essential features that apparently had escaped the attention of mental health professionals everywhere only seven years prior. Though no evidence to support such changes was offered, pathological gambling was purportedly indicated by (at least four) of the following diagnostic criteria, a cursory review of which reveals a strong parallel with, if not duplication of, the newly official symptoms of substance dependence [p. 325]:

1. Frequent preoccupation with gambling or with obtaining money to gamble
2. Frequent gambling of larger amounts of money or over a longer period of time than intended
3. A need to increase the size or frequency of bets to achieve the desired excitement
4. Restlessness or irritability if unable to gamble
5. Repeated loss of money by gambling and returning another day to win back losses
6. Repeated efforts to reduce or stop gambling
7. Frequent gambling when expected to meet social or occupational obligations
8. Sacrifice of some important social, occupational, or recreational activity in order to gamble
9. Continuation of gambling despite inability to pay mounting debts, or despite significant social, occupational or legal problems that the person knows to be exacerbated by gambling.

The most recent edition of the Diagnostic and Statistical Manual for Mental Disorders, DSM IV, was issued in 1994, and again the classification, labeling and diagnostic criteria for substance use was altered significantly. Substance Use Disorders became Substance-Related Disorders, and included 'drugs of abuse, medications (prescription or over the counter) and toxins', for a total of eleven categories. Substance-related disorders were sub-categorized as either 'substance use disorders', which included dependence or abuse, or 'substance induced disorders', which included, among other things, intoxication and withdrawal.

Further, the diagnostic criteria for substance abuse in DSM IV reintroduced the importance of social and occupational outcomes of the behavior as key diagnostic clues. Where DSM III-R had claimed that reliance on such factors was a 'major problem' with DSM III, DSM IV claims the opposite. In fact, all of the diagnostic criteria for substance abuse--recurrent failure to fulfill major role obligations, recurrent use in situations in which it is physically hazardous (e.g., driving), recurrent substance-related legal problems, and continued substance use despite recurrent social or interpersonal problems--revolve around such social outcomes for the definition of abuse. Similarly, the diagnostic criteria for substance dependence have been altered to reflect a newfound (again) relevance of physiological addiction. Tolerance and withdrawal are prominent criteria, as they are once again believed to reflect scientifically legitimate, biological events.

Substance-induced disorders, previously located in the section on substance induced organic mental disorders, include the presumed biological symptoms known as intoxication and withdrawal. Intoxication is defined as "reversible substance-specific syndrome due to the recent ingestion of or exposure to a substance. The clinically significant maladaptive behavioral or psychological changes associated with intoxication . . . are due to the direct physiological effects of the substance on the central nervous system. . ." [p. 183] And withdrawal is explained as "The development of a substance-specific syndrome due to the cessation or reduction in substance use that has been heavy or prolonged. . . the syndrome causes clinically significant distress or impairment in social, occupational, or other important areas of functioning. . ." [p. 185]. What remains unclear regarding these two symptoms, however, is exactly how such problems are to be detected through objective, medical analysis.

Having read this overview of the radical, never-ending changes that have occurred with regard to the definition and diagnosis of mental disorders, and of substance related and impulse control disorders in particular, one's natural assumption might be that such changes were the result of significant improvements in scientific knowledge and diagnostic technologies. After all, we generally assume that, over time, our scientific understanding of issues such as these improves through experimentation and experience and that, as a result, we are continually moving toward some indelible truth about the subject at hand. However, as the remainder of this chapter will illustrate, it is illusion to believe that people gain in knowledge what they gain in experience. The changes outlined above were not the result of improved knowledge borne of objective, scientific experimentation. Rather, they were the result of a continuing effort on the part of moral entrepreneurs, in the face of evidence to the contrary, to define mental

disorder and addiction as 'real' social problems. It is to this process that we
now turn.

"PROCESS ADDICTION":
AMERICA AS AN ADDICTED SOCIETY

"In the modern system, people work out selves with a great deal of
institutional support. The legal, economic, political and religious rules
prescribing and legitimating personhood have standing. As actors form their
own subjective personhood, they are perhaps as much affected by the
institutionalized recipes as by any untutored 'experiences'." [Meyer 1987, p.
242]

It is this author's contention that, along with legal, economic, political
and religious rule sets, individuals increasingly construct their subjective
personhood through the use of a medical set of rules; a set of rules described
above as the disease model of behavior. In particular, the institutionalized
recipe of addiction is utilized both as an explanation of behavior and as a
way of understanding the world and one's place in it. As such, perhaps the
simplest way to understand the 'discovery' and popularity of Internet
Addiction Disorder in the late 1990s is to first examine the social
construction of alcoholism in America.[6] For it is the birth of the alcoholic
that ultimately gives rise to every other form of addiction as disease
commonly accepted today, including Internet addiction.

According to MacAndrew and Peele [1988, 1985], the word 'addiction'
derives from the Latin word 'addictus', and originally meant 'to give oneself
over to any interest or pursuit to which one might have become strongly
attached'. As such, prior to the 1800s, non-pejorative, non substance-related
uses of the word were the norm. Likewise, prior to the 1800s, heavy
consumption of alcohol was both commonplace and widely accepted; it was
neither sinful, nor criminal, nor disease. Social convention (informal social
control) was utilized to control any unacceptable behavior that occurred as a
result of someone having over-indulged. Further, most drinking took place in
a family-oriented tavern, and was seen as an opportunity for 'time out';
people who got drunk were assumed to have chosen that course of action.

---

[6] While this history focuses on the construction of alcoholism as a disease, the reader
   is reminded that parallel arguments were made with regard to a wide assortment
   of other drugs, including cocaine, opiates and the like. For additional history on
   such matters, the reader is referred to Peele, 1985 and 1988.

However, with the rise of the Industrial Revolution, the term took on a
decidedly derogatory connotation. How, and why, did this occur? It occurred
because it was a functional, socially useful argument for those individuals in
charge of defining the moral order of the Industrial Revolution. Shifting a
society from an agricultural economy to an industrial one requires that the
individual participants: 1) believe in the ideals of progress and hard work; 2)
internalize the demands that such an economy makes for efficiency and
structure; and 3) be interested in achieving the material rewards that are said
to result from such socioeconomic organization. As the economy of the U.S.
shifted in this direction, it became apparent that certain members of society
were simply not interested in material rewards and, in fact, appeared to lack
the self-control to conform to this new mode of social organization.
According to MacAndrews [1988]:

> "Because the most visible portion of this minority consisted of chronic
> drunkards, it is to them that this reductionist 'explanation' was first applied.
> How. . . are we to *make* sense of the fact that there are people among us
> who, while seemingly like us in other respects, appear determined to
> destroy themselves? Enter the reductionists, whose solution goes like this:
> They continue to drink as they do because, unlike the rest of us, they have
> become physiologically addicted to the substance and hence are incapable
> of doing otherwise. And what is the empirical warrant for this solution? It
> is simply that if it *were* in their power to control themselves, they would do
> so. And, to complete the circle, because they haven't done so, it is obvious
> that they can't. This solution thus falls into place as a quasi-scientific
> phrasing of a ploy that compact majorities have always relied on to
> comprehend those who affront their sense of the appropriate. The general
> structure of this ploy is' I'm OK; you 're not OK'". [p. 166]

In addition to a changing economic structure, there were other sociocultural factors at work as well. According to Peele [1985, 1989], the
problems caused by such changes in lifestyle were exacerbated by increased
mobility (as the Western frontier continued to expand) and by an
increasingly heterogeneous population, as immigration continued to escalate.
Gone were the traditional social regulations, typically centered around
family and community, that kept heavy drinking in check:[7] "Alcohol took on
a new image–drinking became a male prerogative that symbolized assertive

---

[7] Regulation of drinking was not the only function transferred from family and
community to more bureaucratic institutional structures. Poverty, criminal
behavior, and other forms of social deviance–all became the province of newly
established poorhouses, prisons, asylums and sanitariums.

independence and high spiritedness. Simultaneously, liquor began to be seen by many as 'demon rum'". [1985, p. 30]

As responsibility for the regulation of deviant behavior was increasingly delegated to formal, bureaucratic structures, those involved in forming and maintaining such official organizations were increasingly able to define the moral order of the new economic structure. In the case of alcohol, the American Temperance Society, from its formation in 1826 until the repeal of Prohibition in 1933, was to be the moral authority in charge of defining drinking as a 'social problem'.

According to Gusfield [1975], drinking in America has evolved through three 'non-conforming behavior types'-- the repentant drinker, the enemy drinker and the sick drinker, the first two of which are labels applied at varying stages by members of the Temperance movement. Beginning in the early 1800s, drinkers came to be defined as objects of social shame; as noted above, they did not appear to 'fit in' to the middle class values required by the Industrial Revolution. As drinkers joined together and vowed abstinence, a norm of sobriety gradually replaced the norm of heavy, if informally regulated, drinking. By the 1870s, being middle class meant being 'dry'. However, as moral suasion toward middle class values proved ineffective at wiping out heavy drinking in segments of the population, the movement turned toward legislative initiatives. As Gusfield notes:

> "Efforts to achieve legislation governing the sale and use of alcohol. . . had a close relationship to the immigration of Irish Catholics and German Lutherans. . . They brought with them a far more accepting evaluation of drinking than had yet existed in the United States. . . These immigrant cultures did not contain a strong tradition of Temperance norms which might have made an effective appeal to the sense of sin. . . By the 1850's, the issue of drinking reflected a general clash over cultural values. . . Prohibition came as the culmination of the movement to reform the immigrant cultures and at the height of the immigrant influx into the United States." [p. 94]

As Peele [1985] goes on to add:

> ". . . the entire nation became polarized around the issue of temperance. Wet and dry forces began a century-long battle that ended when national Prohibition went into effect in 1920. . ."
>
> "When Prohibition was repealed in 1933, the goal of national temperance was permanently laid to rest. In its place grew the modern disease theory of alcoholism, as defined and defended by the Alcoholics Anonymous self-help fellowship. . . The AA vision of alcoholism had important commonalities with the temperance vision of demon rum. The chief of these was the utter necessity of abstinence. This point of view was

forwarded by AA adherents with a religious fervor strongly reminiscent of the Temperance movement. . . The issue of abstinence for the alcoholic has thus always been a deeply emotional one, not one that has rested on a body of evidence." [pp. 30-31]

The birth of Alcoholics Anonymous (AA) in 1935 marked the rise of Gusfield's third wave of drinker, the 'sick drinker', through the use of Benjamin Rush's disease model of addiction. In keeping with Rush's theory, AA proponents argued that alcoholism was a condition affecting only those individuals suffering from a genetic 'allergy' to alcohol. As such, only those individuals afflicted with this medical predisposition need abstain from drinking. This (politically astute) rejection of complete abstinence for everyone was instrumental in the rise of 'the alcoholism movement' because it fit the format of the germ theory of disease. It allowed for the comforting possibility of sorting and categorizing individuals as either diseased or not diseased.

As described by Peele [1989] and Rice [1996], this alcoholism movement consisted largely of an unofficial consortium of academic research and intellectually liberal advocacy groups that would support the notion of alcoholism as a disease. Most notable for their contributions to the disease model were the Yale Center of Alcohol Studies (established in the late 1930s) and the National Council on Alcoholism. Founded in the 1940s through the collaborative efforts of the Yale Center and AA, the National Council on Alcoholism (NCA) served as the public relations arm of the alcoholism movement by forming local chapters throughout the country, sponsoring public education programs, conducting advertising campaigns, and presenting the disease concept in magazines and films [Peele 1989].

The empirical evidence in support of the movement from that time to the present has its origins in a 1946 study conducted by E.M. Jellinek, a non-physician researcher with the Yale Center. His research, which consisted of an analysis of fewer than one hundred questionnaires from a mailing sent to about 1600 AA members, lead him to argue that 'certain uniformities' in the experiences of this group could be utilized to construct a typology of alcoholism—the typology outlined in Chapter One that depicts alcoholism as a primary, chronic and progressive disease state in which the victim experiences a loss of control over his drinking. Thus, Jellinek's [1952, 1960] typology of behavior as disease, constructed from the subjective interpretations of individuals who had already self-labeled as 'addicts' and who had collectively reinterpreted their experiences and identities in a manner that fit the AA mold, became the 'objective' standard for defining, categorizing, diagnosing and treating alcoholism and alcoholics across the general population.

Through the next three decades, as medical technologies continued to advance, others turned their attention to research in support of the genetic predisposition and loss of control propositions. For example, in 1960, Kaij conducted the first 'twin study' of alcoholism and reported: "a 74 percent concordance of alcoholism between identical twins. That is, if one member of a pair of genetically identical twins was alcoholic, the probability of the other member's also being an alcoholic was 74 percent. In contrast, the concordance of alcoholism between fraternal twins was only 32 percent." [Thombs 1994, p. 30]. In theory, this difference in concordance rates between identical and fraternal twins is indicative of the large role that heredity plays in determining the 'trait' of alcoholism.

In 1973, Goodwin conducted a study in which he examined rates of alcoholism in adopted children. In general, the theory was that children born to alcoholic parents but adopted and raised by non-alcoholic parents (call them Group One) were more likely to develop alcohol-related problems than adopted children born to (and raised by) non-alcoholic parents (Group Two). The differences in rates of problem drinking could then be attributed to genetic factors, rather than environmental ones. He found that for five of the eighteen variables involved (hallucinations, lost control, morning drinking, alcoholic ever, and treated for drinking ever) there were significant differences in the outcomes between Group One and Group Two. Thus, he argued, there was a significant difference in alcoholism rates (18 percent for Group One and five percent for Group Two) that could be attributed to genetic predisposition. [Thombs 1994, p. 24-26].

Finally, from the mid 1970s through the 1980s, a variety of other studies were conducted in an attempt to support the genetic predisposition proposition, most of which revolved around various forms of metabolic and brain wave analyses. Such projects examined: metabolic rates of acetaldehyde within and among families; alcohol elimination rates among ethnic groups; and wave amplitudes of P3 brain waves in the offspring of both alcoholics and non-alcoholics.

While all of these types of studies purported to find at least some evidence of a genetic predisposition toward alcoholism and the corresponding inability of the alcoholic to control his or her drinking, social scientists have consistently been able to demonstrate that all of these studies were plagued by serious conceptual and technical errors. As Peele [1985] notes, "social scientific studies refuting the disease theory are of four types: 1) laboratory studies showing that alcoholics' patterns of drinking do not conform to the loss of control model, 2) clinical research demonstrating the efficacy of techniques aimed at moderating problem drinking and alcoholism, 3) longitudinal studies both of the natural course of alcoholism and of outcomes for treated populations, and 4) cross-ethnic and cultural studies demonstrating that social and belief systems are a principal component in alcoholism." [p. 32]

For example, in 1962, Davies, a clinician and researcher in England found incidence of safely moderated drinking among a group of alcoholics who had undergone treatment ten years earlier. He was not alone; in 1981, Heather and Robertson's *Controlled Drinking* documented numerous confirmations of people labeled as 'alcoholic' returning to controlled drinking. Further, beginning in 1976, The Rand Corporation, under contract with the National Institute on Alcohol Abuse and Alcoholism (NIAAA), issued a series of reports evaluating the results of NIAAA treatment programs. At the eighteen-month (after treatment) follow-up, Rand investigators found "24 percent of the treated alcoholics were abstaining while 22 percent were drinking normally. Among those the investigators identified as definitely alcoholic, the figures were 25 percent abstaining and 16 percent drinking normally." [Peele 1985][8] And, as noted by Thombs [1994], a 1977 review of alcoholism research literature turned up nearly 60 laboratory studies in which alcoholics demonstrated no loss of control over their drinking, but instead regulated their consumption of alcohol according to perceived costs and benefits.

As for Jellinek's 1946 study (and those that followed) that declared alcoholism as a chronic and progressive disease, countless studies in the years since refuted both of those ideas. Alcoholism does not follow any clear or particular path, nor is the individual defined as an alcoholic 'always' an alcoholic, as AA proponents claim. Researchers found instances of 'spontaneous remission', in which alcoholism disappeared without any treatment; trends indicating that, as people (particularly men) age, alcohol problems decline significantly (a process Peele (1985) called 'maturing out'); and significant numbers of former 'alcoholics' who apparently were

---

[8] Not only had researchers and clinicians come across empirical evidence supporting the notion of moderate drinking among 'alcoholics', beginning in the 1970s, researchers began to successfully apply behavioral modification techniques in order to teach alcoholics to drink moderately. For more detail on such studies, the reader is referred to Chapter Two in Peele's [1985] *The Meaning of Addiction*.

'cured' because they were capable of drinking in moderation without any
signs of a loss of control.[9]
Finally, concerning the studies on genetic predisposition outlined above,
social science researchers have noted a number of problems. For example,
Kaij's 1960 'twin study' was discredited by two separate reviews of twin
studies on several counts. The study was not 'blind' (with few exceptions,

---

[9] Research refuting the fundamental typology of alcoholism as a primary, progressive
and chronic disease is simply beyond the scope of that which needs to be
documented in detail for our purposes here. Interested readers are referred to the
following research for additional detail:
a. Bigelow, W. and Liebson, J. (1972). Cost factors controlling alcoholic
   drinking. Psychological Record, 22, 305-314.
b. Cohen, M. Liebson, J., Fallace, L. and Allen, R. (1971) Moderate drinking by
   chronic alcoholics: A schedule-dependent phenomenon. Journal of Nervous
   and Mental Disease, 153, 434-444.
c. Cohen, M., Liebson, J., Fallace, L. and Speers, W. (1971) Alcoholism:
   Controlled drinking and incentives for abstinence. Psychological Reports,
   28, 575-570.
d. Fillmore, K. M., (1987) Prevalence, incidence and chronicity of drinking
   patterns and problems among men as a function of age: A longitudinal and
   cohort analysis. British Journal of Addiction, 82, 77-83.
e. Fillmore, K. M., and Midanik, L. (1984) Chronicity of drinking problems
   among men: A longitudinal study. Journal of Studies on Alcohol, 45, 228-
   236.
f. Heather, N. and Robertson, I. (1981) Controlled drinking. London: Methuen.
g. Miller, W. R. (1982) Treating problem drinkers: What works. The Behavior
   Therapist, 5, 15-19.
h. Miller, W. R. (1983) Controlled drinking: A history and critical review.
   Journal of Studies on Alcohol, 44, 68-83.
i. Mello, N. K., and Mendelson, J. H. (1971) A quantitative analysis of drinking
   patterns in alcoholics. Archives of General Psychiatry, 25, 527-539.
j. Nathan, P. E., and O'Brien, J. S. (1971) An experimental analysis of the
   behavior of alcoholics and nonalcoholics during prolonged experimental
   drinking: A necessary precursor of behavior therapy? Behavior Therapy, 2,
   455-476.
k. National Institute on Alcohol Abuse and Alcoholism. (1990) Alcohol and
   health: Seventh special report to the U.S. Congress (DHHS Publication No.
   ADM 90-1656). Washington, DC: U.S. Government Printing Office.
l. Pattison, E. M., Sobell, M. B., and Sobell, L. C. (1977) Emerging concepts of
   alcohol dependence. New York: Springer.
m. Room, R. (1983) Sociological aspects of the disease concept of alcoholism.
   Research advances in alcohol and drug problems, eds. R. G. Smart, et.al.,
   vol. 7. New York: Plenum.
Sobell, M. B., and Sobell, L. C. (1976) Second year treatment outcome of
   alcoholics treated by individualized behavior therapy: Results. Behavior
   Research and Therapy, 14, 195-215.

only one twin from each pair was interviewed and that twin's impressions were used to classify the other). The identical twins were more thoroughly investigated than the fraternal twins. The methods used to calculate concordance rates were atypical. And finally, incomplete sibling information was incorrectly rectified. [Thombs 1994].

Goodwin's work on adopted children had technical problems as well. The sample size was small (174 adoptees total), and nearly 25 percent of those either could not be located for or refused to participate in the interviews. What were originally two control groups were merged together midway into the study. And, perhaps most importantly, only five of the eighteen variables listed showed significant differences in alcohol-related problems between the control and experimental groups–meaning that more than four out of five of the individuals who were born to alcoholic parents *did not* become alcoholics themselves. [Thombs 1994] Questionable proof of a genetic link to alcoholism, indeed.

Regardless of all evidence to the contrary, belief in substance use as a disease continued. Throughout the 1950s, the alcoholism movement upheld the psychoanalytic framework that mandated treatment for individuals who were 'ill with regard to conformity'. There was nothing wrong with society or social norms, and the alcoholic had to learn to accept the label and conform to social expectations.

However, during the late 1960s and early 1970s, the therapeutic community took a turn toward a philosophy Rice [1996] terms 'liberation psychotherapy':

> "a set of assumptions and presuppositions–about human nature, culture, and society and about the right way to structure the relationship between the individual and society– that may be and are shared by any number of therapeutic theories and techniques. Chief among these core assumptions and presuppositions is that conventional culture and society make individuals sick by thwarting the development of the 'real self' in the interests of social conformity. To get well, in this view, the self must get out from beneath the repressive thumb of culture and society; hence, 'liberation' psychotherapy." [pp. 28-29]

Rice goes on to argue that, married to this belief that culture makes individuals sick is the assumption that, when functioning freely, people will invariably behave in a constructive and trustworthy manner. When this proved not to be true, and in fact, caused an entirely new set of social problems people had to deal with in their daily lives, professionals in the field of mental health fused liberation psychotherapy with the disease model of addiction in the following manner:

"Although ultimately beholden to liberation psychotherapy truths, co-dependency's creators also were and are all thoroughly schooled in the disease model of addiction. As such, they were uniquely situated between two symbolic systems. As the keepers of two flames, with access to two sets of truths, the advocates were in a position to provide an answer to this turn of events, a way of explaining the public impact of liberation psychotherapy by using the core principles of liberation psychotherapy itself.

"The presumption of innate benevolence is both a statement of the human essence and a model of intentionality. Although AA and liberation psychotherapy hold to almost completely opposed assumptions about the self-to-society relationship, the disease model of addiction provides essentially the same model of intentionality as liberation psychotherapy. . To say that the unmanageability of alcoholics' lives was the result of a powerlessness to do otherwise is to make a statement about their intentions: They did not intend to harm others and only did so because they have a disease, an addiction. Drawing upon that overlap in the causal logic between conventional addiction discourse and liberation psychotherapy but still faithful to the ethic of self-actualization, co-dependency conceptualizes the psychological condition that is caused by cultural repression of the self as an addiction. Thus, such problems as incest, the various forms of abuse, and criminality are all instances of 'unmanageable' behavior resulting from people's 'powerlessness' over their own actions. . . (they) cannot be intentional acts because, 'the basic nature of the human being, when functioning freely, is constructive and trustworthy'. Therefore, those who engage in such acts cannot be functioning freely." [p. 103]

Merging liberation psychotherapy's cultural critique with the disease model of addiction leads to what Rice argues is a revolutionary (rather than evolutionary) change in the conceptual framework underpinning the alcoholism movement as outlined above. The disease model (which emphasized the biological nature of addiction) fuses with the adaptation model (which emphasized environmental factors) and yields a logic in which culture (read environment) causes a disease (addiction) and consequently, all problems in living (in adapting to said culture) are addictions. It is in this way that the co-dependency movement, which arose from the co-alcoholism (Adult Children of Alcoholics) movement of the mid-1980s, utilizes the then newly official conceptualizations of behavior as disease found in DSM III-R to bring to the general public an entirely new way of thinking about addictions.[10] In this new framework, all addictions are 'process addictions':

---

[10] One of the ways in which this movement brought this new way of understanding addictions to the public was by enlisting both licensed and unlicensed practitioners. In 1968, there were 12,000 clinical psychologists in the U.S. at a time when no other country counted more than 400. As of 1990, there were

"Plainly, this is a theory that requires an understanding of addiction that goes beyond the conventional, if tenuous, linkage of addiction with physiological dependence upon some mind-altering substance. . . A process addiction is an addiction (by individuals, groups, even societies) to a way (or the processes) of acquiring the addictive substance. The function of an addiction is to keep us out of touch with ourselves (our feelings, morality, awareness–our living process). An addiction, in short, is any substance or process we feel we have to lie about. . . Process addicts, in a nutshell, are addicted to whatever alters their moods, anything that enables them to ignore or avoid their terrible feelings about themselves. . . The generality of the concept of process addiction also undergirds the 'discovery' of a whole series of 'activity addictions', including: intellectualizing, working, buying, hoarding, sexing, reading, gambling, exercising, watching sports, watching t.v., having and taking care of pets. . . all of these activities can be full-fledged and life-damaging addictions. Each is a way to get so involved in an activity that one is mood altered by doing the activity." [1996, 105-106]

From this brief listing, one understands that in the co-dependent world view, anything, any activity, may become addicting. However, upon closer examination, one learns that the framing of activities as addictions revolves around the presumption that human beings have 'relationships' with these activities. In other words, in order to get around the absurdity of suggesting that people are addicted to eating, the argument is that people have a 'relationship with food', and that such a relationship can be healthy or unhealthy. People have relationships, not only with other people, but with food, work, shopping malls, books, playing cards, exercise machines, televisions, and, most recently, computers. Further, all of these relationships, including those we have with other people, are to be evaluated and labeled according to how well they measure up to a predefined, ideal-type relationship. While a detailed examination of this ideal type is reserved for Chapter Four, such relationships are said to be formed in communities in which people were bound closely together by kinship and tradition, rather than by bureaucratic structure and self-interest. In such communities, relationships with other people were genuine; they were healthy, loving and caring, and certainly were of a higher priority than relationships to material things or activities. In order to understand how Internet addiction emerges

42,000. Between 1975 and 1990, number of psychiatrists increased from 26,000 to 36,000, clinical social workers grew from 25,000 to 80,000, and marriage/family counselors grew from 6,000 to 40,000. The number of unlicensed "paraprofessional" counselors (for example, those who organized and ran AA, CoDA, and so forth) grew rapidly as well: "Virtually non-existent ten years earlier, by the mid 1980s there were more than 130,000 such unlicensed therapists" [Rice 1996, p. 27] from this co-dependency movement, let us first examine the basic arguments of relationship addiction as they apply to other people, and, from there, as they apply to machines.

Perhaps the best overview of the tenets of relationship addictions are to be found in Anne Wilson Schaef's [1989] *Escape from Intimacy: The Pseudo-Relationship Addictions*, in which the author utilizes the framework of co-dependency to argue for the existence of three categories of relationship addictions: sexual addiction, romantic addiction and relationship addiction. These 'pseudo-relationships', Schaef argues, are forms of process addictions and are the norm for our culture. As such, they are as destructive as but even more subtle than substance addictions, ". . . we live in an addictive society. . . we have all been exposed to and trained into an addictive process. This addictive process is not a normal state . . . it is something we have learned." [p. 1]

With regard to sexual addiction, Schaef claims, the addict substitutes a sick relationship to an event or process for a healthy relationship with others. Sex becomes a 'mood-altering fix'. The addict, preoccupied with sex, is caught in the grips of a progressive disease in which she (Schaef claims that most 'pseudo-relationship' addicts are women) loses her sense of spirituality, experiences a breakdown of her personal morality, moves ever-further from the truth, and eventually becomes insane.

Similar problems plague the victims of romance addiction, a disease in which the individual is in love with the very idea of romance, and does not really care about the other person. Her thinking process becomes progressively confused and insane, as she increasingly focuses on the 'make-believe' relationship. She is dishonest in her relationships and seeks only the 'buzz' and risk brought about by new ones. According to Schaef, denial is a critical attribute of this addiction; the real world cannot be allowed to impinge on the fantasy experience. Sufferers are marked by low self esteem and are afraid of real intimacy. The relationship is a 'mood altering fix' and the individual may 'get high' from a song, setting or memory. Like sexual addiction, romance addiction is a progressive and fatal disease.

Finally, there are two types of relationship addictions. In the first, the individual is addicted to being in *any* relationship; in the second, she is addicted to a relationship with a *specific* person. In either case, Schaef argues that efforts to make such relationships last can readily be interpreted as 'protecting the supply', in much the same way substance users are claimed to protect their supplies of drugs. Like the sexual and romance addictions, victims of this progressive and fatal disease lose their moral compass and eventually become insane.

With such problems in living defined as addictions, victims of sexual, romantic and relationship addictions formed Sex and Love Addicts Anonymous, a self-help group modeled after AA, with local chapters around the country. But because these pseudo-relationship addictions presented so much variety in symptomology, offshoot groups were later formed to help victims with their own, specific needs. The 1980s witnessed the creation of: Sexaholics Anonymous, Co-Dependents of Sexual Addiction, Online Sexual Addiction, Renewal from Sexual Addiction, S.A.N.E. (Sexual Awareness Nurturing and Empowerment), S-Anon, Sex Addicts Anonymous, Sexual Compulsives Anonymous, Sexual Recovery Anonymous and Relationships Anonymous.

All of this group formation and membership notwithstanding, there are a number of problems raised by the argument that the types of relationships among people outlined above are addictions. First, Schaef simply offers no evidence to support these claims. A second and interrelated problem is that 'addiction', by definition, cannot be 'the norm' for a society. While removal of the physical body and biological causation from the concept of addiction makes possible such a claim, it is impossible to define those who are addicted unless there is a control group of individuals who are 'normal'. When addiction is the norm, such a comparison is simply not possible, thus making evidence to support the existence of such addictions impossible to obtain. Once again, addiction is in the eye of the beholder.

Finally, and equally troubling, is the problem of separating 'pseudo' relationships from 'real' ones. While a detailed discussion of this particular problem is reserved for Chapter Three, it is well documented (not to mention self-evident) that people are social animals who require ongoing interaction and socialization in order to become and remain human. One wonders how it is possible for one group of people to define, once and for all, a set of relationship properties that could be utilized to dictate to others what makes their relationships meaningful, or 'real'.

In the late 1980s and early 1990s, this argument for relationships as addictions was redirected toward technologically-mediated interaction. While such arguments had been going on for decades regarding television (a discussion of which is reserved for Chapter Four), more recently they have centered on the role that computers play in the everyday lives of individuals. As computer technologies have allowed for interaction at ever-increasing levels of sophistication, some people have started to wonder about the effects these changes are having on the individual and on society.

For example, *Mind at Play: The Psychology of Video Games* [Loftus and Loftus 1983], examines the rise of arcade-type video games–why they are fun and why children enjoy them so much. The authors point out that the fact that children can and do become very engrossed in this type of activity lead others (adults) to assess the activity as 'addictive'. While the authors pointed out that one of the primary attractions of such games was that they offered a gathering place in which children could meet and socialize with others their own age, the official assessment was that such involvement was abnormal and self-destructive; that there was something about the games themselves to which children were inexplicably and inevitably drawn. The machines were addictive. Though concern died down as the video arcade began to lose its place as the 'cool' social scene, it resurfaced with the development of individualized, private home systems such as Nintendo and Sega.

Similar concerns have been raised with regard to computers, particularly as the popularity of the personal computer has grown; if relationship addictions were the 'disease of the 1980s', computer addiction is the disease of the 1990s. As we shall see in the following chapter, the idea of individuals becoming addicted to computers, and to the Internet in particular, is one that takes for granted the truthfulness of co-dependency without actually examining the historic evolution of the nature of addiction. By and large, believers in the idea of computer or Internet addiction simply assume the underlying philosophical arguments of the current definition of addiction to be the true and correct ones, without conducting (and often ignoring) any empirical research that might serve to challenge those assumptions.

Although research in this particular field is limited, one work in particular is worth noting. Margaret Shotton's 1989 book, *Computer Addiction? A Study of Computer Dependency*, is interesting because, while it initially takes for granted the assumptions regarding process addiction outlined above, it still challenges the idea that individuals are, or even could be, addicted to computers. Shotton's investigation is an exploratory one in which she sets out to discover whether 'computer dependency' exists.[11] After evaluating the 1970s and 1980s academic literature on the subject, most of which lacked any sort of empirical research and only discussed people who were 'heavily involved' in computer programming, Shotton's second step was to discover whether people would self-label as computer dependent.

Clearly, such an approach (even in an exploratory study) has a number of problems. For example, with the co-dependency movement firmly in

---

[11] Shotton uses the term dependency rather than addiction, compulsion or obsession because that term is in keeping with the World Health Organization's terminology in 1989.

place, and the general public ready and willing to accept the idea that behaviors are addictions, it is likely that people would quite readily self-label in such a manner. This is particularly true since the label provides the individual with an explanation of behavior and absolves him or her of responsibility for that behavior. Further, Shotton appears to take the label of dependent at face value; she evaluates behavior based upon the number of hours (including work hours) people spend on their computers, with no prior, objective definition of what it means to be computer-dependent. The reader will recall that this is precisely the method used by Young [1996] in her study of Internet addiction.

However, despite such limitations, Shotton's study suggests some basic challenges to the idea of process addiction. In a nutshell, she concludes that computers are, in fact, not the 'desocializing' agents that they are purported to be. When one individual in a relationship chooses to spend increasing amounts of time working with the computer for any reason, rather than spending time with the significant other, it is typically because problems of poor communication plagued the relationship to begin with, and not because of some computer-induced personality change. One partner simply found something better to do with his or her time. And, as with many other purported addictions, Shotton points out that the people included in her survey were there primarily because of complaints by or the initiative of their significant others. The overwhelming majority of those defined as dependent did not want to stop and did not believe they spent too much time with the computer. [p. 253]

The real question posed by this research is, why are computer enthusiasts as a group targeted as being in some way deviant, ill and in need of help when non-technologically oriented hobby enthusiasts, as Shotton's research reveals, are not and in fact are often admired instead? Though we will return to this issue again in later chapters, perhaps Shotton's assessment is the most succinct, if not prophetic:

> ". . . there were logical reasons why some people chose to turn to an interaction with inanimate artifacts for the satisfaction of their needs. What was less clear was why the cognoscenti should have voiced their fears so forcefully, and why alarm was expressed for those who used computers intensively when dedication to other activities was often encouraged.

> ". . . computer dependency was only one of a multitude of computer-related anxieties current at the time this research was initiated, many of which had been well-publicized in the press although not all were necessarily well-substantiated. . . the fear that some people would become socially and psychologically dependent upon computers was merely one of many fears

attributed to computer usage. . . The introduction of this new technology
appeared to have created a climate of apprehension about computers in
general, and any overt behavior patterns associated with their use were
perhaps seen as suspect.

"(such misgivings) have been shown to occur with a certain regularity
when people do not fully understand the ramifications of a new technology.
. . intensive interest in computers differs little from dedication to many
other activities. The difference appeared to lie in the attitudes of others
towards what were considered to be acceptable pursuits." [pp. 235-236]

Chapter 3

INTERNET ADDICTION DISORDER: SOCIAL INTERACTION AS PATHOLOGY

In Chapter Two, I provided an overview of the often radical, never-ending changes that have occurred with regard to the definition and diagnosis of mental disorders, and of substance-related and impulse control disorders in particular. Further, I argued that such changes were not the result of significant improvements in objective, scientific knowledge and diagnostic technologies, but instead were the result of a continuing effort on the part of moral entrepreneurs, in the face of evidence to the contrary, to define mental disorder and addiction as 'real' social problems. To support this argument, I provided an overview of: the sociohistorical framework in which such changes took place; how certain groups of individuals used such changing values to their advantage to create socially functional truths; and the research that consistently refuted this 'common sense' disease model of addiction. Implicit in that entire argument was the suggestion that there is a more fruitful way of seeing the rise of mental disorders and addictions as diseases. And, as alluded to in Chapter One, that way of seeing is through the sociological lens of symbolic interaction.

SYMBOLIC INTERACTION AND THE DEVIANCE PROCESS

Symbolic interaction is the study of the making of meaningful behavior. In general, symbolic interaction theory states that human beings have the capacity for thought; this capacity is shaped by social interaction, in which people learn meanings and symbols that allow them to develop that capacity. Further, these meanings and symbols allow people to carry on action and interaction, and people can modify or alter meanings and symbols on the basis of their interpretation, or definition, of the situation. People can make these modifications because they have selves. That is, they can interact with themselves, examine courses of action and the advantages and disadvantages of each, and then choose one course of action over another. These intertwined patterns of action and interaction are what constitute groups and societies.

Symbolic interactionists assert that meaning emerges from consensus among actors and is established in interaction. That is, meaning is not inherent, it is created and therefore unstable and problematic. [Brissett and Edgley 1975] Within this context, the self is defined as the meaning of the human organism; a meaning which is highly situational. [G. Stone 1970] The self is established by its activity and by the activity of others towards it. It is not inherent in the individual because the "individual" is a shared, interactive phenomenon; self is an outcome, not an antecedent of behavior. What one does establishes who one is, not vice versa; there is no useful distinction to be made between actor and action. Further, interactionists argue that human beings are primarily symbol users; the meaning of the self first and foremost [E. Becker 1962] and all other subsequent meanings are constructed through symbols, which are the primary cultural resource.

Another way of phrasing the statements above is to say that society *is* symbolic interaction. [Blumer 1969] That is, all human interaction is mediated by the use and interpretation of symbols. And, in order for such interaction to occur and be meaningful, each participant in that interaction must be able to take the role of the other through the use of the sign system, or technology, of language. An important consequence of this use of language to bring meaning to the self and the world is that there is no ultimately 'real' world; the world and the self are 'real' insofar as they are known through language. [E. Becker 1962]

Two implications of symbolic interactionist theory are of critical importance for our purposes here; the self as process (rather than entity), and the role of language (symbol systems) in the simultaneous creation of both the social self (socialization) and the social order. Through interaction, one develops a self; the capacity to observe, respond to, and direct one's own behavior (reflexivity). That the self continuously arises out of interaction implies both interaction among individuals and a prior existence of the group(s) within which the self emerges. This process of self development, often called socialization, is a life-long procedure; the self is a process, not an entity, and is neither the product of impinging stimuli, nor a reflection of an overarching and overwhelming cultural system, nor an organism driven by and essentially determined by internal mechanisms. [Hewitt 1984] As Goffman [1959] aptly summarizes, the self is not an organic thing that has a specific location. "In analyzing the self then we are drawn *from* its possessor. . .for he and his body merely provide the peg on which something of collaborative manufacture will be hung for a time. . ." [p. 253] The self is not the possession of the actor, but the product of interaction within a scene or frame.

And what specifically constitutes this scene or frame? According to Blumer [1969], "Symbolic interaction involves interpretation, or ascertaining the meaning of the actions or remarks of the other person, and definition, or conveying indications to another person as to how he is to act." [p. 66] In other words, the self and social order are simultaneously framed through the symbol system of language. Language serves as the basis for everyday social life; it is the cohesive factor for human groups, because groups are symbolic, rather than physical, phenomena. Through the use of language, individuals create their selves and their reality; they indicate to themselves and each other what their responses to objects will be, and thus what the meanings of those objects are. [Lauer and Handel 1983]

Within this process of reality-construction, language serves as a means of socialization for new selves. Language allows for the transition from biological entity to human self through role-taking, and this role-taking process is the basis for society. Cooperative processes are necessary for the maintenance of social order, and cooperative processes can only occur to the extent that individual members are able to apprehend the general attitude and, therefore, predict the behavior of other members of the society:

> "From the standpoint of its individual members, a society is a thing with an existence independent of themselves, even though its continued being depends very much on them and their behavior. A society, in short, is an object toward which its members act, and to a great extent the fact of social order is simply the fact that people act toward, and so constitute, this object in a stable, orderly fashion. What is true of society as a whole also is true of the smaller groups, organizations, communities, institutions and other units that make it up." [Hewitt 1984, 188]

The primary means by which members 'act toward' and 'constitute' community, social order and the self is through talk. As Hewitt observes:

> "This points to the crucial importance of that form of conduct we call 'talking'. For on whatever occasions it takes place, talk is a primary means

by which people sustain the world of objects in which they live, particularly abstract objects such as goals, rules, ways of life, institutions, groups, communities and society itself. Talk thrives best when conditions are in some way problematic. People account for their conduct when others define it as problematic or when they think they are likely to do so. Such forms of talk as accounts and disclaimers themselves make an important contribution to social order. By calling attention to rules, norms, and expectations, these forms of talk allow homage to be paid to the usual, regular, and typical ways people are expected to behave. They call attention to social order, even though the circumstances in which they arise involve apparent failures of that order."[p. 189-190]

But what has symbolic interaction to do with whether or not individuals suffer from some sort of mental disorder, addiction in particular? It is through this process of talking that individuals simultaneously construct 'the normal' and 'the deviant'. And, as we shall see shortly, mental illness and addiction are merely behaviors which have been collectively defined as deviant. In general, deviance refers to violations of social norms. Norms are behavioral codes, or prescriptions, that guide people into actions and self-presentations that conform to social acceptability. All social groups make such rules and attempt, at some times and under some circumstances, to enforce them. Social rules define situations and the kinds of behavior appropriate to them, specifying some actions as 'right' and forbidding others as 'wrong'.

However, whether an act is deviant, whether it violates social norms, depends on how other people react to it; it is the response of the 'other' that is problematic. Variations in response to particular actions occur over time, and depend as well on who commits the act and who feels he has been harmed by it; rules are applied more to some persons than to others. Thus, deviance is not a quality that lies in behavior itself, but in the interaction between the person who commits an act and those who respond to it. Because human action is normative, human values determine what is to be considered a 'problem'.

Howard Becker [1963], an early proponent of deviance as a social construction, argued that social deviance is outside the individual, rather than inside, and that categorization is not an automatic process; social power and negotiation of the definition of the situation are paramount. Others have utilized his typology of deviance[12] to further the argument that deviant

---

[12] Becker constructs a 'typology' of deviance through combining the presence or absence of the action in question with the presence or absence of sanctions. 'Conforming behavior' is that which obeys the rule and which others perceive as obeying the rule. The 'pure deviant' is one who both disobeys the rules and is

behavior is not necessarily that which violates social norms, but is instead behavior which is perceived as a threat to a particular group's values, within a particular situation. [Lauer and Handel 1983; Hewitt 1984] Deviance, as a perceived threat to social values, is also a threat to the identities of individuals involved; one constructs who one is through the values to which one subscribes.

What this means in terms of the place of deviance in society, then, is that deviance does not mark the breakdown of social order. Instead, it marks the specific points at which one may most fully understand the social order. Deviance is constructed as a means of pointing out what the social rules are and the consequences for violating those rules. Thus, constructing deviance is the 'politics of reality' [Hewitt 1984];

> The 'reality' of deviance can only be achieved when people are imagined and successfully labeled as such. Deviance. . .refers to the socially constructed negative moral meanings that are situationally generated to describe behavior and personal attributes perceived as different and disturbing to certain audiences. The unifying factor among all behaviors and attributes named and categorized as deviant is that they are perceived to be at variance with some group's definition of what is preferable or morally acceptable. To create 'deviance' is simultaneously to create 'normality'; we can know one only in relation to the other. [Pfuhl and Henry 1993, p. 22]

Seen in this way, mental disorder is precisely that; a form of social deviance, of *dis-order*, that violates social rules, norms and expectations. In fact, as Kirk and Kutchins [1992] point out, it was precisely this symbolic interactionist argument[13] that threatened the underlying theoretical construct of 'mental disorder' (as discussed in Chapter Two) and ultimately lead to the creation of DSM III in 1980, as the discipline of psychiatry attempted to

---

perceived as doing so. The more interesting cases, in terms of developing an understanding of social order and identity, lie in the 'in between' possibilities: 1) the 'falsely accused', who is seen as having violated the rules, even though he or she has not; and 2) the 'secret deviant', who violates the rules, but no one recognizes it or responds to it as a violation.

[13] Sociologists were not the only people questioning the social construct of mental disorder as a medical problem. Psychiatrists as well, particularly Thomas Szasz, argued that what were being called mental illnesses were not illnesses because they had they had no clear links to any underlying physiological causes. Instead, the criteria for labeling such problems as illnesses were social and ethical, and were used to 'disguise . . . the bitter pill of moral conflicts in human relations. . .' [Kirk and Kutchins 1992]

defend its historically and empirically weak ties to medicine through application of the disease model to human social behaviors:

> ". . . sociologists viewed mental illness as they would any other label for deviant behavior. Mental illness, they suggested, told us not so much about internal, individual pathology, as about the social processes through which certain behaviors became defined by people in authority as instances of insanity. Mental illness was viewed as an arbitrary social label, conveying more about the structure of authority in a particular social situation than about pathology. This view spawned an active sociological literature on the conditions and processes by which some people were labeled as mentally ill and the consequences of such labeling for self-attitudes and the reactions of others. . . (arguing that) behaviors that are labeled mental illness are simply behaviors for which other explanations were unconvincing. Mental illness is merely a residual category of behavior, an explanation of last resort. . . mental disorder is viewed as a label behind which psychiatrists and the public hide their ignorance. . . (and) the act of labeling 'residual deviants' played an important part in encouraging the individual to meet the role expectations of someone who is 'insane'." [p. 21]

Perhaps the most thorough examination of the conditions and processes in and by which people come to be defined as deviant, and the one that I will utilize here to examine the creation of Internet Addiction Disorder, is that put forth by Pfuhl and Henry in their 1993 work, *The Deviance Process.* While the authors offer a very detailed analysis of the specific steps involved in the social construction of deviant behavior, a thumbnail sketch will suffice for our purposes here. Essentially, there are four interrelated phases in the construction of deviance: 1) creation of various deviance categories; 2) creation of deviant individuals who will populate those categories; 3) assessment of the social and personal consequences of that labeling process; and 4) response to labels and the associated stigma.

Consider phase one, the creation of deviant categories. Any rule-breaking behavior one can imagine is nothing more and nothing less than one type of social behavior, all of which are consequences of choice. Rather than being the violation of some universal set of objective laws that results from some internal drive or environmental stimulus over which the violator has no control (as is purported by the disease model of addiction), rule breaking behavior is volitional behavior that breaches some pre-defined, socially constructed norms. Thus, in order to understand how someone is defined as a deviant, one must first understand the process of creating the particular category of deviance into which that individual will eventually be placed.

In short, deviance is what those with the power to influence the rule-making process say it is; it is constructed to reflect the definitions of immorality held by such persons and groups. Such private definitions of morality are transformed into public rules of behavior in a political process that involves four steps. First, a behavior is publicly signified as different. Second, that behavior is negatively evaluated. Third, the behavior is interpreted as a violation severe enough that it warrants condemnation or control in some form. Finally, such rule-making behavior defines rule violators as deviants liable to various actions allegedly designed to control them. Through this activity, which Pfuhl and Henry [1993] refer to as 'banning', an activity is signified as evil, bad, wrong or immoral, and rule-breakers are imbued with guilt.

In this banning process, moral entrepreneurs[14] seek to achieve a moral conversion; they seek to alter peoples' perceptual and cognitive structures regarding a particular issue in order to legitimate their viewpoint. Typically, this sort of project is accomplished through the use of mass media (e.g. television, movies, and the like), folklore, and various and sundry alliances. Moral entrepreneurs select a cultural myth, or at least a portion of a myth, that is in harmony with the dominant social reality and, with the help of mass media, alliances with previously established moral leaders, and testimonials and endorsements from publicly influential figures, exaggerate that myth in order to create a 'moral panic' about a particular issue among the general population. The central notion of such a panic is that a problem exists in society because of a particular group of people, and that that group needs to be controlled in some way if the problem is ever to be resolved.

Naturally, this construction of deviant categories of behavior calls out for the creation of deviant individuals who may then be 'rightly' placed in those categories. This is phase two of the deviance process. In short, this is accomplished by stripping the legitimate identity from selected actors by classifying and dealing with them as a specific deviant type. The four stages in this 'deviant career' are as follows [Pfuhl and Henry 1993]. First, the individual in question is publicly identified as a rule breaker. Second, she or he is excluded from participation in non-deviant activities. Third, the individual comes to define him- or herself as deviant. Finally, the individual attempts to 'manage' this deviant identity in one way or another.

The methods by which moral entrepreneurs classify individuals as deviants and place them into categories include, but are not limited to:

stereotyping individuals and groups; institutionalizing deviance; retrospective interpretation; and status degradation ceremonies [Garfinkel 1956]. Because stereotypes are regarded as valid descriptions of the groups to which they refer, moral entrepreneurs work to utilize these taken-for-granted 'realities' to institutionalize categories of deviant behaviors. Such institutionalization occurs when an official agency of some sort is delegated the responsibility for dealing with deviant types. Prisons, mental institutions and, Rice [1996] would argue, self-help groups, are all examples of such official agencies.

Agents of social control operating within such institutions utilize retrospective interpretation and degradation ceremonies in order to 'prove' that the individual is really deviant and to isolate him or her from participating in non-deviant activities until he or she is rehabilitated. Retrospective interpretation is the process by which control agencies integrate the moral definition of the banned act, the presumed character (stereotype) of the particular rule breaker, and the treatment to be accorded; entrepreneurs select information from the individual's past that can be defined as consistent with, or inevitably leading up to, the newly defined deviant act and build a case that such behaviors were 'indications' that the person was somehow different, or deviant, all along. In many cases, the end result is that the deviant individual undergoes a degradation ceremony, in which the 'true' identity is altered to signify a total change. This new identity implies a lower social status position and is intended to reflect not only what the person has done, but why he or she is supposed to have done it. As Goffman [1959] notes, and as we shall return to momentarily, such degradation ceremonies are particularly salient when the deviant identity under construction is that of mental patient.

Though not all rule breakers are publicly identified and labeled as deviant, those who are labeled find that their public identity is 'spoiled' and are burdened with the consequences of stigma[15]. The process by which people come to be 'the thing they are named', and the personal and social consequences of that process, are the focus of the third phase of the deviance process. The process of labeling, as summarized above, serves to locate

---

[14] Moral entrepreneurs are those individuals or groups who seek, in a heterogeneous society of multiple realities, to have their particular reality defined as the official one.

[15] Stigmata are marks placed on people to indicate their low social position or status as an outsider. They symbolize one's morally spoiled identity or social undesirability and take precedence over other qualities to which one may lay claim.

people in the social order and rank them relative to others. Given the symbolic interactionist perspective that the self is constructed through this sort of interaction, a person's identity, then, consists of the names by which he is known. Regardless of whether he satisfies that expectation, a person known by a given label is expected to display the stereotyped behaviors associated with that label.

Thus, the consequences of labeling move beyond the personal to the social; as an individual comes to accept the label that has been attached to him, he may very well begin to display the accompanying stereotyped behaviors and, in some cases, may 'go along' with this new identity by self-labeling. Whether or not this amplification of deviance and corresponding role engulfment materialize depend largely upon the source of the stigma (ascribed or achieved), whether the labeling process is formal or informal, the socioeconomic status of the deviant, and whether the deviant chooses stigma management or stigma transformation as a response to this labeling process. It is this choice, and the actions taken by deviant individuals and groups to bring it about, that constitute the fourth and final phase of the deviance process.

Stigma management refers to efforts of labeled individuals (or groups of individuals) to control information about their spoiled identity, typically by either avoiding contact with 'stigma symbols' (signs that reveal one's label), using 'disidentifiers' (symbols that prevent one from being conceived of as deviant), or leading a sort of double life (by placing restrictions on one's choice of associates). So, for example, a gay individual may choose to avoid the stigma of being labeled as such by the larger society by avoiding certain bars, by keeping his gay and straight circles of acquaintances separate, or even by getting married.

If such information control is not possible for whatever reason, the labeled person may choose the path of 'stigma transformation'. Such transformation involves either altering the meaning of the label or reducing its perceived relevance to who one 'really' is, and may be accomplished in a number of ways, including: purification and transcendence, deviance disavowal or avowal, use of accounts (justifications and excuses for behavior) [Scott and Lyman 1975], or use of 'covering'. This notion of stigma transformation is particularly relevant for the analysis of addiction because, as will be discussed in detail momentarily, the rise of the disease model of behavior as it has been applied in the process addiction movement is in large part the result of efforts on the part of the labeled group to not only transform the stigma of addiction, but to transform themselves from rule breakers to rule makers. It is this transformation that begins the cyclical deviance process again, as the labeled have worked to redefine reality in their own terms and for their own purposes.

As noted above, in the discussion of phase two of the deviance process, the population of the deviant category 'mentally ill' is particularly relevant to the addiction label under examination here, as it is this second generation of illness that lead ultimately to the view that a series of behaviors could be defined as an illness in the medical sense. Symbolic interactionists who study the deviance process have devoted considerable attention to the assignment of the 'mentally ill' label, with perhaps the most cogent examination being that of Erving Goffman [1959, 1963, 1969]. For example, in his *Moral Career of a Mental Patient*, Goffman examines the pre-patient, inpatient, and ex-patient phases of the 'careers' of individuals who have been labeled as mentally ill and put through the hospitalization process. Noting that many patients are 'unwilling', and have been forced into such a process by family threats, police escort or trickery, Goffman examines how hospital staff and the deviant's significant others work in concert to define the individual in question as one who needs help; they stereotype, institutionalize, and utilize retrospective interpretation and degradation ceremonies to make the label the 'real' identity.

However, Goffman notes, there are a number of 'career contingencies' involved in determining whether this new label will 'stick'. Such contingencies include socioeconomic status, visibility of offense, proximity to a mental hospital, and so forth. Additionally, if and when the individual is hospitalized, other career contingencies pop up and impact when and if he or she is to be discharged, including the desires of the family, the availability of a job, and so forth. Thus, Goffman concludes, mental patients suffer not so much from mental illness, but from *contingencies*, and it is these contingencies, and the rule maker's social distance from them, that produce the so-called 'sick behavior'.

Additional empirical evidence of this labeling process has been found by other researchers. For example, Rosenhan [1975, p. 302] asks: "At its heart, the question of whether the sane can be distinguished from the insane. . . is a simple matter: do the salient characteristics that lead to diagnoses reside in the patients themselves or in the environments and contexts in which observers find them?" In order to answer this question, Rosenhan conducted an experiment in which eight 'sane' people gained admission to twelve different mental hospitals. To do so, each arrived at a hospital and claimed to have heard voices, but made no other alterations in significant life events, relationships, thoughts or feelings. Upon admission, the 'patients' ceased simulating any symptoms of abnormality. Regardless, none of the 'normal' patients were detectably sane to the hospital staffs. Not only were the original labels of mentally ill 'sticky', hospital staff engaged in retroactive labeling; they reinterpreted previous acts and behaviors in light of the patients' admissions of hearing voices.

Regarding addiction, these notions of a deviance process and corresponding deviant careers have been used to empirically examine many of the substance-related and impulse control disorders outlined in Chapter Two and to refute the idea that such series of behaviors can be legitimately defined as illnesses. For example, in his examination of how individuals 'become' marihuana users, Howard Becker [1963] argued that, in order to become a regular, a person must, through interaction, learn to perceive the effects of marihuana use (i.e. that he is 'high') and learn that these effects are pleasurable. Perceiving the 'high' is only accomplished in a social setting, but even after the high is perceived, it is not universally defined as pleasurable.

Thus, he concludes, research on drug use that focuses on the question 'why do they do it?' and attempts to use a psychological framework of traits inherent in the individual that predispose or motivate (especially those that focus on need for fantasy or escape) provide inadequate explanations. That is, deviant motives do not lead to deviant behavior. Rather, a person engages in a behavior. Someone else defines it as deviant, and motives are attached after the fact as a form of an 'account'. Such motives serve as functional explanations for the individual doing the defining, and are often adopted by the labeled individual as a matter of course. When the deviant individual does not accept the label (and the corresponding motive), they are said to be 'in denial', which, in itself is another symptom of 'disorder'.

Similarly, in his work on heroin use, Stephens [1991] analyzes how persons become socialized into the social role of street addict. Focusing (in much the same way as Becker) on the user's expectations and interpretations of the drug's effects and on the sociocultural settings in which the drug is used, he argues that, over time, the individual becomes increasingly committed to the identity of drug user and then proceeds to organize his or her behavior around this 'master status' in a six stage process. First, the individual is recruited into initial heroin use. Next, the individual actually uses the drug. If his or her expectations and interpretations of this initial drug use can be defined as pleasurable, then what Stephens refers to as the 'honeymoon' phase begins. In this phase, the individual increases his or her involvement beyond experimental stage. Phase four consists of what Stephens calls 'first addiction', the point at which the individual 'recognizes' that behaviors and choices reflect 'physical dependence' as defined by mental health professionals and those in his social circle who have adopted this label. In phase five, the individual is fully involved in 'life as a junkie'; he is committed to the identity of drug user and lives a life in which his activities revolve around drug procurement and use. Typically, the individual will eventually enter phase six, which is marked by the point when the individual decides that the lifestyle is too demanding and chooses to abandon the role.

Finally, Rosecrance [1985] applies the same framework to a study of regular gamblers in an off-track betting establishment. In this work, Rosecrance sought to understand why regulars are so persistent in their gambling, despite the financial and (sometimes) interpersonal costs. He examined how they define their social worlds and how they adopted the social role of 'regular', and discovered that they do so in much the same way as street addicts adopt their role in Stephens' work. That is, regular gamblers, like heroin users, follow a 'career line' which consists of seven basic phases. The first, or 'acquisition', phase is the one in which the now-regular acquired the behavior pattern. Acquisition typically occurs only for those gamblers who begin gambling early in life (in the teen years) and who also achieve a 'big score' early on.

The second phase is 'modification'. In general, the gambler's goal in this phase is to avoid losing contact with the behavior pattern and the social world of gambling that he considers to be exciting. He gears his future life course toward maintaining contact, even though he learns that the 'beginners luck' experienced in phase one is atypical. In phase three, the regular works to develop a gambling strategy; he develops both a specific method of play and the money management techniques that allow him to continue participation. Such strategic planning usually leads, at some point, to a second big score, which in turn increases his commitment to the social role of gambler. However, in phase four, that strategy inevitably fails, and he must decide how to transcend losing streaks in order to maintain the desired level of commitment. This disillusionment-resolution process, which marks phase five, marks the point at which the regular decides on his proper level of future participation. The decision is based on his win-loss ratio, financial resources, family and employment concerns, and social relationships with other players.

Should he choose to continue as a regular gambler, he will eventually reach phase six, what Rosecrance terms the mid-life phase, in which he experiences a renewed self-evaluation. Again he compares his performances with other regulars, re-examines gambling strategy, and re-examines the social and financial rewards of participation. Finally, the regular eventually reaches phase seven, retirement age, at which point he decides that he can no longer sustain participation and quits the role.

Rosecrance argues that this career is a socialization process in which social interactions with other gamblers become increasingly important. Regulars see their gambling as a rational, task-oriented, worthwhile, stimulating, all-engrossing and non-competitive activity in which they choose to participate and in which interaction with fellow gamblers is the primary attraction. In fact, when questioned, what those who have considered discontinuing participation feared was not the loss of 'action', but the loss of social contact, group membership, and the accompanying benefits of social interaction. So, while outside observers see regular gamblers as 'addicted' to gambling, Rosecrance argues that such an assumption is a misunderstanding of what is actually going on: ". . . it can be concluded that in this instance it is not gambling per se that the participants fear losing but the rewards of group membership." [p. 73]

Regulars disavow the labels of 'deviant' and 'compulsive' (one of Pfuhl and Henry's 1993 strategies for stigma transformation, to which we will return momentarily). While they are aware that many regulars lose more money than they can afford, the loss is attributed to poor strategy, not to uncontrollable urges. Regulars argue that the label 'compulsive gambler' is one formulated by outside observers who are unfamiliar with actual gambling situations: "Those shrinks don't know shit about gambling." [p. 110] Interestingly, they do see themselves as 'addicted' to the behavior, but in a non-pejorative way. The regulars align themselves with the original meanings of addiction discussed in Chapter One; they see it as an intense commitment and a strong preference—addiction is a common response pattern, not an aberration. Thus, Rosecrance concludes, "Continued participation represents a commitment to a difficult enterprise, not a compulsive drive. . . The basic assumption of the compulsion model, that losing gamblers have an 'unconscious wish to lose' is not in accord with the ethnographic data developed in this study " [pp. 110, 126]

In 'disavowing' the labels of deviant and compulsive, the regular gamblers in Rosecrance's study seek to transform the stigma attached to their behaviors. That is, they deny that their behavior is in some way abnormal, and argue that their non-pejorative 'addiction' to gambling is a normal, natural response to an activity so exciting and engrossing. In much the same way, this is the strategy adopted by participants in the co-dependency movement. While co-dependents do not directly claim that they are 'normal', they do argue that, because process addiction permeates a fundamentally ill, addicted society, the response of co-dependency is a normal one under the circumstances. In so doing, they seek to transform their stigmatized behaviors by themselves becoming the moral entrepreneurs, thus beginning the cycle of the deviance process anew. In order to accomplish this redefinition of the situation, co-dependents must *become* co-dependent. That is, they must select the co-dependent career line in much the same way as the regular gambler, marijuana user and street addict select their lines of behavior, for, as Rice [1996] notes:

> "co-dependency is not something one 'has', but, rather, something one believes. . . co-dependency is a discourse, a symbolic system, a set of beliefs, about the self in relation to society. The co-dependency movement, in turn, is the product of people selecting those beliefs as a way of conceiving of, talking about, and acting upon the problems they encounter in their lives. By 'having' (that is, selecting) co-dependency . . . (people) have an explanation for their actions." [pp. 10-11]

Of what, specifically, does this co-dependent career line consist? According to Rice, newcomers to the co-dependent movement are not yet assimilated into the norms of the group: "Becoming co-dependent demands that they acquire and cultivate the ability to conceptualize and talk about themselves in the requisite ways, and acquiring that ability rests, in the first instance, upon deciding that that is the course of action they want to pursue."[p. 142] Typically, this decision is made when newcomers are able to identify with the experiences of other group members; drawing connections between the comments of regulars and their own situations is the first step in the process. The newcomer must be able to 'relate' to what is being said: "The co-dependent, the process addict, is a social role, defined by a set of obligations and privileges. . . The first set of obligations are biographical. Falling under the twelve-step rubric of 'getting out of denial', the biographical obligations entail admitting powerlessness over an addiction and the unmanageability of one's life. At one level, this means acknowledging that one is sick; at another, it entails fitting one's life story with the discourse's symbolic system." [p. 144].

In this way, people undergo "conversion". An important factor in doing so is to adopt a new "universe of discourse" through a three step process. First, one must engage in a biographical reconstruction in which one retrofits one's life story within the new symbolic system. Second, one must adopt a master attribution scheme through which one may frame all life troubles in terms of the co-dependent model. Finally, one must suspend analogical reasoning and believe the model literally, rather than merely metaphorically.

As with all other varieties of mental illness and addiction, the creation of co-dependency was originally the work of counselors, or what Rice terms "symbolic specialists", seeking to place issues and problems in living within a clinical, addiction-oriented frame of reference, as was originally done with the problem of heavy drinking. However, as Rice [1996] aptly notes:

> "This analogy between alcoholism and virtually all problems in living is a somewhat fragile rhetorical construction. Throughout the various treatises on co-dependency, particularly in their discussions of the newest categories of process addiction, the advocates appear to recognize this fragility, taking considerable pains to assure that people take seriously the analogy that the discourse draws between the new categories and more conventional, and publicly accepted, forms of addiction. . . unmistakably trying to establish an analogy between process addiction and alcoholism and thereby to achieve legitimacy for process addiction on the same grounds as for alcoholism: the inevitability and unintentional nature of people's conduct."
> [p. 124-125]

The co-dependency movement is not the only arena in which such fragile arguments are constructed or in which such pains are taken to assure that people take the creation of a new 'addiction' seriously. If co-dependency was the disease of the 1980s, then Internet Addiction Disorder is the disease of the 1990s. For it is during the 1990s that computer-mediated communications and interactive computer technologies such as the World Wide Web, Usenet, Internet Relay Chat, and Multi-User Dungeons have become increasingly sophisticated and popularized. And it is during the 1990s that such technology has become the victim of its own success; symbolic specialists, utilizing the same unexamined framework and methodologies as had been used to create other forms of addiction, have now worked to create a new 'illness' known as Internet Addiction Disorder. It is to this creative process that we now turn.

CREATING A NEW PATHOLOGY: INTERNET ADDICTION DISORDER

The notion that people could become addicted to the Internet is not an entirely original one. Prior to 1995, when the Internet was in its infancy, arguments regarding dependence on technology were formulated in the more general terms of computer dependency. While researchers like Shotton [1989] attempted to theorize about and empirically research the existence of computer dependency from an academic standpoint, legal and mental health practitioners worked to legitimate the concept in the 'real world'. Perhaps the most striking examples of this legitimation process are two court cases in which the defense was 'not guilty by reason of computer addiction'. The first case was that of Kevin Mitnick, who, in 1989 pleaded guilty to stealing a DEC (Digital Equipment Corporation) security program and to illegal possession of long distance telephone codes belonging to MCI. Mitnick's career as a hacker began at age 16, when he hacked into his high school's administrative system just to 'look around'. Some time later, he was caught stealing telephone company technical manuals from Pacific Bell's computer center in Los Angeles. Still later he hacked into a local university, again to look around.

Though he faced a maximum of 20 years in prison and fine of $750,000 for the crimes against DEC, he served no jail time. Based upon his history as a hacker, his defense team convinced a judge that he was addicted to computers and could not stop himself. He was instead sentenced to a year in a rehabilitation center where he could be treated for his addiction. Harriet Rossetto, the director of the rehabilitation center said that Mitnick would benefit from the program because "(his) hacking gives a sense of self-esteem he doesn't get in the real world. . . This is a new and growing addiction". [Papai, 1993] However, it appears that the 'treatment' was ineffective. After undergoing rehabilitation, Mitnick was recaptured in early 1994 in North Carolina in possession of approximately $1 million worth of stolen data and was labeled the world's most wanted hacker; he had been 'on the run' for three years before he was captured in North Carolina. This case is believed to be the first in which a person indicted for a computer hacking-related crime was treated as an addict. [Quittner, 1994]

The second hacker - addiction case took place in London, and ended in the acquittal of Paul Bedworth, again the result of a computer addiction defense. In 1991, a sting operation was set up to capture Bedworth and other fellow hackers. In court, the two co-defendants pleaded guilty to the charges, but Bedworth refused. Instead, he claimed that he was addicted to computer use and by virtue of that addiction was unable to form the necessary intent. "The defense claimed that Bedworth's inability to engage in normal social relations lead to his isolation from his peer group and resulted in his becoming addicted to computer hacking. . . The hacker ethos of individuals against the system certainly resembles other addict subcultures and the concept of repetitive behavior leading to some kind of intermittent reward can clearly be seen to be habit forming. In the case of computer addiction, it could be argued, the particular action may be, for example, attempting repeatedly to crack a password. . . In Bedworth's case, he was said in his psychological assessment interview to have made unprompted statements such as 'I believe I am addicted to hacking'. Evidence was also presented that he spent abnormally long hours in the computer laboratory, that his computer activities took precedence over all other activities, and that he had made statements to the effect that he felt uncomfortable and frustrated when not able to hack and that he had a need to hack even when he perceived that this might be antisocial or illegal behavior." [R. v. Bedworth 1993]

In court, the defense called an expert witness in compulsive behavior who tested Bedworth and concluded that "he was an obsessive person, totally besotted by computers. . ." Said the expert, "That side of the case wasn't made up. Even today, while he is studying artificial intelligence, Paul spends all his nights up to midnight in the computing labs and his weekends too. He's hooked on computing. . .The child, whose best friend is a computer rather than a person, is not going to function normally in society. We need to be able to predict how he will behave and what treatments will restore him to normal health." [Gold, 1993]

Not long after the conclusion of the Bedworth case in 1993, what would become one of the defining moments in the creation of Internet Addiction Disorder occurred. Psychiatrist Ivan Goldberg created a set of diagnostic criteria patterned after the 1994 edition of the APA's Diagnostic and Statistical Manual of Mental Disorders, and claimed that they were indicative of a new pathology, Internet Addiction Disorder. Not only that, Goldberg started an online support group, the Internet Addiction Support Group (IASG), for those afflicted with this new disorder. The diagnostic criteria, listed below, are nearly identical to those outlined in Chapter Two regarding Substance Use and Impulse Control disorders.

Are you suffering from Internet Addiction Disorder?

As the incidence and prevalence of Internet Addiction Disorder (IAD) has been increasing exponentially, a support group, The Internet Addiction Support Group (IASG) has been established. Below are the official criteria for the diagnosis of IAD and subscription information for the IASG.

Internet Addiction Disorder (IAD) - Diagnostic Criteria

A maladaptive pattern of Internet use, leading to clinically significant impairment or distress as manifested by three (or more) of the following, occurring at any time in the same 12-month period:

(I) tolerance, as defined by either of the following:

(A) A need for markedly increased amounts of time on Internet to achieve satisfaction

(B) markedly diminished effect with continued use of the same amount of time on Internet

(II) withdrawal, as manifested by either of the following:

(A) the characteristic withdrawal syndrome

(1) Cessation of (or reduction) in Internet use that has been heavy and prolonged.

(2) Two (or more) of the following, developing within several days to a month after Criterion 1:

(a) psychomotor agitation

(b) anxiety

(c) obsessive thinking about what is happening on Internet

(d) fantasies or dreams about Internet

(e) voluntary or involuntary typing movements of the fingers

(3) The symptoms in Criterion 2 cause distress or impairment in social, occupational or another important area of functioning

(B) Use of Internet or a similar on-line service is engaged in to relieve or avoid withdrawal symptoms

(III) Internet is often accessed more often or for longer periods of time than was intended

(IV) There is a persistent desire or unsuccessful efforts to cut down or control Internet use

(V) A great deal of time is spent in activities related to Internet use (e.g., buying Internet books, trying out new WWW browsers, researching Internet vendors, organizing files of downloaded materials.)

(VI) Important social, occupational, or recreational activities are given up or reduced because of Internet use.

(VII) Internet use is continued despite knowledge of having a persistent or recurrent physical, social, occupational, or psychological problem that is likely to have been caused or exacerbated by Internet use (sleep deprivation, marital difficulties, lateness for early morning appointments, neglect of occupational duties, or feelings of abandonment in significant others)

What was not immediately apparent to the casual observer was that these criteria, and the associated support group, were completely made-up. What Goldberg had attempted to do was to force the psychiatric community to introspect; to evaluate the usefulness of creating new 'disorders' out of what are essentially problems in living. What he in fact accomplished was the launching of an entirely new area of specialization within the mental health professions – that of Internet addiction treatment specialist. But Goldberg did not accomplish such a feat alone. He had help from popular press journalists around the country; journalists who, despite being told by Goldberg himself that the entire idea was a ruse, reported their 'findings' *as if* they were 'real'.

Academics and mental health professionals, in turn, took such popular press articles at face value and utilized them not only as catalysts for their research agendas (which in and of itself might have been entirely appropriate) but as evidence for their conclusions. Thus, in effect, researchers decided what they wanted to find, and then utilized DSM guidelines (themselves filled with a host of unexamined assumptions) to fit their 'data' to their pre-determined conclusions. As the following chronology illustrates, it was in this manner that reality was socially constructed – that IAD was made 'real'.

As noted in Chapter One, IAD made its first appearance in a significant popular press forum in a March 1995 article in the New York Times entitled, "The Lure and Addiction of Life On Line". The article, while it did not use the IAD label or cite any specific scientific research that had been conducted, made the argument that increasing numbers of individuals were spending a great deal of time online—so much time, in fact, that the Internet was interfering with other aspects of their lives. Quoting addictions specialists and computer industry professionals, the article likened such Internet use to compulsive shopping, exercise and gambling.

For example, Dr. Howard Shaffer, the Associate Director of the Division of Addictions at Harvard University Medical School was cited as stating that: "the on-line habit is generally a relieving experience, like low-level alcohol use. . . But in some cases, users start showing tolerance and increase their on-line time. They become isolated and ignore other aspects of life. . . Unlike stamp collecting or reading, computers are a psycho-stimulant, and a certain segment of the population can develop addictive behavior in response to that stimulant." The article also pointed out that, in response to a query posted on the Internet by a reporter as to whether people felt that time spent on line interfered with other aspects of their lives, nearly half of the approximately 100 respondents self-labeled as addicts, and 22 reported experiencing 'a cocaine-like rush' from their mastery of online technology. By the end of that same year, the formal label of IAD was firmly attached to the new malady. Due in large part to the work of Kim Young, psychologist at the University of Pittsburgh at Bradford, word of IAD had spread throughout the Internet community via popular media. For example, in a December Newsweek article, Kendall Hamilton and Claudia Kalb focused on the work of Kim Young and her estimate that two to three percent of the online community have serious Internet addictions. The article also cited pages on the World Wide Web, such as 'Webaholics' and 'Interneters Anonymous' as evidence of the veracity of Young's claims. While the authors point out that IASG, started by Goldberg, was intended as a joke, the thrust of the article is that IAD is 'real'; various first-name informants who have self-labeled as Internet addicted are quoted as making claims such as "People who don't deal with it just don't understand. It's as addictive as alcohol or drugs." [Hamilton and Kalb, 1995 p.60]

What the article fails to note, however, is that the World Wide Web pages cited as proof of IAD are actually parodies of the idea, constructed by veteran Internet participants to mock what they see as the latest attempt by the uninitiated to denigrate online activities. For example, the home page of Interneters Anonymous is a knock off of the AA styled self-help group and, among other things, parodies the 12 step process as follows:

1. We admitted we were powerless over the Internet and online services - that our computers and modems were overused.
2. Came to believe that the almighty webmaster could restore us to sanity.
3. Made a decision to turn our will, lives and mouse pads over to the almighty webmaster.
4. Made a searching a fearless inventory of our hard drives.
5. Admitted to the almighty webmaster, to ourselves and to the Internic the exact nature of our addiction.
6. We are ready to delete the collection of bookmarked URL's.
7. Humbly asked the almighty webmaster to remove our web pages from Lycos, InfoSeek and Yahoo.
8. Made a list of chat rooms visited and admitted our addiction to members of each.
9. Made amends to all our chat room friends we have lied to about our looks and appearance.

10. Continued to take inventory of our hard drives and delete all the useless files we collected via FTP.
11. Sought through Wired and other Internet reading material to improve our conscious contact with the almighty webmaster.
12. Having had significantly lower AOL, CompuServe and electricity bills as a result of these steps, we tried to carry the message to Interneters, and to practice these principles in all our affairs.

By the end of 1995 then, one can see that academics, mental health professionals, journalists and individual Internet participants are beginning to work in concert to define the new deviant category of Internet addict. Academics and mental health professionals lend credibility to the notion by conducting research and reporting findings. Regardless of whether such research is based upon plausible assumptions, or whether the methodology is in any way scientific, it is defined as legitimate by those whose interests are served.[16] In turn, journalists provide the vehicle for spreading the word about this newly discovered disorder to the public. Citing sources who self-label as Internet addicted, counselors who conclude that such a disease exists based upon limited interactions with those self-labeling 'patients', and Web pages that are clearly (upon only a cursory examination) mocking the idea, reporters churn out article after article. As the idea fans out from its central starting point, it becomes more real. Internet participants themselves, seeking an explanation for their activities that is easily legitimated [Rice 1996] begin to select IAD as their disease of choice.

By mid-1996, IAD was in full flower. As additional scholarly research was conducted and results presented and fed to the public through print media, Phase One of the deviance process became more firmly entrenched. As noted in Chapter One, Young began studying Internet addiction in 1994, after her interest in the concept was kindled by personal experiences with friends and clients and by anecdotal reports (like those above) which claimed that some on-line users were becoming addicted to the Internet ". . .in much the same way that others become addicted to drugs or alcohol. . ." [Young, 1996, p. 1] And in August, 1996, at the annual meeting of the American Psychological Association, she presented the results of her research in a

---

[16] In Young's first official presentation of research findings, at the annual APA meeting in August 1996, she points out the flaws in her methodology. Regardless, she presents the findings of that research, both at that conference and to the popular press, with no further examination as to their validity or reliability.

paper entitled, "Internet Addiction: The Emergence of a New Clinical Disorder."

In this research, Young asked volunteers from a number of sources to respond to a survey consisting of eight questions about amount of time spent online, preoccupation with Internet use, feelings about that Internet use, its impact on other significant relationships, and so forth. Respondents who answered 'yes' to five or more of those eight criteria were classified as addicted Internet users, and those who responded 'yes' to fewer than five were classified as normal Internet users. Based upon the results, Young reached several conclusions. First, addicts had, in general, less computer experience and expertise and had been online for a shorter amount of time (usually less than one year) than normal users. Second, addicts spent a significantly greater number of hours per week online than normal users, and had built up this high usage habit over time. Third, the more interactive the application, the more addictive it is. For example, participating in chat rooms and newsgroups is more addictive than surfing the Web or working with more traditional information protocols (e.g. gopher and ftp). And finally, while normal users reported few or no adverse consequences of Internet use, addicts reported academic, relationship, financial and occupational problems similar to those reported by pathological gamblers, alcoholics, and people suffering from eating disorders.

Young is not the only researcher who has become interested in Internet addiction. Other academics, following her lead, have theorized about or conducted their own studies of IAD in order to contribute to the body of knowledge surrounding this new disorder. In the spring of 1996, Oliver Egger, a researcher in Switzerland, conducted an online study that asked questions similar to those asked by Young. For example, he asked respondents about the specific Internet applications used and their reasons for doing so; duration of and changes in Internet usage; feelings regarding that usage; and experiences while online (e.g., staying on longer than intended, losing track of time, and so forth). The survey yielded 450 valid responses, which were analyzed and compared to other available studies.

Not surprisingly, he reaches many of the same conclusions that Young reached:

"Ten percent of the respondents considered themselves as addicted to or dependent on the Internet. Some of the questions were based on the addiction criteria from the Internet addiction researchers and on common symptoms of addiction. The results show a significant difference in the answers from addicted versus non-addicted users. This leads to the conclusion that addictive behavior can exist in Internet usage. On the other hand, the answers based on the common symptoms of addiction questions are not so strong in the addicted group that one can speak of an addiction, in which for example, continued persistent use of the Internet appears in spite of negative consequences. Interestingly, people consider themselves as addicted or dependent to the Internet independent of gender, age or living situation. Common signs include: preoccupation, loss of control over use, concerns expressed by others, persistent use despite negative consequences.

Those respondents who self-described as "addicts" reported: negative consequences of Internet use; feelings of anticipation about and guilt over Internet use; complaints from friends or colleagues about the amount of time spent online; and increased participation in online self help groups." [King, 1996] Viktor Brenner, a Ph.D. Candidate at Marquette University, also conducted a study in early 1996 in order to "address issues of Internet use, abuse, and its potential for a behavioral addiction". [Brenner, 1997]. Again, the survey was administered online and asked questions in a true/false format, each of which was designed to assess the extent to which Internet users' experiences paralleled those of other substance-related and impulse control disorders already accepted in the most recent version of the Diagnostic and Statistical Manual of Mental Disorders. (1994) According to Brenner, the results (which he states should be interpreted cautiously) indicate that ". . .the skewed distribution and base rate of endorsement of more severe interference is consistent with the existence of a deviant subgroup who experience more severe problems due to Internet use. This is also preliminary evidence of phenomenon that can be interpreted as tolerance, withdrawal, and craving." [1997, p. 881].

Again journalists took up the cause of IAD. In a March article in the Seattle Times entitled "Is the Internet Addicting?", Diedtra Henderson pointed out that more and more people are spending time online, often to the detriment of other life roles and that some therapists have added 'computer addiction' consultations to their practices. The article centers around the experiences of one individual, a student at University of Washington–how she began using email, and eventually expanded into other online activities. As a result, this individual lost weight, began skipping her classes, and started neglecting other life roles. Says Henderson, "The computer-addiction phenomenon is so new that people don't agree on its characteristics." The article goes on to claim that the affliction is growing; it is moving from male 'techies', who were the traditional stereotype of computer addicts, to students, women, retirees, and so forth. Citing Judith Klavans, Director of the Center for Research on Information Access at Columbia University, who states that, "The communicative aspect of computer use is very appealing.

So chat rooms are a big draw. . .", Brenner's study, and clinical psychologist Michael Green, who 'treats' computer addiction and claims that he is an ex-computer addict, Henderson posits that this disorder, though new and poorly understood, is growing, and could strike anyone, anytime.

Interestingly, as background for this article, the online Seattle Times Web page cites testimonials from the Webaholics Web page. This site was (it has now officially signed off of the Internet) actually a forum for people to construct tongue-in-cheek confessions of Internet addiction and to ridicule the idea that anyone could 'really' be addicted to the net, as the following samples make clear:

> "I admit it. I am addicted to the Web. I had a life somewhere but where it is now I don't know. And I am proud!

And:

> "I can't quit!! Help me, please!! Jesus, I've pawned all of my furniture, books, TV, stereo...I'm coding on my living room floor, because all I have left is my PC...I've gotta stop before I lose it all!"

And finally:

> "The first step to recovery is admitting that you have a problem, right? I have a problem and I DON'T CARE. Mwahahahahahaha. I'll wear it proudly, like a badge or perhaps a scarlet W would be appropriate. I haven't earned the nickname "cyberbabe" from my co-workers for nothing."

And in a May article in Computer Currents Magazine entitled "Webaholic: Compulsive Computing on the Rise", Art Shriver states: "Computer addiction is difficult to define. Even professional therapists and counselors cannot say exactly when or how one person's passion becomes another's problem." Quoting Michael Green (again), who is a recovering technology addict and who claims to treat addicts as a 'spiritual consultant', the article states that surfing offers a psycho-stimulant much like gambling and that this is why a *certain segment* of the population becomes addicted; virtual reality can become a substitute for real life because the pain of rejection is less with computers, they are more responsive, and one can "connect with another person using an altered persona."

The article goes on to point out that we are not all at risk for computer addiction. That is, while the disease is spreading beyond the white male computer 'techie' population, the rest of the Internet population is not equally at risk for developing IAD. Counselors claim that people with other addictions and compulsions (gambling, alcoholism, and so forth) are more likely to develop Net addiction. Says Claudia Evenson, Director of Addiction Services at Linden Oaks Hospital in Naperville, Illinois, "We're just beginning to realize that when we ask a person what their hobbies are and they say computers that that can be something we need to watch out for later on."

Note two factors at work in statements such as these. First, the classic disease framework is being used to claim that there is some fundamental difference between 'us and them'; those who 'have it' and those who 'do not have it'. Second, as Pfuhl and Henry [1993] and Rice [1996] have noted, individuals who become indoctrinated into the disease model of behavior in one instance are increasingly willing to adopt that same sort of self-labeling mechanism to explain other behaviors. Mental health professionals are hard at work on Phase Two of the deviance process; populating the socially constructed category of Internet addict.

As time moves on, certain populations of Internet participants are targeted and labeled as 'very vulnerable' to a behavioral disease. For IAD, one such target population is college students. In a June article in the APA Monitor entitled "Computer Addictions entangle students", Bridget Murray focuses on how vulnerable college students are to net addiction. Quoting Young, the article states, "Substitute the word 'computer' for 'substance' or 'alcohol' and you find that Internet obsession fits the classic Diagnostic and Statistical Manual definition of addiction". How this is possible remains unclear, as 'addiction' has not been in the DSM terminology since the original 1952 version. The article continues to cite Young: "People seek the same escapist, pleasurable feelings from the Internet that they seek from drugs, gambling or alcohol. Gambling gives them a high, alcohol numbs them and the Internet offers them an alternate reality. Just as people struggle to keep from taking a drink or popping a pill, they struggle to turn their computer off." And Kathleen Scherer, psychologist at the counseling and mental health center at the U of Texas at Austin says: "Internet social interactions can start to replace real social relationships." Finally, Kandell, psychologist at the University of Maryland, states that: "Students visiting chat rooms or playing MUD games can assume new, glamorous identities. Some start to believe that they're loved and cared for in their new identities - an illusion that these online relationships are the same as the real thing. Online you have the freedom to talk to anyone, be anything you want and not be censored for it. It's a sort of unconditional acceptance unusual in flesh-and-blood relationships that makes you less used to dealing with real life."

As will be discussed in later chapters, the two key points being asserted here, that online relationships are not 'real', and that online interaction provides unlimited freedom to do, say and be anything one wishes, are simply not true. However, arguments such as these are the fundamental basis for the construction of IAD as a social problem. It is the belief that the Internet is an anarchistic, anonymous, non-real format that makes possible its demonization by the uninitiated.

In fact, in a July article in Computerworld Magazine entitled "Just One More Click...", Daniel P. Dern attempts to get at this underlying assumption by pointing out that the research on the subject, to date, is inconclusive at best: "Computer-oriented obsessions are far from new. During the 1970s and 1980s, computer games such as Adventure, Zork and Rogue brought many a department to a productive standstill for days or even weeks." Dern argues that the same thing is happening now, as Usenet MUDs and IRC are becoming more sophisticated and accessible. Ultimately, however, Dern's argument went largely unnoticed, as the push to move through the deviance process continued.

In December of 1996, perhaps the most sensationalized article on IAD (before or since) appeared, again in the New York Times. The article, entitled "The Symptoms of Internet Addiction" began by describing the so-called withdrawal symptoms of someone going off the Net "cold turkey"; the account provides a description of the same physical symptoms as so-called drug withdrawal. The article then cites the story of the woman whose husband divorced her, claiming she was spending too much time online, rather than devoting herself to the care of the house and children. This story, (and one other similar story), is covered over and over again in popular press articles as 'proof' that the net really is addicting. And, as the reader is by now beginning to note, the Young and Brenner studies are cited over and over again as well, even though their methodologies are flawed and results inconclusive. It is not so much the veracity of the claims that is relevant, as it is *who is making them and how useful they are* in perpetuating desired myths within a given cultural framework.

Further, the New York Times article claims that there are a number of online sites to help people with their addiction, such as Netaholics Anonymous, Interneters Anonymous, and the IASG. These pages are cited as legitimate (and legitimating) sources, even though they are quite clearly structured to parody the idea of IAD. Again, this story notes that while Goldberg may have been joking when he listed symptoms and started his support group, for the people who have become regulars, IAD is real. In support of this argument, the article quotes Young and Kandell, respectively, as saying: "When pathological gambling first started, no one was taking it seriously." And, "Many addicts aren't yet seeking help because they are in denial. I think we're about a year away from having people recognize it's really a problem. It's out there. There's no question."

Of course, another way of understanding this argument is to state that "we are about a year away from completing phases one and two of the deviance process, and thus having IAD officially defined as 'real'". In a December article in Wired magazine entitled "'Internet Addiction' Meme Gets Media High", Janelle Brown makes this point precisely: "The media have discovered a new problem: Internet addiction. But reports about the alleged disease from The New York Times to CNN to PC Week - are primarily based on hype and misconstrued jokes." Brown points out what others in journalism already knew; that Goldberg started IAD and the IASG as parodies of the DSM IV and the psychiatric profession. She critiques the methodology and conclusions of the Young study, points out that Goldberg himself sees IAD as the latest incarnation of Internet paranoia, notes that a select few theorists and mental health professionals are quoted repeatedly, and states that most web sites dealing with the issue are purely satirical, even those referred to in the New York Times article as 'resources'.

And again in a December article in Newsweek entitled "Breathing is Also Addictive", Steven Levy also critiques New York Times article outlined above and the entire idea of addiction: "The problem with that article, and dozens like it that ran in 1996, is that 'Internet addiction' doesn't really exist. This disconnect between reality and reporting was symbolic of the general media's inability to convey the boggling changes that society is about to undergo, all because of our impending connectedness. The media declared 1995 the year of the Internet; in '96, we tried to explain it to you. The measure of our success, sadly, may one day be judged by the Internet-addiction scare." As Levy argues, and as Chapter Five discusses in detail, what keeps people online for hours is not web surfing (as even the limited studies outlined above point out), but unrestrained contact with other human beings.

But arguments such as these hold no sway in a culture that is firmly entrenched in and committed to the co-dependency movement and the accompanying self-help revolution. By the end of 1996, several mental health professionals around the country, convinced that IAD was 'real', had set up specialized practices to treat computer-dependent individuals and their significant others. For example, Maressa Hecht Orzack, of McLean Hospital in Massachusetts, has a Web page for her Computer Addiction Services practice, which includes treatment for addicts, significant others, educational outreach programs, and employee assistance programs.

In her overview of IAD, she states that the new disorder may be called computer addiction, Internet addictive disorder or cyberaddiction. Claiming that IAD is very similar to pathological gambling or compulsive shopping, she lists psychological and physical symptoms, states that it has been identified by some professionals and the media, and suggests that the addicted one is not the only one affected (noting that family therapists often hear about IAD because significant others are usually the ones who bring complaints to a therapist).

Orzack, who uses cognitive behavior therapy to teach the patient to identify the problem and to learn coping skills to prevent relapse argues, "We are just seeing the tip of the iceberg. Our society is becoming more and more computer dependent. . . This trend is a potential problem affecting all ages. . .Computer addiction is the use of computers in order to change an individual's mood." Interestingly, just as Young's research into (or construction of) IAD was sparked by personal experiences, Orzack states that she, too, noted a 'problem' with her own behavior regarding time spent online, which she then began attributing to clients: "I noticed that I was spending too much time on computer games. This led me to realize that behavior of this kind could be an addiction. I made a connection between my own computer experiences and my research in addictive disorders and treatment of addictive behaviors and impulse control disorders."

So, by the end of 1996, despite people like Brown, Dern and Goldberg pointing out that IAD was a complete fabrication, Phase One of the deviance process was essentially complete. The socially constructed category of Internet addicted had been firmly implanted in the minds of the general public, and in the minds of enough academics, researchers, and clinical practitioners and journalists to sustain it as a 'real' disorder. However, a very important piece of work remained; that of constructing the deviant population in such a way as to simultaneously sustain the notion that IAD could strike 'anyone', while suggesting that certain 'types' within that population were more susceptible than others. In other words, people must be made to feel vulnerable, in such a manner that they monitor their own behavior closely for potential problems. But at the same time, they must be afforded the opportunity to believe that there is something fundamentally different about their natures (essential selves) that makes them less likely to fall victim. Such criteria allow for a central step in the process of constructing a social self; that of creating 'in' groups and 'out' groups. It was to this step, Phase Two of the deviance process, that 1997 was largely devoted.

According to research and popular press articles, those most likely to be afflicted with IAD are children, students and housewives. In an April article in the Cavalier Daily entitled "Caught in the Web", Geoffrey Maurer focused on vulnerable college students with free Internet access on campus. Citing Young's study as evidence that IAD is "a significant disorder which negatively impacts social, occupational, family and financial functioning", Maurer argues that university students can easily fall prey to addiction and that the convenience of free online services panders to the compulsive user: "IAD surfs its way through communities, claiming victims who cannot resist the WWW temptations . . . people can retain anonymity, hide their true identity. . ."

And, in a June article in The Cincinnati Enquirer entitled "Internet blamed for neglect: Police say mother addicted to web", Tanya Bricking cites another case of a housewife accused of child neglect due to excessive online use: "Internet addiction led a 24-year-old mother of three to leave her children in conditions so filthy that police took them away, police said Sunday. The playroom of her apartment had broken glass, debris and child handprints of human feces on the walls." And again, the article quotes psychologist David Greenfield as saying that 'people can become addicted to just about anything. . . the addiction is similar to that of gambling. It's potent. There's instant gratification. It becomes a pretty powerful drug." Comparisons are drawn between this case and the one in the Pacific Northwest (cited above) in which another mother 'spent too much time online' and her husband sued for custody of the children. The underlying suggestion of such analyses is that 'empirical evidence' of IAD is in keeping with Young's preliminary findings that housewives are one of several groups who are particularly vulnerable to Internet addiction.

Grohol, coordinator of the online Mental Health Network, is one who has continued to reassert the point that, "the problem is that we don't have any research", and has noted that 'that kind of research takes years to do— and that professionals in the psychiatric community do not 'come up with' diagnoses after single case reports'. He suggests that net-skeptical traditional media have taken every opportunity to feed net hype and fears regarding pedophiles, and now addiction. Thus, articles such as those in the Enquirer continue to flourish, and belief in IAD continues to grow. When Young presented her findings from her original study in more detail during the August 1997 meeting of the APA, outlining the specific 'types' of people vulnerable to IAD in more detail, reports ricocheted through the media.

On August 15th, an article appeared in c/net news online which cited Young's study, outlining her findings about who is most likely to be addicted, how much time addicts spend online, and so forth. Interestingly, the article does point out that, because her colleagues in the mental health community loathe calling it (IAD) an addiction, Young was forced to change the label to 'pathological use'. However, she continued to use addiction in her survey and reports.

Another article appeared on August 15th, this one in Wired Magazine. Entitled "Shrink Speaks: The Net is Addictive", the piece focused on Young's 1997 APA presentation, and claimed that her findings were no different than in the previous study and she was simply rehashing old data in order to secure media exposure. As did the article above, this piece noted that Young switched to the 'pathological Internet use' label, because, to date, there had been no formal acceptance of her proposal to put Internet absorption on the same footing with gambling or alcohol addiction.

And on August 18th, another article cited Young's latest 'findings' from the APA meeting. In this piece in the Computer News Daily, entitled "Internet Addiction Starting to Wreck Lives", author Bill Hendrick appears to take the study at face value, avoiding any examination of the methodology or underlying assumptions. Summarizing Young's findings, Hendrick states: "Net addicts establish virtual relationships that feel close but really aren't." Those findings, in essence, detail Young's perception of the rewards that 'drive' people to Internet addiction, and the types of people most likely to fall victim.

For example, articles in the August 28th and September 3rd editions of USA Today state: "Three rewards drive what Young calls Internet Addiction Disorder. . .(first) community - meeting friends online. Overdoing it can be a sign of neglected real life personal relationships. . . (second) fantasy - adopting new personas or playing out sexual fantasies. . . (third) power - instant access to information and new people, a positive that can go bad." Interestingly, this second presentation of findings from her same study generated far more publicity for Young, despite the fact that she had been forced by that time to re-label the disorder as 'pathological Internet use'. Because of a refusal by those officially in charge of constructing the DSM to equate Internet 'absorption' with pathological gambling or alcohol addiction, Young chose an 'official' label of pathological use. However, she continued to use IAD as the label in her presentations.

Continuing with the theme that children and students are particularly vulnerable, Joyce Kasman Valenza of TechLife magazine authored a September article entitled "Lonely and Bored Children May Use Computer

As Escape". Again, Valenza relies primarily on the experience of Orzack, who claims that children and college students are most vulnerable to IAD. She also cites Young, who claims that "Internet addiction has now gained credibility among mental health professionals as a clinically significant disorder which negatively impacts social, occupational, family and financial functioning." What remains unclear is why, if this is the case, Young altered the label of this disorder from IAD to the milder 'pathological Internet use' as noted above.

Further, an article in the September/October issue of Stanford Today (Online) entitled "The Lonely Planet: Computers Make Our Lives Easier - And Pull Us Further Apart" focused on work of Sara Stein, a psychiatrist at Stanford's medical center. Stein, who believes that adolescents are very vulnerable to IAD, says ". . . the anonymity of the net renders the majority of normal users indistinguishable from the small minority of insidious, sociopathic and dangerous ones. But computer addiction may be the more prevalent problem. Humans can become physiologically and psychologically addicted to substances or habits, ranging from heroin to shopping. . . Why not computers and the Internet?" Stein goes on to outline the symptoms, which include a preference for online relationships and recognized addiction symptoms of tolerance and withdrawal: "Computer addiction can have serious consequences: major depression, psychotic disorders, sleep disorders and even drug abuse."

What is interesting to note is that professionals in the mental health field such as Stein continue to rely on the traditional symptoms of tolerance and withdrawal, even though such symptoms have no basis in biological fact and have been so watered down in the DSM as to be irrelevant. Further, as Grohol [October 7, 1997] notes, definitions of pathological use are problematic because, quite simply, there are no baseline measures of what 'normal' use might be: "The most taken-for-granted concept is that there is an absolute definition for what is 'normal'. . . (there is a tendency for) mental health professionals to misunderstand and mis-diagnose overuse of the Internet with little to no baseline data. How can one talk of 'overuse' when the data which exists today is very preliminary in terms of 'normal' Internet use. . . What are we left with in terms of a disorder specifically caused by the online world? Exactly where we were originally. No such disorder at this time has been proven to exist. Research to date is still muddy, inconclusive, preliminary and contradictory. Until much more careful research is conducted, overuse of the Internet may exist. . . but it is not a disorder."

Orzack, too, in a November article in the Middlesex News entitled "Web Junkies: When does interest cross the line to addiction?", claims that IAD is 'as real as alcoholism' and that the symptoms include withdrawal, loss of control and compulsive behavior. And she goes on to point out that, "A lot of computer addiction that we see is brought to our attention by the spouse's partner." As the reader has by now noted, it is primarily those who Pfuhl and Henry [1993] call the 'moral entrepreneurs' who 'recognize' the symptoms of IAD in their significant others and attempt to control that behavior by labeling it from a clinical framework. Such efforts serve to complete phase two of the deviance process, the population of the deviant category with specific individuals.

Not surprisingly, with this type of media attention devoted to it, IAD has truly become the disease of the 1990s. Young people and students continue to be defined as the population most likely to fall victim to IAD, as evidenced by such articles as:

1. "Internet Addiction Growing on College Campuses" [Liebert Publishing], which cited Kandell's article in the inaugural edition of the new Cyberpsychology journal, a publication devoted entirely to the psychology of online interaction; 2. "Net Addiction a Campus Problem?" This piece also focused on Kandell's article in Cyberpsychology [c/net news online], in which the author asserts that Internet addiction on campus is a rapidly growing epidemic and cites studies by various universities that estimate the average time students spend online; and 3. "Internet Addiction", a February 18 article by Bill Maxwell, which also cites the article by Kandell as 'proof' that Internet addiction is real, and that students are particularly vulnerable to this illness. The article defines IAD as "a psychological dependence on the Internet, regardless of the type of activity once logged on", and claims that its victims drop out of school at a higher rate than non-addicts.

The reader by now begins to get the idea that, even though the evidence to support the notion of behaviors as addictions is non-existent, the popularity of the idea of Internet addiction continues to grow. By the end of 1998, self-help IAD groups and 'treatment' centers staffed by mental health professionals had popped up all over the United States, and all over the Internet. Young's Center for On-Line Addiction (COLA) is billed as first online counseling service, consultation firm and training institute for Internet addiction. The site offers personal counseling, corporate and professional services for executives, mental health practitioners and educators, customized workshops, and so forth.

Lay people are getting in on the act as well. A February article in Jacksonville Business entitled "Internet Addiction: Local Support Group

Forming to Help Those with Web Obsessions" chronicles the story of a Jacksonville man who has organized a local self-help group for people who spend too much time online. He calls it Online Anonymous. He is not a mental health professional, but says he is "struggling with online addiction" and that struggle has given him insight into what it takes to kick the habit. He plans to model the group after AA and its 12-step program and says, "Once I gave up trying to do it as a human being and invited God in, then I started doing all right."

By the end of 1998, much of the deviance process with regard to Internet Addiction Disorder was complete. The deviant category had been defined as real; if not 'real enough' to be included in the DSM, it was at least legitimated by and legitimating of countless research projects, news articles, counseling centers and self-help groups. Further, a rough sketch of the common 'potential victims' (students, children, bored housewives) had been established; the category had begun to be populated. As we shall see in the following chapter, in keeping with the philosophy of liberation psychotherapy, much of the work of populating this deviant category was accomplished by the 'deviants' themselves. In a sense, the popularity of 'addiction' as an explanation for a wide range of human behaviors, coupled with a program of medicalizing human social behaviors and a generalized apprehension regarding mediated communications, lends itself in the instance of Internet addiction to the compression of the final two phases of the deviance process (consequences of labeling and the transformation of stigma) into this second phase. In short, many of the 'victims' of Internet addiction have readily adopted that role; they have selected the label for themselves, and have used it as 'the real explanation' of their behaviors. A brief history of the cultural framework which has encouraged this selection, as well as the specifics of how such an identity is established in interaction, are the subjects of the next chapter.

Chapter 4

AN EASY MARK:
TARGETING ONLINE INTERACTION

As has been implied throughout the course of this work, many aspects of the Western cultural framework were instrumental in the deviance process outlined in Chapter Three. That is, while humans do, in fact, construct the standards of normalcy and deviance in interaction, they rely to a certain extent on a foundation (or culture) set in place by other human interaction well in advance of the current campaign. Regarding the construction of IAD, perhaps the two most significant factors were the trend towards medicalization of deviant behavior and a generalized sense of fear of (or at least ambivalence about) mediated communications of all forms. This chapter is devoted to an overview of these trends and to a detailed account of the ways in which such factors permeate the legitimation of IAD 'in the minds of individuals.

A BRIEF HISTORY OF MEDICALIZATION

While previous chapters provided a brief summary of the medicalization of behavior, a more detailed examination is in order if we are to understand the link between medicalization, mediated communications, and the re-definition of social interaction as a 'disorder'. Medicalization of behavior is rooted in the 'germ theory of disease'. Developed in the late 1800s, this theory gave rise to what we think of today as scientific medicine. Scientific medicine, in which the body is viewed as a machine, is based in part on the 'doctrine of specific etiology', meaning that each disease is caused by a specific germ or agent. The framework focuses on the internal environment (the physical body) and ignores the external *social* environment. As this doctrine has, over time, has been applied not only to physical ailments, but to mental, emotional, and behavioral issues as well, the focus has shifted to the medicalization of deviant behaviors specifically. Thus, in short, medicalization is the defining and labeling of deviant behavior as a medical problem, usually an illness, and the mandating of the medical profession to provide some type of treatment for it. This process has two steps; the social construction of an illness, and the social construction of deviance as a special type of illness.

Consider first the social construction of illness in general. At its core, illness is nothing more and nothing less than a negative human social judgment of existing conditions in the natural world. When such negative social judgments, based as they are on the germ theory of disease, are applied to human behavior, the end result is a redefinition of devalued behaviors as illnesses (step two). In contrast to deviant behaviors defined as crimes (of which there are relatively few today), behaviors defined as illnesses "locate the source of deviant behavior within the individual, postulating a physiological, constitutional, organic, or occasionally, psychogenic agent or condition that is assumed to cause the behavioral deviance . . . usually mandating intervention by medical personnel with medical means. . ." [Conrad 1980, 25] Thus, while willful deviance is equated with crime and dealt with by agents of social control such as the police and court system, unwillful deviance is equated with illness, and the appropriate agent of social control is medicine.

Historically, this disease model was applied to unexplained behaviors, and lead ultimately to the emergence of 'mental illness' as discussed in Chapters One and Two. Mental illness, which in previous centuries was labeled 'madness', 'occurred' largely through humanitarian efforts to 'treat' the mad and cure them–they were redefined as ill and not criminal.

As Conrad [1980] notes, "Medicine has not always been the powerful, prestigious, successful, lucrative and dominant profession we know today. Its status is a result of medical politicking and therapeutic expertise. . ." In ancient societies, disease was given supernatural explanations and 'medicine' was the province of priests or shamans. Though Hippocrates in ancient Greece rejected such explanations and developed the first theory of 'natural' causes of disease, his work was largely ignored through the Middle Ages, when Christians viewed illness as a punishment for sin. The Renaissance in Europe brought renewed interest to Hippocrates' theory and marked the drift toward natural explanations of disease and the emergence of medicine as an occupation separate from the Church. Medical theory in Europe developed slowly, and diagnoses were often inaccurate, based as they were upon the patients' descriptions of symptoms, the physicians' observations of symptoms and the patients' appearance and behavior. Rarely was a medical exam of any sort administered. Medicine was by no means scientific. Colonial American medicine was even less well developed. There were no medical schools and few practices–further, there were no regulations on who could call himself a doctor. There was virtually no medical theory. Only in the early 19th century did medicine become a full-time vocation–before that, it was practiced part time by teachers, clergymen, and the like.

In the first half of the 19th century, important changes took place. Educated physicians convinced state legislatures to pass laws limiting the practice of medicine to persons of a certain training and class. However, those laws were repealed in the late 1820s and early 1830s because they were considered elitist, and a number of different medical sects developed, based upon which types of therapies they utilized. Such sectarianism, combined with lack of medical theory and ineffective and often harmful medical treatments contributed to the low status and lack of prestige of early 19th century medicine. Better-educated practitioners were concerned about such problems, and in 1847 founded the American Medical Association (AMA) to "promote the science and art of medicine and the betterment of public health". The AMA was also designed to enforce standards and ethics of what was considered 'regular' medical practice (with homeopathic and botanical physicians defined as 'irregular'), thereby striving for exclusive professional and economic rights to medical turf. The AMA was the crux of the attempt to professionalize medicine; through this organization, physicians sought to constitute, consolidate and control the market for their expertise. A medical monopoly was created. [Conrad 1980]

In the second half of the 19th century, the medical profession was frequently involved in various social reform activities. Physicians became medical crusaders, attempting to influence public morality and behavior. This crusading often led them into the moral sphere, making them advocates for moral positions that were only marginally related to medical practice. They sought to change people's values.[17] The lines between sickness and

---

[17] The interested reader is referred to Conrad's discussion of the role of physicians in issues such as abortion, birth control, eugenics and social hygiene.

deviance were sometimes not clearly drawn; some diseases were considered deviance, and some deviance became defined as disease. With the rise and relative success of the germ theory of disease (compared to procedures such as bloodletting, blistering, purging and the like), the social status of the medical profession began to improve. This was true even though the most significant reductions in diseases like smallpox, malaria, and cholera were largely the result of better nutrition and housing, and improved public sanitation. With this added clout, the AMA continued its drive to restrict medical practice to the 'regular' methods, to the exclusion of the irregular procedures mentioned above.

By the end of the 19th century, significant medical breakthroughs had been made in surgical medicine and hospital care. It is at this point that the germ theory of disease was born, and gave rise to scientific medicine under a unified paradigm that viewed the body as a machine and promoted the doctrine of specific etiology as outlined above. New licensing laws were established, which sealed the monopoly on the practice of medicine. Not only was there a monopoly on medicine, but it was a self-regulating monopoly, in which the members were insulated from external evaluation. Members defined the territory of medicine and set the standards for treatment without interference from any outside groups. Since that time, the medical sector of society has grown enormously, and in the 20th century has become the second largest industry in America. [Conrad 1980]

Like the history of physical disease, the history of mental illness has its roots in the belief that supernatural powers were at work in the mind of the mad, and that madness was some sort of punishment for sinful behavior. And, like the history of physical disease, this notion of madness as supernatural was first uprooted by the medical model of madness in ancient Greece and Rome. However, when the Roman Empire collapsed in the 5th century, belief in madness as supernatural returned and lasted through the Middle Ages. Again, the Renaissance in Europe revived the medical model of madness; madness became 'mental illness'. Four significant changes between the 16th and 18th centuries brought about the ascendance of the medical model of madness: the 'great confinement' of lunatics and other deviants; the separation of the able-bodied from the lunatics; the entrance of physicians; and the emergence of a unitary concept of mental illness. [Conrad 1980, 44]

The Great Confinement refers to that period in the mid 17th century when harmless mad people who had roamed the countrysides and towns of Europe under a feudal system and were seen as the responsibility of local communities were first 'hospitalized' and formally excluded from the community. Such confinement was required in order to accommodate a shift to the capitalistic enterprise. However, the institutions in which such individuals were placed offered no actual treatment. Rather, these places served as the legitimate means by which 'mad' people were confined (along with criminals, beggars, prostitutes, the unemployed and the poor). Further, such institutions mandated that occupants work; they provided cheap manpower in periods of full employment and reabsorption of the idle in low employment times.

After a time, the grouping together of such social outcasts began to lose its economic utility. For the sake of efficiency, the able-bodied and lunatics were separated from one another. This separation gave rise to special institutions like the workhouse, madhouse and the prison; the mad were separated from the other deviants, not for treatment, but to protect the others from 'contagion' of madness and to impose order in the workhouse.

Throughout the 17th and 18th centuries, physicians played a small role in the confinement of the mad and provided little treatment. However, with the rise of optimism about medicine's ability to solve problems, the germ theory of disease was transferred to treatment of the mentally ill as well. By the end of the 18th century, the physician was essential to the madhouse; it was the physician who was capable of certifying people to be confined in such a manner.

Central to the rise of the physician's role in classifying and treating the mentally ill was the emergence of a 'unitary concept of mental illness'. For the first time, the concept of the *mind* came in to being, and was used as an explanation for madness; a person's 'state of mind' caused deviant behavior. Thus, 'illness' came to include misconduct and the deviant behavior commonly known as madness; what started as a myth was reified and later used to justify medical involvement and authority over madness. ". . . scientific empirical knowledge of the origin of madness and the physician's ability to 'cure' mental disease played at the most a small role in the development of a popular concept of mental illness   by the late 18th century the concept of mental illness was becoming the dominant definition of madness" [Conrad 1980, 48]

The American's mimicked the Europeans in both thought processes regarding madness and the process of institutionalization of the mad and their gradual separation from other able bodied workers. During the 19th century, there was an 'epidemic' of asylum building–in 1824 there were only two state asylums, but by 1860, 28 of the 33 states had public institutions. As noted in Chapter Two, a number of social forces, including an increase in social mobility and political participation, an increase in religious and intellectual freedom, and greater geographic mobility, all served to create a sense of anxiety among citizens about the future of their fledgling republic. Many saw these trends as an overall erosion of discipline, as something that needed to be corrected–as the primary cause of deviant behavior. In this view, mental illness is caused by social forces; forces of great social change. And because the environment can cause mental illness, the environment can also be used to cure it. Specifically, a structured environment, in which the ill were isolated from the healthy, was the means to the cure. By 1880, there were 75 state asylums.

However, the cure rates purported by asylums were never met, and optimism for the system waned. Institutions reverted to custodial care and abandoned treatment and cure plans. In terms of the history of the medical conception of madness, the 19th century was a significant period. In the United States, as in England, madness moved once and for all into medical turf. Alienists (as physicians of the insane were called) were able to gain a monopoly over the definition and treatment of madness. All new asylums were run by medical superintendents. Medical men did not have 'scientific' evidence of mental disease, nor did the asylum as such offer a medical cure. In fact, both their causes and cures were social. Medicine was embraced as much for its humanitarian 'moral treatment' as for any technical expertise. By the time the early optimism of asylum cures had waned, medicine had secured control over the domain of insanity. Again, this was accomplished without physiological evidence for cause and before the advent of successful 'medical' treatments. In America as in Europe, medical dominance of madness was a social and political rather than a scientific achievement. As Conrad [1980] explains:

"In the early 20th century, the discovery of general paresis reinforced medical conceptions of madness and gave rise to a hope that the organic causes of all mental illness would be similarly discovered. The wide acceptance of Freudian ideas in the first half of this century both muted and expanded the medical model of madness. A psychogenic model was grafted onto the medical model. In the 1930s, with the advent of shock therapy, lobotomies, and genetic theories, somatic conceptions of madness reemerged. By the 1950s, partly through efforts of the mental hygiene movement, public attitudes toward mental illness changed in the direction of medical ones. The public, however, still maintained a narrower view of what constitutes mental illness.

"In 1955, because of the introduction of phenothiazine drugs, mental hospital populations began to decline. The diffusion of drug treatments aligned well with medical concepts of madness, since psychiatrists could now give medications for the 'illness'. The drug revolution, the declining hospital populations, and an increased interest in the social aspects of madness preceded a major change in social policy: the development of community mental health centers. The community mental health movement, and its professional arm, community psychiatry, were an attempt to turn psychiatric concepts to community problems. Although community psychiatry encompassed a range of opinions, in its extreme forms it was the psychiatricization of everything. The 1970s have seen somewhat of a decline in interest in community psychiatry and a resurgence of organic and biomedical theories of madness.

"There are a few recurrent themes in our history of the medical concept of madness. Medical theories have located the source of madness in a variety of somatic organs: the humorous, the stomach, the nervous system, the brain. Every era seems to have its own reform movements that lead to an increased optimism, which several years later, after the movements fail to live up to their promise, reverts to a pessimistic view of madness. This has often taken the form of a 'somatic pessimism', locating the causes of madness in physiology. Medical involvement with madness, historically speaking, emerges more as a humanitarian reform than as a biomedical accomplishment. It is worth repeating that medical concepts became the dominant conceptions of madness long before there was any evidence that madness had any biophysiological components, and before any medical treatments, other than the non-medical moral treatment, made any impact on madness. The development of the medical model of madness was a social and political rather than a scientific achievement." [pp. 71-72]

CRITIQUES OF MASS ELECTRONICALLY-MEDIATED COMMUNICATIONS

Combining with this medicalized view of human behavior to produce a 'disorder' out of what might otherwise be considered 'just talking' is a general apprehension about mass, electronically mediated communications. As the brief history that follows will detail, this apprehension stems largely from the belief that there is some fundamentally 'real' form of communication (face-to-face), and that all other forms are lacking this 'realness' by comparison. Beginning with the birth of print media, this argument has most recently been applied to electronic media such as television and, finally now, computers. The following statement by Ernest van der Haag [1968] is representative of the basic argument critics have made about mass, electronically mediated communication:

> "All mass media in the end alienate people from personal experience and, though appearing to offset it, intensify their moral isolation from each other, from reality and from themselves. One may turn to mass media when lonely or bored. But mass media, once they become a habit, impair the capacity for meaningful experience." [p. 5]

From this perspective, such communication is seen as a social problem, and ultimately not real communication at all. Although this argument has been made about print-mediated communications such as newspapers, books and magazines [Snow 1983], the critique in the recent past has focused on television. As noted by James Anderson and Timothy Meyer [1988], such critiques generally fall into the 'traditional' or 'effects' oriented theory of media and follow what Denis McQuail [1994] calls the social disintegration framework. That is, such critiques of mass, electronically mediated communication "locate the cause of media effects in the text itself, establish the agent of action in the individual responding to the text and find the effect in the behavioral acts attributed to the individual acting under the influence of the text." [Anderson and Meyer 1988, 311] Further, these social disintegration critiques hinge upon two basic arguments: first, people lose a sense of 'who they are' or personal identity; and second, people lose a sense of real community and meaningful interaction with others.

This notion of people 'acting under the influence' is exemplified in the critiques of people such as Bernard Rosenberg [1971] who suggests that, "television is an hallucinogen. . .the masses are victims of a merciless technological invasion that threatens to destroy their humanity. . .it anesthetizes people and they are tricked into believing everything they see on television." [pp. 4-6] Similarly, Dwight MacDonald [1968] claimed that because of this effect, viewers become 'passive consumers' who lose their human identity because they are no longer related as members of a community. According to this critique, results are two-fold; people lose their sense of self and must look to television for a confirmation of self-image

[Mills 1968], and, ultimately, the television is a tool of political domination, of tyranny.

Perhaps the most forceful critique comes from Jacques Ellul [1991], who, in his analysis of the effects of mass, electronically mediated communications on personal identity and community, suggests that the world is not a global village (as McLuhan suggests) for four reasons. First, people no longer know each other person-to-person. That is, people do not know the personality, nature and ideology of the individual transmitting the information. Second, the human relationship is greatly altered when information is transmitted through technology because words are dissociated from the people who say them; it is impossible for this to be otherwise. Third, in the real village, the information transmitted was relevant to people's lives and they could change a course of action as a result. This is not the case with mass communication. Finally, Ellul argues that ". . .only technicians use the mass media, and it is out of the question to penetrate their domain. The amateur has only his hobby. He is more eager to accept the information, because he feels he is taking part in the big game. The belief that anyone can send information is only a wish and a myth; not reality. . . . the proliferation of media seems to be fundamentally anti-democratic." [Ellul 1991, 353]

Most recently, communication mediated through computer technology has suffered criticism similar to that described above. In general, such critiques may be subsumed under one of four basic and interrelated arguments, which claim the following: first, interaction on the Internet is anonymous and thus unlike real social interaction; second, no one can be held accountable for the statements he or she makes; third, because there is no formal government, the Internet is in a state of anarchy; and fourth, because of these factors, the Internet does not constitute a real community.

Turning first to anecdotal critiques [Gravino 1995] made by people who participate in the Internet to varying degrees, one finds these arguments made regularly. Consider the following examples. Andre Bacard, a physicist at Stanford, comments on a tendency for excessive computer use in some people, "Their entire social world is vicarious, it encourages and cultivates psychosis in many people." [p. E2] James Donley, medical director of outpatient psychiatry at the University of Kansas Medical Center, comments, "It lets people have a fairly simple relationship, where you can kind of predict or dictate what happens. . .you don't have to put up with all the things about human relationships that are both exciting and unpleasant. It can be used as an avoidance of social relationships." [p. E2]

This notion of predictability and simple relationships is common among critics of so-called 'virtual' communities. Michael Heim [1995], a philosophy teacher and author, suggests that virtual community seems to be a 'cure-all for isolated people who won't give up their isolation'. He comments that "I know people in rural communities who hear wishful thinking in the phrase 'virtual community'. . . For many, real community means a difficult, never-resolved struggle. It's a sharing that cannot be virtual because its reality arises from the public places that people share. . . For many, the 'as-if-community' lacks the rough interdependence of life shared." [p. 3] Heim, taking this distinction between so-called virtual community and real community as an appropriate one, goes on to suggest that people can and should learn to juggle those worlds, that the 'worlds of the primary body and the cyberbody need to reinforce one another'.

Other critics of the Internet suggest that there are a lot of 'fringe group' elements on the Internet, and that the lack of government combined with anonymity shield these users from law enforcement, unlike the real world. Walter Mossberg [1995], columnist for the Wall Street Journal, says:

> Virtual communities are clubs for the technically adept. They must become more like open, democratic societies where people take responsibility for their actions and welcome the participation of others. The on-line community is not a digital democracy because discussion occurs in a climate where people hide behind assumed names and can smear others with impunity and censor those they don't like. [p. B1].

He goes on to say that there are three main problem areas. First, there is anonymity; participants do not have to use 'real' names and thus it is impossible to figure out the 'true' identity of someone making claims. This so-called lack of true identity supposedly makes it easier to engage in malicious activities, such as smearing people, concocting financial scams, and victimizing people sexually. Mossberg claims that this problem applies to Bulletin Board Systems (BBS) and chat-room discussions and that, even though these constitute a large part of the Internet, nothing can be done because no one is in control. The second problem cited by Mossberg is incivility; it is too easy to 'flame' people and on-line discussions too often break down into name-calling that would not be tolerated in a real-life meeting or social setting. There are no limits to expression except to be 'flamed' or canceled through vigilante justice.

Finally, there is the problem of censorship and intimidation; any participant may attempt to scare or gag people with whom he or she disagrees:

> This vigilante justice finds wide approval or at least absence of condemnation. It is the digital equivalent of dictatorships. Hackers can get in anywhere because there is no security and no one is in control. For the same reason, there is no personal privacy. Further, because there is no central authority, and people do not want security which interferes with the cultural dictates of free and open communication, vandals won't be stopped until bounty hunters are recruited to hunt them down. [p. B1]

Bart Ziegler and Jared Sandberg, also columnists for the Wall Street Journal, liken the Internet to talk radio, "Internet sessions can be like talk radio, with participants making strident or even subversive arguments just to get heard. The comments can be anonymous, and their accuracy hard to verify. These discussions are no-holds-barred gripe sessions. This is a problem because people play on human fears and a willingness to believe everything that passes over electronic networks" [p. B1]. Continuing this analogy between talk radio and Internet communication, Michael Halloran, a professor of communication, suggests that the computer medium itself may be the determining factor in the ability of participants to communicate effectively.

Halloran [1995] proposes that, in its current state of development, computer users are limited to words and emoticons.[18] Thus, Internet flamers may simply be frustrated by their situation, and their frustration may express itself in the creation and excoriation of villains. In the virtual spaces of the airwaves and the Internet, I can become a transparent ego. The rantings of flamers on talk-radio and the Internet maybe the spontaneous overflow of strong feelings, untempered by either the tranquility of recollection or the constraints of sociality. By placing people where they are morally alone and audible to thousands, these media may be releasing the dark feelings we once learned to conceal from all but our closest intimates, even from ourselves. [p. 11]

Two of these comments in particular are most relevant to the issues at hand here. The first is the notion that interaction through computers is a

---

[18] Emoticons are symbols generated through combining keyboard symbols into forms that resemble human actions or expressions. The most common emoticon is the 'smiley', which can take on many shapes, but is usually indicated as :-)

social problem; it pulls participants away from so-called real social interaction and limits their ability to deal with others because they are accustomed to being able to manipulate situations involving the computer. The second is the idea that people are indiscriminate in their choices of what information to believe or what interactions to engage in simply because such information has passed through the computer medium. Traditional critiques of television claimed similar outcomes when they suggested that people are 'tricked into believing' everything they see on television. Whether these claims are, in fact, true is left for Chapter Five. However, it is worth noting that, within the relatively limited body of scholarly analysis of CMC currently available to us, some people who study the Internet and claim that there are groups which constitute communities, still do not really dispute the suggestions that the CMC involves a high level of anonymity, lack of authority and understood norms, and anarchy. In fact, they seem to argue that the Internet contains communities in spite of these obstacles, without challenging this common sense understanding of interaction through computers.

For example, in his study of interactions on the Whole Earth 'Lectronic Link, or WELL, Marc Smith [1992] claims that because virtual interaction is aspatial, asynchronous, acorporal and astigmatic, it is anonymous. That is, there is no necessary link to 'who one is' in 'real life', even though he argues that people do construct computer-specific identities.

In her analysis of Internet Relay Chat (IRC) chat-rooms, Elisabeth Reid [1991] uses Geertz's definition of culture to argue that chat-rooms do, in fact, constitute communities. However, simultaneous with this claim, she utilizes the analytical framework of Kiesler, Siegel and McGuire [1984] to argue that, because chat-rooms suffer from an absence of regulating feedback, 'dramaturgical weakness', few social status cues and anonymity, IRC as a whole has few widespread norms, etiquette is not readily apparent, and computer mediated communication is thus uninhibited and non-conforming. What remains unclear is how culture, as defined, develops under the circumstances proposed in this framework.

Still other analysts of computer mediated communication, while not directly arguing the extent to which on-line community is so-called 'real' community, imply the virtual/real community dualism in the very way in which the problem is set up to be discussed. In their discussion of the social consequences of CMC, Chesebro and Bonsall [1989] contend that ". . .socially, computerized communication is clearly a double-edged sword. It can function as either a social or an antisocial force. The strategies we develop to deal with computerized communications need to be our own and to promote our own ends." [pp. 121-122] Chesebro and Bonsall suggest that people 'overcompensate' for the incompleteness of the computer contact through various means, such as using more informal and expressive language that would otherwise be used or through developing computer friendships. The authors go on to cite numerous works which claim that interaction through computers restricts access to the full range of communicative insights possible in face-to-face communication. In short, it is a nonsocial experience that can remove individuals from real human communication and displace the uniqueness and humanity of more traditional modes of communication.

Having outlined the process by which human behavior has become medicalized, and the basic critiques of electronically-mediated communications, I now turn to examples, all taken from an online Internet addiction self-help group, of how such interpersonally functional and socially legitimated arguments are used in the deviance process to support the notion of human interaction as a disorder. In general, there are three major contributors to the social construction of Internet Addiction Disorder online; academic researchers, 'significant others', and the 'victims' of IAD themselves.[19] What follows is an examination of how these three groups work in concert to define and legitimate not only the general social label of Internet addict, but the specific role expectations of those who adopt that label. As the reader will note, members of each of these three groups rely heavily on one another to accomplish this task.

Consider first the role of the academic researcher. As explained in the previous chapter, academics have played a vital role in the construction of IAD. Ignoring for the moment that it was an academic who started IAD and an accompanying on line support group as a joke, other researchers (and even aspiring researchers) in the field of mental health have been instrumental in moving IAD past this initial phase. Of course, the most notable of those has been Kimberly Young. However, Young's role has not been limited to writing academic articles based upon online surveys of self-labeling Internet addicts, nor even to operating the Center for Online Addiction (COLA). She is also a fairly regular contributor to Goldberg's

---

[19] Journalists often 'lurk' silently in such groups, looking for story material (as noted in previous chapters) but rarely contribute anything directly to group members through online communications.

Internet Addiction Support Group (IASG). Within this group, Young appears to play a dual role; that of recovering Internet addict and that of counselor (though she denies this latter role to her online companions, insisting that she is just another group member).

Regarding the role of recovering addict, consider the following posts, in which Young describes her personal experiences with online addiction and how they compelled her to begin researching the problem professionally:

From: "Kimberly S. Young"
Subject: Clarification

Given a few of the recent posts, I wanted to clarify what I feel is an important issue. As I mentioned before, I am not the moderator of this list and my role here is not as a *professional* but as a group *member*. Therefore, please do not refer to me as Dr. Young, it is Kimberly (which I sign in my emails).

While I do study Internet addiction, I have tried not to offer my opinions as an authority but I share my views as a fellow participant. As many of you know, I struggled with my *own* addiction to the Internet. Especially when I began to study this phenomenon, I had a difficult time pulling myself away from chat rooms and found that on-line relationships filled a void in my life. Therefore, I personally find this group helpful.

I first thought about studying Internet addiction when my friend called me whose marriage almost ended due to her husband's obsession with chatting. However, it was my own experience along with those I began to interview early on which motivated me to devote my field of study to on-line behavior. As I spoke with more people, it quickly became clear to me how serious compulsive Internet use was as their lives had become completely unmanageable (lost jobs, divorce, parents worried for their children, students failing school, financial debt). In also speaking with family members, I saw how cyber affairs broke up marriages and the pain for the entire family this caused.

Many complained that little information on the topic was available which inspired me to write "Caught in the Net" and build my web site. But even as I caution in the book, these things are only a first step for further discovery with more research and clinical study needed. And I am glad to see that continued work is being done.

While I am rambling here, I did want to publicly thank all of you who have privately emailed me for your kind comments about how helpful these materials have been to you. I am glad to know that my work has made a difference. And thank you for listening.

Sincerely,

Kimberly

And:

From: "Kimberly S. Young"
Subject: Re: online relationships

On Sat, 26 Sep 1998 WriterRad@aol.com wrote:

> *My experiences with online romance have been that they are just too* >*thin and unrealistic. I have never had an online romance with a person who* >*lived in my local area. All of my experiences have been with women who* >*lived beyond driving distance. They have included some romances that were* >*superior in their own moments to any offline relationships, but only in those* >*moments.*

You make an excellent point. The ability to break geographic barriers can be a useful means to initially meet people online, but your point on how unrealistic they can become is important. I found many online who pretended or exaggerated parts of themselves - trying to be more impressive then who they were in real-life. Plus, since you only know others through text-based conversations, it is easy to create an "idealized" version of that individual in your mind while chatting. I found myself easily trusting others or believing what they told me, only to later discover something different. One friend of mine met a man from England and they fell in love over the net. He moved here to the states to live with her and they were to be married, until she discovered that he had a criminal record back in England and he was physically abusive.

Kimberly

However, even as she describes herself as a group 'member', struggling with the same sorts of issues as every other group member, she continues to reference her professional status and publications. Further, she utilizes that status to legitimate her argument that IAD is 'real', often referencing attendance at academic conferences and citing other academic articles as proof:

From: "Kimberly S. Young"
Subject: Re: I am not sure if I am addicted

On Tue, 9 Jun 1998 Sydelyne wrote:

> On diagnosis--
> True, it's not official. However, it may just be a matter of time. Caffeine >dependence is now acknowledged in the Diagnostic & Statistical Manual (DSM- IV).
You make a good point. A growing body of research, new journals, and treatment programs have emerged over the past few years related to computer/Internet addiction. For example, a poster was recently presented at the American Psychiatric Association on the topic and I know of a few symposia to be presented at the upcoming American Psychological Association (in August). Furthermore, I conduct training workshops for various affiliates of the National Council of Alcoholism and Drug Dependence and the National Council for Sexual Addiction and Compulsivity, and they have seen a noticeable increase in cases related to Internet abuse.
I have heard that mental health professionals have already discussed the possibility of a task force to evaluate various "Cyberdisorders" for future inclusions in the DSM.
> I think Tony Thomas had a good point about our culture--there may be >serious deficits in our culture which create a vacuum which is too easily >filled by the Internet, and we have little in the way of guidelines on how to keep balance.
Excellent point again. I too believe culture and society play a role in how we have come to use technology in general. I have seen several cases of those who appear to use the Internet to fulfill psychological needs not being met in real life (which contributes to compulsive use). I am not sure if others have this same sense in terms of their own Internet usage, but it might be something to discuss.

Kimberly

In the post above, Young references a group member's point that, while IAD may not be an "official" disorder yet, it may well be in the future because caffeine dependence is now in the DSM. Young references her professional research into online behavior to claim that such a conclusion is logical. Further, as the post below points out, Young also uses her status as an academic to argue that those who disagree with the label of 'addict' are incorrect and do not fully appreciate the nature of the problem:[20]

On Fri, 12 Jun 1998, driven zen wrote:

> Is this because professional audiences find the use of "addiction" inappropriate? Addiction is the appropriate term, but generally viewed as a lay term. That is, the term addiction is not a formal diagnosis, but rather a description of a pattern of behaviors.

Some critics argue that the term addiction should only be applied to cases involving the ingestion of a drug. However, many researchers have previously applied the same term to high-risk sexual behaviors, excessive television-viewing, compulsive gambling, and overeating without such controversy. It is true that unlike chemical dependency, the Internet offers several direct professional benefits. Therefore, it is easy to understand why people will respond with such skepticism when a term that carries such a negative connotation as addiction is juxtaposed with a positive tool as the Internet. Yet it should not ignore that there is an unintended consequence of this technology that can impair an individual's ability to function properly at home, school, or work.

Furthermore, scientific evidence has suggested that it may be possible to experience habit-forming chemical reactions to behavior as well as to substances. Scientists believe that levels of dopamine, a substance of the brain associated with pleasure and elation, may rise not only from taking alcohol or drugs, but from gambling, eating chocolate, or even from a hug or word of praise. When something makes our dopamine level rise, we are more likely to engage in addictive actions to gain more of it. Therefore, linking the term addiction solely to drugs creates an artificial distinction that

---

[20] In the IASG, there is an ongoing debate between Young and a group member named 'driven zen' as to the legitimacy of the term addiction, particularly as it is applied to online interaction.

strips the usage of a term for a similar condition when drugs are not involved.

Again, I think the diagnostic issues raised are being addressed among professionals, but as I also mention it will take time before more clinical study has been conducted.

Kimberly

While the veracity of claims such as "many researchers have previously applied the same term to high-risk sexual behaviors, excessive television-viewing, compulsive gambling, and overeating without such controversy" and "scientific evidence has suggested that it may be possible to experience habit-forming chemical reactions to behavior as well as to substances" is dubious at best, the most important point here is that, as Rice [1996] notes, those who are schooled in the disease model of addiction, and simultaneously devoted to the philosophy of liberation psychotherapy, are uniquely positioned between symbolic systems. They are situated in such a way as to render their thoughts on the topic of addiction highly relevant, by definition, and regardless of their insistence that they are merely 'one of the gang'. This is particularly true in the inner workings of a self-help group, the entire premise of which is that individuals adopt ready-made (by the professionals) labels, the legitimacy and 'real-ness' of which they accept at face value.

However, Young is not the only academic involved in online support groups. Other aspiring researchers, ranging from Ph.D. candidates to high school students, also play this dual role of recovering addict/addiction analyst, as the following posts suggest:

From: "Storm A. King"
Subject: intro

Hi. My name is Storm (that's my real name :-)and I am a net addict.
I was actually one of the very first members of this list when it was created in 1994.
I have read the messages here only from time to time. Things seem to have gotten very interesting lately, and it looks as if this list may be starting to function as a true self help group for once. Congratulations to you all!
I, like Kimberly, am also a researcher of net stuff. I have done a lot of participant/observations in online self-help groups, and am doing my

dissertation on that topic. Do not be alarmed - I am not here to study this group per say. If fact, in 94,I was published suggesting guidelines for researchers that, if followed, protects not only the members of the group but the group it's self.

After 4 and a half full years of being online - I still get over 75 messages a day. :-(

Part of what I want to share is how I partially recovered from my net addiction. I know that I had it bad, in late 96 early 96, cause my wife was fit to be tied and very very upset with my online behavior, and, I could not change it. It took some time for me to realize that I was ruining my marriage. What finally happened is we took a vacation. It turned out, in my case, if I was not around my computer, I really didn't experience much of an urge to go online. So, when I got back after a week, I was able to unsubscribe from a bunch of emails lists, and started to pay attention to my wife when she needed me to - not just when I felt like it.

To this day, she knows better then to try to talk to me while I am online here - she know that if I don't stop, turn completely away from the computer, and face her, then I did not really hear anything she said.

I hope this group will continue on this track of rejecting media hounds looking for a sensational story - at one point the number of posts here from the media and researchers looking for subjects out numbered the supportive ones.

I have met a ton of people for who the net became a powerful, easily accessible source of sexual gratification. Net porn is rampant and hooks a lot of people in. I don't know what to say to people that get hooked on net porn. Any ideas?

Take care,

--

Storm A. King

And:

From: Ingske
Subject: Depression and Internet Usage

Because my thesis is about this I read about everything I can find on the subject. The study will be published in 'The American Psychologist', this is a journal from the American association of psychologist. In my thesis one of my hypotheses will be that net surfers are more likely to have a trait, a personality to develop a depression. It's not that I want to bring different types of personalities in scale. Not at all! But I think that if you have for example a lower self-esteem that there will be a bigger chance that you'll become a net addict. So I can really imagine that if you already have a basis to develop a depression that Internet than makes you even more depressive.

Maybe I should mention that I don't think that everyone on this list is for example depressive. But recent study has shown that about half of the people on the net (50%) had or has a depression. (Normally it's about 5 or 10%).

Inge

And finally:

From: pravda80
Subject: Introduction

Hi to everyone!
I've been 'lurking' on this list for a while now and I guess it's time for me to introduce myself. I've 17 and I've been using the Internet for almost 2 years now. At first, I was only browsing and using e-mail, but even then I was spending over 10 hours per week on the Internet. I didn't have any financial problems with that because I had free access. I only really realized I was addicted at the beginning of the year. Basically, it was getting to the point where once I got on, it was difficult to get off. On some days, I would spend up to 8 hours on-line (more during holidays) and even more time thinking about the Internet off-line. My addiction, however, is not too bad compared with some stories I have heard.

My friends often asked me what I did on the net and I couldn't really answer them because I myself didn't precisely know. Nowadays, I spend most of my time playing MUDs (most addictive thing in the world, including chocolate). The reason I like going on MUDs is because I can be completely anonymous and yet have fun because of that anonymity. I also maintain 3 web sites and use the Internet to communicate with people all over the world.

My school work, thus far, hasn't been effected but I don't think I can keep doing well if I continue to spend 10+ hours per week on-line. I tell myself each time I connect that I'm doing research for school and sometimes I genuinely am. I'm in my final year of high school and I have to sit my leaving certificate pretty soon. The stress is mounting but I always make time or delay doing school stuff to go on-line. I have a computer in my room so my parents don't always see me on the Internet.

You might have read the first post I made to the list about a survey. Well, I'm certainly not a professional. This being my last year of high school, I have the opportunity to do an independent research project and I decided to do something on Internet Addiction. In a way, I'm using this list as a support group and as a source of ideas for my project. I certainly will not use anyone's comments in my project without asking first. It's been really great to read about everyone else's introductions and advice on how to cut down on Internet use.

Thanks for putting up with this terribly long e-mail.

Adelina

While academics are instrumental in legitimating and "officializing" computer-mediated interaction as a disorder in general terms, the task of making such a generalization relevant to specific individuals is the responsibility of those individuals themselves, as well as their significant others. Let us examine first the role of significant others in the deviance process; a role which is most significant when the 'victim' of IAD refuses to acknowledge the 'problem'.

Consider first the following series of four posts, in which group members (some new and some regulars) discuss and debate IAD and its effects on their lives. Each of these four individuals considers him- or herself a significant other involved in a relationship with an addict of some form:

From: BigWolfe
Subject: Areas for research Net Addiction

What are the best sites for researching stories of Net addicts? I would like to find a site where a listing of news & mag articles could be listed...also what about TV and Radio... any good programs.

I HATE AOL and its chat rooms... my 15 yr. marriage has been sent over the edge by this haven for lonely hearts...

(just venting)

I'm a 39 yr. Male with 2 children and a 38 yr old net addict for a wife

-thanks

From: "Craig C"
Subject: Re: BigWolfe

BigWolfe,

>What are the best sites for researching stories of Net addicts?
There's quite a few I've seen, but unfortunately don't have a listing of the
sites. If I run across them I will post them.
>I HATE AOL and its chat rooms... my 15 yr. marriage has been sent
>over the edge by this haven for lonely hearts...

>(just venting)
>I'm a 39 yr. Male with 2 children and a 38 yr old net addict for a wife
>-thanks
I understand your hatred. Myself, I hate MSN and its chat rooms. I'm
47, been married for 18 years, with a 43 year old addict wife, also have 17
and 13 year old children. It's almost ended my marriage, but I'm hanging in
there for now anyway. Try to find some good things to do for yourself, I've
found that helps. There are quite a few spouses and significant others of
addicts who follow this list and have corresponded. I've found talking to
them can be helpful, and at least it gives a place to vent.

Take care, Craig

From: WriterRad
Subject: Re: BigWolfe

Without speaking about the personal life of specific people who I don't
know, I think there is an over emphasis on "my wife the Internet addict."
I noticed that this has become a national concern long before net
addiction etc began to be discussed. In fact, I first heard it bruted about
about four or five years ago from a coworker who religiously reads Ann
Landers column daily. Ann seemed to be booked with males writing in
worried about this.

I think the danger of the addiction model is to remove any notion of social and societal questions in behaviors. I do not believe that marriage, in particular, relations between women and men in marriage in this society is a socially or sexually neutral area. Rather, from a feminist perspective marriage allows for much abuse, much oppression, much closing in of women in particular. I don't find it surprising that women who have been involved in long term marriages suddenly turn to the internet as a new form of communication outreach, or search for fulfillment. I think it speaks to the inadequacy of marriage, or of their particular marriages and to the restrictions and limits that still face women in our society.

I am 51 and know many women who have been locked in 10-20 year marriages that were awful, abusive, neglectful, or in marriages that had just outlived their time (as most marriages do in this society), most marriages end in divorce). A rather common trend was the need for a great outlet in life than what their marriage provided. This seems true among friends I have whose marriage over this number of years and longer has not had problems. All this seemed to be a far too common set of circumstances before anybody heard of the net, chat rooms, cyber sex or whatever. If anything I believe the net has facilitated this coming out into the open.

I don't find the web addiction model completely useful in my own case. I have had a very close family member who WAS ADDICTED to heroin and another who WAS (I say was because he is deceased) an alcoholic. The dynamics of that situation were simple. Anyone who takes heroin regularly gets addicted and their physical need for it powers all sorts of behaviors. An alcoholic cannot drink period.

I have found that since I have become conscious of my net abuse, that I have used the internet in more positive ways--joining this list, finding mental health oriented information, because I am writing, working with other writers, editors etc on my work, etc. I would hardly think this type of change would be possible for heroin or alcohol addicts. Dealing with these circumstances has forced me to deal with the circumstances of my life and my thinking that caused this behavior. The circumstances of the lives of the heroin addict or the alcoholic don't matter ion regard to the nature of their addiction and its eventual tendency to be destructive to life, health, and livelihood. I can remember the one relative who was an alcoholic finding nothing but disaster in the 1950s and the early 1960s when the general opinion was that alcoholism was a behavior rather than a disease and an addiction and that alcoholics could change into being social drinkers, that solutions other than stopping drinking could help etc.

The internet is not addictive. You can use it properly to enhance and enrich your life.

It is not the problem. What is the problem is the circumstances of our lives, and our emotional and mental problems. We have all sorts of theories of that within the list, religious, spiritual, various psychological, just plain quit etc,. I don't want to go into that. We all have different views, and I think arguing about that now isn't going to help any of us. The point is that dealing with net abuse requires dealing with the real problems of our lives that encourage us to exhibit that behavior, not simply saying "the net made her do it. "

I think that complaining about internet addicted spouses can be a means of masking the problem that may exist either in the particular marriage, or marriage in general. I doubt if in such marriages if the net were to disappear that the problems would be solved. I think blaming net addiction in these circumstances may be a form of denial. I am also very wary of reading online information where one spouse accuses another spouse of things when that spouse is not here to defend themselves.

I think this list aims to help those of us struggling with net abuse. If such a wife were to read this kind of letter, I wonder if she would feel this is a place she could come to open up about her real life problems that led to her net abuse, or would she feel that she was coming to a place where women like her were being condemned by folks who don t want to look at their real problems and needs.

I hope this site doesn't become a place where people come to accuse other people of being net abusers and put them down, but a place where we can look into our problems and experiences to help each other positively

TTFrom: Sydelyne

Subject: Re: BigWolfe

I think you have very sensitively pointed out a variety of factors related to this issue.

I have mixed feelings about what you are saying, because I am a spouse writing in about my husband. While this may clear me of the issue involving feminism, I do wonder about balance of power, as I have been the major wage-earner thus far, with my husband just starting his own business (although he has potential to make more). This list is kind of an amalgam of spouses and Internet dependents, which has both advantages and disadvantages. It may help us to see each others' points of view. But of course, these are different perspectives. Although spouses may be considered co-dependents, as well.

I understand your point about women looking for escape. However, I do believe there is something addictive about the Net, after seeing my husband essentially lose his offline personality once he became attached to the Net.

Also, not all wives are become addicted in a context of escaping a troubled marriage; there may be other personal issues besides the marriage itself, which nevertheless relate to the marriage, and which make certain individuals more vulnerable to Net addiction--e.g.:

Intimacy issues Self-esteem issues Phase of life issues (e.g., kids growing up, etc.)Trauma history Tendency to self-sabotage Difficulty establishing stability/happiness (e.g., anxiety that 'anything good that happens to me will be lost'; 'my mother could never be happy, so what right do I have to be happy in my marriage?'

The list could go on.

I agree that this issue could be used to justify dominating/disqualifying a spouse. On the other hand, men whose spouses 'disappear' 'Through the Internet' need support as well. It is very painful to lose a spouse this way. There is a lot of grief and loss involved, and all the stages of loss, including anger. I don't think this kind of loss justifies abusive expression of anger; but this is not the majority of what we see. I see mostly spouses who are confused, hurt, bereft.

I hope it is not daunting for members who themselves are struggling with Internet dependence to hear about this kind of hurt and anger. Of course, worst case scenario is that it could feel invalidating. On the other hand, I have had some very positive responses about my issues with my spouse, from members who are themselves struggling with the same problem which he has but has not acknowledged.

It may also be useful for spouses and those working on their own Internet attachment to have this kind of feedback--kind of a reality check in both directions.

We may eventually want to split into separate groups; but it may also be important to keep in touch, so as not to get too entrenched in our own point of view, and miss the big picture. For now, this is such a new area, we don't know exactly what we are dealing with. My belief is that it makes sense to work together.

--Syd

This particular series of posts begins with two group members discussing problems with 'net addicted' spouses. They seek not only to console one another, but to locate sources of information on net addiction that serve the purpose of legitimating IAD, of making it real. In the third post, another member attempts to challenge the idea that these spouses are 'net addicted', but does not deny that 'net abuse' exists. Rather than calling the addiction framework itself into question, however, challenges such as these (and they appear on a fairly regular basis in this group) serve largely to strengthen the conviction of others that IAD is 'real'. This point is illustrated in the final posting in this thread.

This same framework can be seen in the following series of posts (and in countless others like it). Here, significant others discuss shared experiences of being involved with 'net addicts':

From: PPCa1
Subject: Introduction from a Cyberwidow

I am a Cyberwidow. My wife has been addicted to chat rooms and subsequent long distance telephone calls for 1 and 1/2 years. It has been the hardest period of my life. I am looking for a support group for others going through the same thing. I want to save my marriage, which is fragile right now.

I am a 35 year old male, a successful businessman, with 2 children, 9 and 4. My wife is a teacher but stopped working 7 years ago to take care of the children. My wife and I have been married for 13 years and have been together for 17 years. Her addiction began shortly after we signed up for an on-line service in March of 1997. Within one month, it was causing problems as her usage increased, her secrecy increased, the phone was always busy, and she began to lie (she was never a liar before this.) At the high point of her addiction, she could be on-line for 12-14 hours a day and frequently came to bed at 2-3 in the morning (before this her bed time was 9:30 - 10:00) I can remember some mornings where she signed off at 6:30 am.

The situation came to a head in August of 1997 when I found out she had graduated to talking to a man in another state on the phone. She apologized profusely and promised it would never happen again. She got me to marriage counseling which didn't last.(long story) The next 7 months we were in limbo until April of 1998 when I discovered the second long-distance phone relationship (I ended up paying for both - all the calls were initiated by my wife).

We finally got to counseling with an excellent counselor and are still in it. We had a couple of very good months but she became upset recently because my trust in her isn't returning fast enough. It takes a long time to undo 18 months of lies, deception, and cyberaffairs. I am having trouble trusting her with anywhere she goes, etc but I keep telling her that I know I will get my trust back, I just need time. So we are currently in a backslide and I am afraid she going to slip back into her old ways.

Well, there's my intro - I know it's lengthy but I've been holding it in along time. I hope to find others to go through this with and help each other.

I would like to know more about how this group works - Chats, e-mail, etc.?

From: "Craig C"
Subject: Re: Introduction from a Cyber widow

I can feel for you cyberwidow.

I have been going through much the same. My wife has been addicted for about a year with the chat rooms, cybersex and telephone sex. I've been married for 19 years and have two teenage children.

I think it's good that you want to save your marriage. Whether you can or not, I don't know. Two things I have learned through this, and other groups: 1) The addiction/behavior had nothing to do with me, and 2) I cannot control my wife's behavior (it is up to her). I have thought from the beginning, when I first discovered it, that this would cause an end of our relationship. I still think that way sometimes, but hope that it won't.

Like you, I think the hardest part for me was the lying and dishonesty. I told my wife on so many times that if she wanted to do those things, if it was so innocent and just harmless banter, to tell me the truth, be honest, and not try to hide things. What I got were lies, denials, minimizing and hiding things. The only time anything was ever admitted was when I presented her with concrete proof, in black and white, of her activities. Well, she was always to "embarrassed" and "ashamed" to tell me the truth. I think this is par for the course, as I have heard so many similar stories from others.

The apologies? I heard numerous apologies, but they were all followed by "slips" back into the behavior, some within a day of the apology and vow never to do it again. I don't know whether the apologies are sincere and these are just slips, or whether the apologies are just a way to placate us, with no real sincerity. Like to believe but when they are not followed up on, makes them sort of shallow.

I know it is a very strong addiction. Why, I don't know for sure, and think it varies with the person. My wife says she likes it because of the attention she gets, and for the control. She feels she can control these men like "puppets on a string." She has low self-esteem, so I think this may be part of it too for my wife.

I think it is good you are in counseling. I've tried to get my wife to go, and she says she needs help, but poo poos the counseling idea, saying it won't help and she just needs to stop. Sometimes I wonder whether she is just using the "I need help" thing. I tried to get her help, but she didn't follow through with just a simple phone call to confirm the appointment, so she doesn't seem too serious about it, and it makes me wonder if she is even sincere. But I think counseling is a necessity, and good that you and your wife are going.

I think it will take you some time to get your trust back. I think your wife is being unrealistic to expect it to come back instantly. What happened, happened. There were lies and dishonesty. I think regaining trust is a gradual thing. I know I haven't gotten mine back yet. I would love to have my trust back, would give anything to have it back. It feels terrible not to have it. But I can't just will it back, it has to return in my mind and heart. I think you are being honest when you tell her you are sure it will come back in time.

I would not be surprised if your wife slips back. I hope she doesn't, and try to keep the faith that she won't. But don't be surprised if she does. It is a very very strong addiction. What are you doing for yourself? Are you doing things that you enjoy doing? I was so consumed by this for a number of months (sometimes still am) that I thought I was losing my mind, I was obsessed with it. So I was letting my wife's behavior control me, in a way becoming co-dependent. So I've been reading more, taking walks, got back into meditation after a number of years, trying to do things for myself, realizing that I can't control my wife, can't even help her with it, it is her addiction and only she can deal with it if she wants to. Letting go. Experiencing my moments, living my life. It's hard, I know, but realize you can't control this, only your wife can. Support her in her efforts to overcome this, love her, but realize it is up to her.

Some in this group e-mail each other. If you want to e-mail me, that is fine. I have found that this group, and the e-mail, helps, because it gives me people to talk to about it, even to vent on occasion. This group, and others, also offers me insights into both the addicts behavior and thinking, and the spouses/significant others. Another good site I found, which deals strictly with online sexual addiction is Online Sex Addiction. The site address is http://www.onlinesexaddict.com/index.html. It deals a lot with pornography, but there are some with chat/sex problems, and spouses and significant others. So good luck to you, your wife, and your marriage. I know this was long, but your note brought up so many things in my mind, and I think we can all help each other.

From: Cydlyne
Subject: Re: Introduction from a Cyberwidow

Thanks for writing. I agree with what many on the list have said. I am also a cyberwidow, and your story is very similar to mine with my husband. It's very sad, and I know what you are going through, at least to some extent. I have seen enormous deterioration in my husband over a relatively short span of time, coinciding with when he began to be online all night (as you describe).Also dealing with cyber affairs he has had (and is having--starting with role-play, and now, "adult" sites). So far, he is in complete denial, and feels my concerns are "bizarre."

I hope you find this list helpful it has been great for me. I am still struggling with much of this (we got our computer last fall, and it has been seriously downhill since then--we are now separated, still in couples therapy, but he is still online, even more than before, now that he has his own place).The only things I have found useful so far have been--setting limits, but not rashly trying to recommit to investing in my own life--exercise, work, creative enterprises, friends couples therapy (we also have a new therapist who is better than 2 prior ones we had--still in infancy stage, re: dealing with Internet addiction) Sharing experiences here

I am curious about how you found out about your wife's activities online, and how you began addressing it with her. I wish you the best. Feel free to e-mail me, as Craig also suggested. I also think we will all get a lot out of Sheri's new list (just add an "s" to cyberwidow (=cyberwidows) in the web address.

I can see why it would be hard to reestablish trust. I find a similar pattern in my husband, although it sounds as if your wife is way more acknowledging of her problem than he is. I notice that my husband does not seem to take responsibility for his own actions any longer, and can't see my perspective at all--he can have all the harsh criticism & doubts about trust in the world towards me, but any suggestion of doubt about him is "criticism" (and undeserved criticism, at that). I wonder if that is at all like what you are seeing in your wife. Sometimes, I feel my husband expects me to be as easy to control as his online relationships, where he can just push a button and make them disappear. I wonder if the computer sets up real relationships, in a variety of ways.

Well, take care, and welcome to the group--hope to hear more from you! --Syd

From: Mike Wimbish
Subject: Re: Introduction from a Cyberwidow

On Sat, 19 Sep 1998 WriterRad@aol.com wrote:

->For example, I have seen people speak about the cyber relationships... I bring all these things up because in the cyber relationship a woman who might get involved with me doesn't see all of this, she sees a picture I have sent of me standing between 2 internationally known poets (2 years and about 20 pounds ago). They imagine me ... as a writer...

One of the things my wife kept telling me about her online romances was that I didn't have anything to worry about with them because they were all with women! When asked how she could tell she'd only respond that she could tell. Maybe women have a secret code and decoder ring? Actually, I didn't have a tremendous problem with her internet dalliances except I felt her pulling away. I was begging her for marriage counseling since October of 1997. I did have a tremendous problem in that our children were taken away because she rarely cleaned the house and, because (I'd finally noticed) she started spending money on these relationships, bills did not get paid and the gas and electricity were turned off.

My wife used to go to sleep watching TV late night. Life seemed drained from her. Then she discovered her internet access and began falling asleep at the keyboard playing Scrabble on MediaMOO. My wife is an exceptional writer and a very creative person. It hurt to see her seemingly waste away. I found some MOO sites dedicated to creations of one of her favorite authors.

I led her to PernMOOs. I do not have to accept responsibility for her actions since the introduction, however. The secrecy -- switching screens when I'd walk into the room, early morning\late night phone calls, sudden increase in trips to her sister's home who just happens to live near an online companion and another who lives en route, and other things -- The secrecy led me to mistrust her which led to more secrecy on her part. When I'd invite her to sit with me while I'd MOO, she'd have no part of it. Probably because she'd not want to be obligated with having to ask me to sit with her. No, the problem I had with her was her -- not the internet. The internet did however facilitate what happened to our relationship.

---Mike

From: Cydlyne
Subject: Re: Introduction from a Cyberwidow

Mike--

Re: some of your descriptions of your wife--I can resonate to many parts of your experience, as I have found in the past--the secrecy, the use of TV to sleep, prior to Internet involvement, the creativity in search of an outlet, the pulling away from real relationships.

I suppose we as spouses need to be careful of degrading our spouses, when we are angry. I think your account is very respectful of her, and the loss you experience (very familiar to me) is clear from your description.

--Syd

The reader will note that many significant others have sought therapy for the net addiction problem. However, rather than alleviating the problem, therapy has tended to exacerbate it. Therapy allows the significant others to learn to apply a clinical, disease framework to their experience and to bring such a framework into the online group setting. Interestingly enough, it is unclear why, if these significant others are insisting that online interaction is not as 'real' as face-to-face, do they find such comfort in participating in this online group. Regardless, the act of medicalizing such problems in living by and large serve to seal one's fate; once an individual is ensconced in the role of addict, he can never be redeemed. He is doomed to a life of perpetual 'recovery'.

Of course, significant others do not accomplish such a reality without the aid of IAD victims themselves. As the following series of posts demonstrates, significant others and unrelated victims often work in concert to legitimate one another's understanding, or definition, of the situation:

From: Cydlyne
Subject: Re: Depression and Internet Usage

I heard that there is a book coming out on personality styles and Internet use--that might be useful when it comes out. I don't have the author's name as yet.

I believe there may be something that Internet use does to damage interpersonal boundaries (I think so from observing my husband, and from what others have said).

What I have observed is that my husband and others become ultra-sensitive to real contact, and feel intruded on. Of course, some of this is related to needing privacy for activities that he wouldn't want others to see. But it seemed to be more than that. And he and others who are in denial have such blankness and nonchalance about hurting other people, as if the computer interactions with other people were just an extension of fantasies in the mind. Somehow, it can be completely consuming (replacing all close real relationships), yet seem to "not count." I think it affects real boundaries with other people as time goes on--I see my husband relating to me in a frighteningly primitive way, which would be more acceptable in 2-dimensional (interpersonally, I mean) role-playing. I don't believe I seem real to him anymore--I'm just another projection, convenient to act on like any other nearby role-play character, yet inconvenient in that he cannot just push a button and get rid of me and my reactions to him. The real world has in this way been negated and replaced!

Well, so much for soliloquy. If others who have been addicted or net-attached have insights into how this happens, and how they broke through denial, I would like to hear about it. Thanks for listening!

--Cyd

Someone on this list told me about a movie, Strange Days, based on virtual reality, which in part portrays a similar kind of addiction.

From: Tina Bolli

Subject: Re: Depression and Internet Usage

I just give some feedback to your observations. A lot of this applies to me. First of all, I suffer from depression It wasn't caused by the internet, however, since it's been going on since I was a kid. But I guess I fit the stereotype of someone who can easily become addicted to the net.

Second, I recognize myself in your description of your husband. It's causing many problems with my boyfriend. I feel like he's smothering me when all he wants is a normal relationship. And I'm very insensitive to his needs. I also wish he had an "off" switch

Thanks for your observations. It's helpful to see what a net addict looks like from a non-addict's point of view.

--T

From: KT
Subject: Re: Depression and Internet Usage

Hi,
My mother who was/is addicted to the internet suffers from depression too. She has for as long as I can remember. What I want to know is why people who suffer from depression are likely to become addicted to the internet and chat lines. I tend to think that they would want to withdraw from everything. Maybe Tina you can shed some light on this for me.

Thanks
KT

From: Tina
Subject: Re: Depression and Internet Usage

Hello
It's hard for me to say why people who suffer from depression are susceptible to net addiction. I can just speak from personal experience. As

*for myself, I'm an introvert (I wonder if people with depression tend to be
introverts), so I like doing things by myself. I don't feel a need to go out and
connect with people. So it's easy for me to spend hours online. I don't get
bored or tired. But I think that would drive an extrovert crazy. I'm starting to
wonder if the real connection is introversion and net addiction. Just a
thought.*

- Tina

*From: Cydlyne
Subject: Re: Depression and Internet Usage*

*Hi--
My husband also has some history of depression, although he wasn't
obviously depressed when he started online (now I wonder if he may be
manic). He is extroverted, but doesn't have friends now, as he had in the past
(he lost friends when he got divorced about 7 years ago, and hasn't really
made new ones).
I suppose there are a lot of aspects of our culture which are very
alienating, and leave us at a loss for community. That recent article suggests
that the Internet is a very poor substitute, however.
My husband is also a trauma survivor--I don't know how much that has
to do with it. The part that seems relevant for him is the sense of emotional
safety, which is compromised for him. And the control he experiences, where
he has had severe experiences being helpless, in the past. The rough part for
me is that he has lots of control now, and isn't helpless in his current life, but
I know these experiences are sustained over time. So that may make him
more susceptible--I'm not sure. He is also a creative person, and perhaps
fantasy-prone (although prior to this, he seemed to like to be pretty
grounded in most respects). He used to be very into television to help him
mellow out; and he also used to like video games a fair amount, especially
the ones where you build a community or mini-culture.
Well, I have to say, I am kind of obsessing about him. So maybe he has
become my addiction! Co-dependents (myself for example) need to develop
our own lives more, so that we're not dominated by our family member's
emotional absence/addiction, etc. So it's a similar need, to develop a fuller
life--I am trying to do this through exercising more (joined the local Y),
seeing friends more; and there is more I want to do, e.g., work on creative
projects, work on a project in my work life which I have been neglecting.*

Clean the house (not a very creative enterprise, but unfortunately necessary). Play with my dog. etc., etc. I suppose we should all encourage each other along those lines?
    Catch you later! --Cyd

From: KT
Subject: Re: Depression and Internet Usage

well...my mother who is net addicted and suffers from depression is not an introvert. She is outgoing and when not in a depression enjoys other people's company a lot. I'm just trying to understand why she would find the net so attractive. Perhaps it was the closeness to other men on there that she wasn't getting from my dad? That thought bothers me but it could very well be and likely is, the reason. Thanks for your insight Tina.
    -KT

From: Mwzoeplace
Subject: Re: Depression and Internet Usage

I think you make a good point (re: depression, introversion, and closeness).However, it probably varies--with my husband, we were very close (I thought)before he got online, and he distanced as soon as he got into the Internet(and couldn't tolerate real closeness). So--I suppose it can be a matter of titrating and controlling the intimacy (which could make intimacy more workable, although probably not as healthy--I guess it's not true intimacy, more of a facsimile, like plastic intimacy, surrogate love, etc.--given the article that recently came out about people being more lonely and depressed as the use the Internet more).
    I hope that as we discuss the variations, we'll keep seeing patterns.
    Incidentally, how old was your mother when this started? And how soon after getting the computer did she get addicted? For us, my husband was 50, but it was very shortly after we got the computer (within 5 -6 weeks of getting online). He also became anxious and had trouble sleeping a few weeks after he got online, and I don't know whether that's a coincidence that made him more susceptible, or whether the online activity stimulated his anxiety.

    --Cyd

From: KT
Subject: Re: Depression and Internet Usage

Well my mother had fallen into a depression in May (a couple of years ago)the ironic thing was that my father brought a computer home from work and got an internet hook-up for her to explore the use of computers. Before this, she was computer illiterate and hated them. My father works with computers and thought that if she had a chance to play around with it, she'd gain some confidence and not be so afraid. She started on the computer in August and by the middle of September to October she had a serious problem. The real ironic part is that I suggested to her that she try IRC. A girlfriend of mine introduced me to IRC in 1st year university (a couple of years prior) and I thought it may offer some enjoyment and interaction for my mother during her depression. WRONG MOVE!!! It's odd though, because it's almost as if some people are predisposed to internet addiction (I speak primarily of IRC abuse). Because I have been on before and I never have gotten so involved that it interferes with real life. Some chats I enjoyed but I left them online and that was that. I just wonder why some people are more prone to be lured into IRC addiction.
-KT

From: "Craig C"
Subject: Re: Depression and Internet Usage

KT wrote:

>It's odd though, because it's almost as if some people are predisposed to >internet addiction (I speak primarily of IRC abuse). Because I have been on >before and I never have gotten so involved that it interferes with real life. >Some chats I enjoyed but I left them online and that was that. I just wonder >why some people are more prone to be lured into IRC addiction.
From what I could gather from my wife, who is a chat addict, she enjoys the attention she gets when chatting, and I think that is it primarily. She also says cybersex gave her a sense of control that she could control men "like puppets on a string", so I think that is a part of it too. I have read that people with low self-esteem tend to be drawn to chatting on the net, and I think that's part of the attention seeking thing also. Boredom may also play a part.
I did not think my wife was depressed when she started the net, or became depressed because of the usage. It seemed like she actually got high

from the chatting. She does suffer from manic depressive illness though, tending towards the manic, not the depressed. A soon to be published study, as I understand it (and without actually having read it), found that people who used the internet excessively tended to become depressed, and not that they were necessarily depressed when they started.

From: Cydlyne
Subject: Re: Depression and Internet Usage

Hi--the idea of predisposition is a good one--it would be interesting to know what triggers it. Someone I know said she went to a conference where they discussed Internet addiction, and she heard that people who are bipolar feel soothed by the kind of light the computer emits. That would be very interesting (although I doubt it's something that simple?).

I guess that in purely behaviorist terms, there must be high reinforcement value to the computer--something about pushing buttons and getting whatever you want, pretty much right when you want it. It obviates the need for delayed gratification.

I just remembered a passage from My Dinner with Andre (the movie)--about an electric blanket-- Wally says he likes his electric blanket; Andre says that the electric blanket is dangerous, because "As soon as you turn it on, you enter the dream world"--it takes away the sensations of cold, numbs you to your own response to the real world. He says, "I like it when it's cold!...I can snuggle up to you more because it's cold!..." and words to that effect--that it somehow hones our awareness to not always be gratified immediately, but to need to experience the cold, and seek comfort from it, which then creates new kinds of bonds, and intimacy. Wally then says he won't give up his electric blanket, because, (paraphrasing--I haven't memorized the whole thing--) "Let's face it--New York is cold in the Winter! And if I can have a little more comfort, then I'm going to have it!" So--this seems like a dialectic that applies to computer gratification as well:

1) How cold is our real world (or our perceived world, maybe, as affected by our histories)?

2) How much comfort is actually helpful and rewarding rather than numbing?

3) When does this immediate gratification and comfort become something that shuts us down rather than advancing us? That leads us to tune out the world around, with concomitant loss of contact with others in our lives?

While significant others play an important role in bringing the medical model to bear on computer mediated communications, as one might expect in a self help group environment, it is the victims themselves who are most active in the deviance process. Given only the bare essentials of the disorder's symptoms, causes and consequences, the regulars in this group are quite capable of retrospective interpretation, of aligning their past behaviors with self-selected labels and role criteria. This ability stems largely from personal experience within the clinical framework. That is, it is immediately apparent to the casual observer of interaction in this online group that the regulars are schooled in the addiction model. They have had experiences in self-help groups for other 'problems', they have been involved in one-on-one therapy, and they are very aware of all of the current academic research and phraseology that offers legitimated explanations of their problems in living. As the next two posts illustrate, the regulars use their skills in these areas to make IAD real:

> *From: "Piet Slaghekke"*
> *Subject: Built on the Ashes of a Joke*
>
> *driven Zen wrote:*
>
> *As I keep reminding people, this listserv was originally a joke by Ivan Goldberg. As are his "proposed" criteria for the disorder.*
>
> *Piet Replies:*
>
> *My experience with Jokes is that many times there is a serious truth lying within them.*
>
> *driven Zen wrote:*
>
> *I agree that it is a support group. But, it is built on the ashes of a joke. So, a new name might be good. The authors of "Alcoholics Anonymous," the first major self-help book for addictions (also applicable to impulse control disorders) was written with meticulous attention to the meaning of each word.*

Piet replies:

So all IASG mailing list members do we vote on a new name?? Lets come up with a few? Here is one: Compulsive-Obsessive Internet users support Group

I was thinking... driven zen wrote in a prior posting:

"This is understandable. However, it doesn't justify perpetuating a misleading name."

"Using the term "addiction" for every form of impulse control problem, compulsive behavior, or actual addiction, eventually renders the word useless. Sort of like overusing an antibiotic. When you really need to be able to use it specifically it may have lost its power."

I agree on this. But (as driven zen stated earlier) the term addiction is so embedded in our pop culture that if we change the name of the list now, people may not be able to find the list. The term "Pathological Computer Users Support Group" sounds very heavy to me. I would not describe myself as "Pathological" I would much more easily describe my self as "addicted", in a pop culture kind of way. The idea is that as many people who need this list should be able to find it. "Addicted" is most probably what people will label themselves and will therefore search using this term. Also I think the term "Pathological" would scare many people away.

Until there is a better name, that has also become a popular name, I think we should keep the name of this list as it is. This list has gained a momentum. A change to the name would most certainly disrupt that momentum.

The Phoenix has already arisen from the (ashes and) the Flame.

Greetings to all,

Piet (- ;

And:

From: "Craig C"
Subject: Depression and Internet Usage

Chris wrote,

>*By the way... I have an appointment at CAPS (Counseling and*
>*Psychological Services), a department of University Health Services. I*
spoke >*to my academic advisor today, and she said she has read about the*
>*condition. He says IAs also are susceptible to depression because they*
can't >*perform academically and because we suffer from short-term memory*
also.

I just read an article in the paper last Sunday. It was about a major
research project on internet usage. It found that people who use the internet
get more depressed. This surprised the researchers, apparently because of
the social interaction aspects of the internet, e-mail, chatting, etc. The article
said the results will be published in the next issue of a major psychological
journal. I think it may have been the journal from the American
Psychological Association (?) but am not sure.

Of course, the regular addicts in the group use such legitimating
'evidence' not only to reinforce the legitimacy of IAD among themselves, but
to provide significant others of net addicts who frequent the groups an
official explanation of their experiences as well. Thus, for the significant
others, Internet addiction must be the real explanation for behaviors they do
not approve of; not only do experts in mental health claim that IAD is a
legitimate social problem, but the victims themselves are prepared to testify
that their first hand knowledge of the issue supports such claims. It is in this
way that a scientific discovery of a new disorder is said to have occurred:

From: JMDREIT
Subject: Hello

Well, this is my first shot at breaking my Internet addiction. I have been
online, for the last 5 years. All was well initially, being online was costly,
and I refused to pay additional charges, so I never went into a chat room, or
did extensive web searches. About 18 months ago, when AOL became one
price, a friend suggested that I create a screen name to "play" on. I had no
idea at that time what "playing" online meant, but I figured I would give it a
try. I quickly learned that playing online was exciting, and now know its
dangerous. At that time, my husband was working evenings, and never came

home until almost midnight. Once the kids were in bed, I was alone, and very lonely. I quickly learned thru AOL that I didn't have to be alone, there were people out there, who were itching to talk to me, and anytime I signed on, there were a variety of chat rooms for me to go into, I quickly became a "regular" in some of them, I met lots of people (men mostly) who I chatted with for endless hours. Sometimes I would make "dates" with them, and be online talking until 2 am, or later. I discovered the "rush" of cybersex.....and that was the beginning of the end. My online friends knew me better than anyone else, so I began to be online at work, and at home, always signing on just to see if my "friends" were there for me to talk to. Online conversation led to phone conversations, and ultimately to meeting, I became so hooked on talking to people online that my real life began to suffer. I would justify being on line "just to check my mail". I was ignoring my kids, and my husband, my friends, and my job.

I have finally woken up, and am trying to take charge of my life once again. I have dumped most of the people on my buddy list, and ultimately will be changing Internet services. I will email my new address when I get it.

It has been a difficult road, but the fact that I finally can admit that I am addicted, that has made all the difference in my life. I am somewhat comforted to see that there are others out there in the same boat. I would love to hear from some of you... I would help me greatly.

Its kinda funny that you equated having an online addiction meeting online to having an AA meeting in a bar, because that's what I said to my therapist when i first heard about this. I guess its a place to start, and if I have to be online, this is a good reason

Thanks for letting me tell my story.

From: Sydelyne
Subject: Re: Hello

Thanks so much for sharing your story. If you want to, it would be great to hear how you (and others on this list) came to recognize the addiction. As a spouse of someone seriously Internet addicted, I am having trouble really grasping how much denial I see in my husband, who is online all night, although he needs to go to work in the a.m. He seems to have no concern at all about how this affects our family life. So--would appreciate any observations you may have on why it is so hard to recognize, if you have any thoughts about it. Welcome! --Syd

From: JMDREIT
Subject: Re: Hello

Syd

It was hard for me to recognize. I have been in therapy for almost a year, and although my therapist has mentioned it, and suggested a change, I denied it. I guess it kinda came to me when I pushing my husband to try some alternated sexual experiences, swinging, threesomes, and when he finally agreed, I was sick to my stomach. I began to see what I was doing, how I was manipulating him, how I needed him to be involved in my addiction to justify it. I kinda hit me like a ton of bricks. I also have to say, he and I have been in therapy for the last few months, and that has helped me refocus on the relationship. It wasn't easy, its still not, but I don't thing you can push him, he has to see it. I suggest you tell him, gently, how much you miss him. how much you need him, and want him to be around. He might get the hint. I hope this is helpful

Janet

Finally, considerable amounts of time and resources are spent in this online group to indoctrinate newcomers into the medical framework. Online groups such as this one serve as the newest style of confessional (not unlike the television talk show), and allow the self-labeling newcomer to reinforce his or her belief in the real-ness of the disease. While some newcomers confess their sins and are seldom heard from again (as the next three unrelated posts illustrate), more often such confessions serve as a rallying point for the group regulars. They allow for fresh opportunities to strengthen group beliefs about the legitimacy of their shared experiences:

From: "Linda Clayborn"
Subject: Hello all my name is linda

Hello to everyone who is reading this my name is Linda and I am a 17 year old female, who has become very addicted to the internet. I am on it all the time, it has took place of my regular life, instead of going out with my friends to meet people I get online to meet people. I have several people online who think that there are in love with me and this makes me fill good, but I know its not normal I should be meeting guys in real life. I have several home pages that I work on hours on end, and I go crazy when the server goes down and I can not get online. My family ask me why I spend so much time on the net and I have no real reason to explain this .When I am not around my computer I think about all the things happening online that I am missing. It seems like I have quite doing everything I used to like, like going out, watching t.v., listening to music, talking on the phone, etc. just to be online all the time. I mean here it is 12:49pm and I am still up and still online. well I am sorry to have bored you all to death but they told me to tell you about myself and there I did

And:

From: "Christopher J. Caraballo"
   Subject: Hi.. I'd like to introduce myself.

Hi Everyone

My Name is Chris Caraballo I'm 19, and a freshman at Penn State.
   I realized that I am addicted to the Internet a few weeks ago when I took a survey at the Online Addiction Clinic (some think like that anyway) The results of the survey showed that not only am I addicted but it is affecting my life in a negative way.
   I finally realized today that I really need to go get help. This week was our first week back at school. I knew that my online addiction was preventing me from succeeding at my studies when I was moving back to school from home. So as an attempt to cut myself off I canceled my America Online account, and begin using my Penn State Access account for internet access. For about a week I was fine. School just began this past Wednesday, so I didn't have much work. I woke up at about 1pm like most college students who just came back from a night of partying. Then I went online at gay.com and I just started to chat and chat and chat... I had an agenda for the day too, I was suppose to clean my room, kitchen, and bathroom, do the laundry, and then I was suppose to do a small written assignment for my geography that was due today (Monday). Saturday passed by and at about 6pm I took down my to do list from the refrigerator and said... well I'll do it tomorrow, I'm too tired to get started doing all this now. Saturday passed by and then I woke up on Sunday and began to chat on gay.com again. Never actually intending to spend the whole day out on the internet, I did. I never

got the house work done, and I began working on the assignment at 10 pm last night. Then my friends came over and we went to hang out for awhile and I got back at 2am. The assignment was still not done. When I got back I continued to work on the assignment till 3:45am. At that point I was so incredibly tired I could not stay up to revise the paper. So I went to sleep when I was done with the first version and woke up at 7am to begin working on it. It ended up taking a little longer than I expected and I ended up missing my first class of the day at 9am. I went back to sleep for an hour (I was done with the paper at about two hours before my second class. So I went to sleep for an hour and then woke up and went to my second class. I was totally groggy and found myself dozing off during the lecture. Then I went to my third class, feeling a little better because I had had something to eat after the second. Then I went home to go to bed to have a short nap so I would feel better before my first day at work began. My shift was scheduled to work between 5:30 and 9pm, so that gave me about two hours to rest before I had to go to work. I set my clock and went to bed. I woke up at 6pm as my now former employer left a message on my answering machine. That's when I decided I need help, and I went on to the net to research what treatment is available and what I can do.

Even though this sounds like a really bad day... this has LONG been a problem for me. It really began when America Online released their unlimited usage plan. For me, the potential for Internet Addiction was always there... because as soon as they made the plan public, I was practically the first person in line to SIGN UP! That was when it began to interfere with my life. From that day on the phone line at home (I was then still living with my parents) was almost always busy. My parents complained, my nuclear family complained. Once or twice there where emergencies and no one could reach up because I was online chatting on AOL. I would get in trouble with my parents constantly because I was online too much. Though no one ever took it seriously, and neither did I. My mother has been telling me for over a year now that I'm addicted to the Internet, though the thought of Online addiction was not really serious. Though I have begun realizing that it's not the actual act of being addict that's the problem but not doing what I should be that is.

This email has probably already gotten too long... though there is another aspect of my academic life, which is totally screwed up because I spend too many hours on the Internet. Last year was my first year of college. I want to try to keep this as short as possible but what happened is I ended up flunking 4 out 5 classes and withdrawing from my second semester I am not eligible for financial Aid this semester.

Now I know that I am an intelligent person, and do well and focus very well when I am not torn from it with distractions. I find that the hours I spend of the Internet are the greatest problem that I encounter.

My life off the internet, some things about me... As I have already noted, I'm 19, a second year freshman at Penn State. I was born in Brooklyn, raised in Queens, NY. I am very social by nature, very friendly, easy to get along with and talk to as well as popular.

My life online, Well I used to go by the screen name NYCityKid2 on AOL, I used to chat in mostly gay youth/local chat rooms such as queensnym4m or18to21m4m. Now online I tend to be using gay.com's browser based chat rooms, and I usually go to the Pennsylvania room as PSUkid. I'm not into cyber sex or anything like that so I don't believe It's the sexual aspect of IA that I have a problem with.. I believe it's the social aspect.

I'm happy to have joined the list serve. I am attaching a picture of myself when I was at Penn State Erie (where I went to school last year).

I'd like to hear from you any of you. Thank you for listening.

Chris

And finally:

From: "Gaebryl Firuz-Zamri"
Subject: welcome all newbies,

i used to go to an actual 12-step program dealing with internet addiction on 12th street in New York, which was rather cool, `cept we had more of a coke-binging, acid-trippin' corporate IT programmers assemble there. `course, there was also a nintendo-addicted 15 year old reformed crack dealer (no kidding), but other than him and me, there was little interest or acknowledgment on the subject of internet abuse. When i moved back home to Malaysia a year ago (i sorta emigrated to the States to stay with this girl i met on the irc), i just went around the 12-steps circuit, doing Narcotics Anonymous, Alcoholics Anonymous, Marijuana Anonymous, and even Alanon meets. i don't talk much about my net addiction there, and don't really plan to. i mean, how do you rate when someone has a 'relapse' or 'slip' *with our ailment? However, when my fiancé threatened to break off the engagement and i started taking sick leave from work due to marathon runs d/l stuff off the net or goofing off on MUDs (or even just preparing spreadsheets and powerpoint presentations for the next session) then i sorta figured out i musta have had something akin to a 'relapse'. i still miss my old group though, `course most of us just sat around bragging about what we used to do on-line and how many warez sites we were leecherz of, or even comparing the longest periods we spent on-line.*

U could say we weren't really in 'recovery', but we weren't 'actively using', which to me, means shutting down all social activities and getting wired to a virtual world for 12-36 hours. i work with puters now, so i am technically on-line 10 hours a day, but i try to limit that to work-related activities only. Anyway, my boss just walked in, so i'm gonna stop rambling now and get back to work. To all the newbies, welcome. If there are any MUD or MP3 abusers out there, do drop me a line. It kinds of get lonely thinking you're unique in your addiction.

c y l8r guys

While there are plenty of single-post confessions of Internet addiction in this online group, as noted above, it is more often the case that such confessions generate compassionate responses on the part of group regulars, as they simultaneously welcome newcomers into the fold and reassert the real-ness of Internet Addiction Disorder:

From: "Lsfsdfsd Jgggjfdf"
Subject: Introduction: 18 yr. old male from California

I would like to introduce myself, anonymously. I am 18 years of age and from San Diego, California. Basically, my dad left my mom when I was 12 and I hardly ever see him since. Also, I've moved a couple times during my life which has totally RIPPED me from any long-term friendships. I have always had trouble making friends. Right now I have hardly ANY friends at all. I just try to find people online to fulfill that emptiness. The internet / computer addiction in general is F**CKING up my life completely. I just dropped out of college because I didn't want to get bad grades on my records so possibly if I can beat this net addiction I can go back and transfer to a good 4yr University. I DO work however, but still the internet has totally made me depressed just like the new study says. I now go to a

counselor who is a PhD and yet he has NO CLUE about this internet stuff. I try to explain to him about it and about Dr. Kimberly Young's research, he is still learning about it.
Anyway, that's my story really summed up.

THE INTERNET IS THE CREATION OF THE DEVIL.
It is worse than any hardcore drug in my opinion, as it totally RIPS you from your social skills. I have hardly any social skills now, I used to before I used the net. I have never had a girlfriend in my life, nor sex, and I am on the verge of ending it all since I see nothing in my future as the internet has made life suck.

From: DLC2757
Subject: Re: Introduction: 18 yr. old male from California

Hi:
You are too young to let the Internet take over your life. Don't ever give up hope, because there are people out there who will listen to you. I know the pain you are feeling is probably unbearable right now, but it does get better in time. I grew up in a divorced and dysfunctional family and I know how it feels to have no one to turn to. I'm 40 and have been married for 13 years and the Internet is destroying my marriage. My husband has been in denial and refuses to see he has a problem. I sent him Dr. Kimberly Young's web site and he keeps deleting it. I have found phone numbers of women here in the town where we live and all sorts of things. Addiction is the same whether it is the Internet or drugs or alcohol. Try and stay away from the things and the people that tempt you and to find other interests to keep you busy. Just remember there are people out there praying for you and if you want to chat e-mail me sometime.
{{{HUGS}}} to you Donna

From: Frahan Ahmad
Subject: Re: Introduction: 18 yr. old male from California

Hello,
I just read your mail and as I was going to do my Home Work but when I read your mail, I just stopped and thought that I think that I can help you. First, my introduction is that I am also a computer/internet addict. I am 15

years old and male from Midland, Michigan. I think this much introduction is enough. My suggestion is that all what you can do is yourself and its a fact that no one can do that for you. Its all that you should make a schedule for every day. In which you should not give more than1 hour to computer. And I know that's hard to do. But if you want to have a good future you should do that. I know that its easy to say but its hard to act because I am also in the same kind of situation. And still I am suffering with the addiction. I am also interested in these kind of problems. Because they are very very hard to solve. If you have any questions please feel free to ask.

Or consider the following series:

From: "Olivia H"
Subject: Introduction

Hi,
I would like to introduce myself to the members of this support group. My name is Olivia. I am 31 years old, married, and have 4 children ages 14, 12, and 6 yr. old twins. I work full time outside of my home.

I am, without a doubt, addicted to the internet. I fancy the social scene in particular. I spend an average of 7 hours per day online using programs such as IRC, Mplayer, ICQ, Powwow, etc. On any given day, I can be found staying online until the early hours of the morning. I have been so sleep-deprived, that I have fallen asleep while at work, or worse, while driving home. Needless to say, my marriage is falling apart as I am disinterested in my relationship with my husband; I would much rather communicate with one of my cyber friends which, by the way, are all male. I have also neglected many areas of my household; chores, bill-paying, etc. I don't spend the time with my children that I should and if they interrupt me I usually don't hear them or become very agitated that they have taken my attention away from the screen.

I thought about ending all of my online relationships cold-turkey, but that would be seemingly harsh on me as well as my cyber friends. These people make me feel good, and I in turn do that same for them. Maybe that's what I'm looking for, I'm not sure.

My hope is to relate with people who have the same problem, and to maybe shed some light on why I am doing this. My family needs me.

Olivia

From: Geoff Silverstein
Subject: Re: Introduction

Olivia and the group-

Nice to hear from you...I'm looking for the same things...I've tried and tried to eliminate chat from my life. So far, I've deleted ICQ and IRC...and I'm trying to stay off Yahoo Chat...
How have others of you out there dealt with your chat addictions? Please provide some insight...thanks,
Geoffrey

From: "Guobryl Firuz-Zamri"
Subject: Re: Introduction

This is in response to the query by Geoffrey

Hi there!
I'm a firm believer in the adage 'abstinence is not a substitute for recovery', but it has it merits. I wouldn't want to go and junk my modem, I work in the IT business and that would tantamount to professional suicide, but I try to recognize areas of high-risk in my on-line interactions.
MUDs for me is out, and so is IRC. My office communicates by ICQ because of the distance between all the relevant branches, but I limit it to receiving orders and invoices and responding to them. I avoid chats, and I find myself setting 'away' on the toggle just in case I get tempted to indulge in anonymous cyberchat.
For me, and this is just my way of dealing with it, I try to recall my low bottom with the internet (the worse of which was finding myself in America, I'm from Malaysia, in a Ramada Inn somewhere in Tennessee with a married woman I met on the Internet, and discovering that I was in love with her on-line persona but not her in RL. Not that I found that out immediately, though. It took joining a 12-step group and bumming jobs in New York City for two years before I even considered giving up on this cyber-romance.)
I know why I want to quit. RL is good, and I live in RL. The net is kewl, it's cerebral satisfaction and fulfils deep social needs, but it isn't RL, and RL is where I live the rest of my life. I want to get wired, like permanently (put an IV modem jack up my veins and strap me to a T3 connection, heh) but I

want real emotions and experiences more. I'm on a trial run with my fiancé again, not that it would 'really' make me want to go abstinent, but I feel it's important that I give RL a chance, despite all the misgivings I might have to RL due to unfulfilled needs stemming from past experiences.

I find trusting another human being, especially someone off the net and without my addiction, helpful. I log on because I don't trust, and trust is an important factor in my recovery.

Jeez, there I go again flooding the screen. Have waaaaaaaaaay too much time on my hands without MUDs nowadays... heh. Good luck and God bless

to everyone else.

-Gaebryl

From: "Gaebryl Firuz-Zamri"
Subject: Re: Introduction

This is in response to Olivia

Hi!

Hey, great to hear from you. It's always gratifying to find out I'm not alone with my addiction. I was on the IRC for a number of years myself, then abstained for a few years due to IRC-related factors in RL, then rejoined via another client, MUDs. I have a great number of friends and 'allies' on MUDs, good people I wish were my friends in RL, and vivid almost-real experiences shared with these people of on-line interactions. I hate going cold turkey, I don't believe in going cold turkey, but I find I have to just to save my relationship with my RL fiancee. But it's more than that, as well. I have friends in RL who I have conflicts with now due to constantly comparing them with my MUD buddies, and it's not fair on them. They can't compete with people who largely exist in my own head. People who in RL I might have less in common with than my good, loving RL friends. This is from my own personal experience. I still check e-mail, I still do company work on-line, but for leisure, I find myself doing weird things like reading a book, or calling up my fiance and actually talking to her instead of just nodding off at everything she says and then logging on for a few hours afterwards. And I find when I'm 'clean' from MUDs, I can actually talk to my friends with less judgement, and am actually open to what they say and find myself enjoying their company. Not all the time, but then, even on MUDs there are always lamersz and lags to bugbear me, and those aren't even valid human experiences. 3 days 'clean' today, my head feels kind of groggy like I'm really withdrawing from the intense MUDding... but I also feel good about myself. I really really loved smelling the air outside on the way to the office today, and I have been reading this great book which had been lying beside my home PC for the past three months. Today was a good day... :o)

-gaebryl

From: Mike Wimbish
Subject: Re: Introduction

On Wed, 8 Jul 1998, Olivia H wrote:

>I thought about ending all of my online relationships cold-turkey, but >that would be seemingly harsh on me as well as my cyber friends. These >people make me feel good, and I in turn do that same for them. Maybe that's >what I'm looking for, I'm not sure. My hope is to relate with people who >have the same problem, and to maybe shed some light on why I am doing >this. My family needs me.

Hi Olivia,

From everything I know of cyberlife, you're only important to those online while your text is scrolling across their CRT screen. If you should lose access, while your input would be missed for a short time and there might even be a couple frantic passionate emails sent, you would be forgotten and another would take your place as easily as you slipped into their lives before.

In the Virtual world - you can be replaced as easily as a blown fuse. In Real Life - you cannot be replaced. You are more than simple text to your husband and your children. I'm glad you understand your family needs you. Understand, those online do not.

I wish you well on your recovery.

Mike

It is in this circular fashion, then, that interaction through computers has been re-presented as a social problem—as an addiction. Given a cultural framework that allows for, and in fact demands, the medicalization of behavior, moral entrepreneurs in the field of mental health have succeeded in utilizing peoples' apprehensions about new technologies to make IAD 'real'. Perhaps more importantly, they have done so with the aid of journalists, 'victims' of IAD, and those victims' significant others. For, contrary to the common assumption, 'victims' of deviant behaviors (and their significant others) do not succumb to circumstance. Rather, they play an active, critical role in selecting which truths and which realities they will apply to themselves. Searching for absolutes in a world of uncertainty and change, all parties involved use the tools available to them to construct meaningful, socially useful, and, above all, plausible explanations for their behavior. As Shotton [1989] aptly notes:

"The introduction of computers into our society occurred with great rapidity with the development and widespread use of the microchip, and was often poorly executed without adequate information being given to those who were expected to use them. This lack of knowledge and understanding appeared to some extent to have been influential in the development of many and diverse anxieties being associated with the use of new technology. Many within the population were extremely skeptical, if not specifically fearful, of computers; therefore any people who showed a serious interest in new technology were viewed as atypical and perhaps somewhat suspect, especially if they were the type who were generally not well understood by others. . . the anxieties associated with computer dependency and the effects arising from it may be no more unusual than many others which have been attributed to new technology."

"The introduction of any new technology may be considered cyclical; from the development of the science and its application, to the mass production and widespread dissemination of the machinery. This appears to be followed quickly by concern about the possible negative results flowing from its use; concern about the environment, society and the individual. However, most older technologies only directly affected a few people at their inception, and most systems were well accepted for their benefits before they became the common property of society. This appears not to be so with computers; their introduction was extremely rapid and seemed to affect the lives of those who have never directly used or even seen them. . . Quite regularly the press bring computer-centered scares to our notice and few can be thoroughly disproved to the satisfaction of society. . . The new, unknown technology is frequently seen as more threatening than older mechanisms which have been proven to be dangerous but are now familiar. . .

"Any potential psychological effects are less tangible, and therefore more disturbing than the more obvious accusations of physiological damage caused by computerization. . . Generalized fears seem to concentrate upon the belief that new technology strips people of their freedom and privacy. . . Computers have been accused of causing such psychological and sociological effects as the de-skilling of labor, job stress, redundancy and unemployment, social isolation, powerlessness and alienation. Further, the use of computers has been charged with altering personalities, with changing the socially gregarious into recluses and destroying relationships. . .

". . . described new technology and some of its applications as potentially 'obscene', 'morally repugnant' and 'dangerous', and attacked the dehumanizing aspect of computerization and its impact upon society. . . The fears cited appear not unrelated to the new anxiety, that certain people seem to become 'addicted' to their interaction with the computer. . . This differs little from the fears expressed thirty years ago with the advent of another revolutionary technology into the home, the television. The television was accused of affecting children in very much the same way that the computer is today. . . the common fear. . , was that they were being adversely influenced and affected by violence on the screen.

"A more pervading fear lay with the fact that many people seemed to be cutting themselves off from other forms of recreation by watching television excessively. . . Although apparently extreme, the fears directed towards the computer were not entirely new and differed little from those expressed towards television. Further research was able to show that such negative reactions had been expressed for centuries with reference to the introduction of other older technologies.

". . . at some time or another each (invention such as the steam engine, motor car, wireless, telephone and television) has been accused of damaging those who come into contact with them, either psychologically or physically. Gas lighting was almost universally considered dangerous and even impossible by many. However its social benefits were quickly accepted after its inception, subsuming the more irrational fears. . . Even the introduction of the telephone led to a great deal of resistance, the common fears being that its use could lead to deafness or electrocution. . . most of the apprehension and resistance was due to the new mental barrier which was created between the speakers. . .

"Thus many apocryphal tales abound, but most are difficult to substantiate. At one time traveling at more than 20 miles an hour in a train was thought to make the body disintegrate. When people survived at this speed, traveling at more than 40 miles per hour was said to lead to suffocation as it was thought that the air would be sucked from the carriage. . . Mistrust has always existed and has always to find an outlet. These examples hardly differ from the present fears that working at a computer can lead to ocular damage, miscarriages or computer dependency; anxieties are voiced and suspicions are aroused, and they are rarely disproved to the full satisfaction of society.

"One may conclude that it is not at all surprising that the computer has engendered anxieties, either rational or irrational. History has shown that many major innovations through the ages have created similar fears. The technological changes brought about by computerization have the potential for influencing the course of society far more than has any other mechanism in our history, and that the computer has been accused of causing physical, emotional and psychological change should not astonish us. However, the modern technologies of television and computers have perhaps created the only truly new fear, the one which accuses them of appearing to create an 'addiction' to their use, to the detriment of the psychological and social lives of the individuals concerned. Although 'television dependency' seems to be accepted as part of modern life, computer dependency still causes concern." (pp. 236-243)

Chapter 5

ON BEING HUMAN:
ONLINE SELF AND COMMUNITY

The belief that mediated communication is somehow less real than face-to-face communication has been a driving force in the social construction of IAD. A brief review of the stated motivations and assumptions behind the limited research on IAD, combined with an examination of this readily accepted assumption on the part of self-labeling Internet addicts, will serve to illustrate this point.

As noted throughout this work, Kim Young has been a key proponent of Internet interaction as a disorder. Intrigued by her own online experiences and those of close friends, she sought to investigate whether Internet usage could be considered addictive and to identify the extent of problems created by such misuse:

> "I first sought to determine a set of criteria which would define addictive from normal Internet usage. If a workable set of criteria could be effective in diagnosis, then such criteria could be used in clinical treatment settings and facilitate future research. However, proper diagnosis is often complicated by the fact that the term addiction is not listed in the DSM IV. I viewed pathological gambling as most akin to the pathological nature of internet use. By using pathological gambling as a model, I defined Internet addiction as an impulse control disorder which does not involve an intoxicant. Therefore, I developed a brief eight question questionnaire which modified criteria for pathological gambling to provide a screening instrument for addictive Internet use."[1996, p. 2]

Young concluded that Internet addiction exists and that its causes and consequences are the same as those of other addictions. Arguing that Internet interaction is an addiction with the same qualities as substance ingestion related addictions, she claims that IAD impairs real life relationships; this is the number one problem caused by Internet addiction.. Internet addicts, she claims, "form an emotional attachment to the on-line friends and activities they create inside their computer screens. Internet addicts enjoy those aspects of the Internet which allow them to meet, socialize and exchange ideas with new people through highly interactive Internet applications (such as) chat rooms and MUDs. . .These interactive areas form a type of virtual community amongst its members. . . allow an internet addict a vehicle to escape from reality and seek out a means to fulfill an unmet emotional and psychological need."

Mark Griffiths [1997, p. 81] concurs with this assessment, stating that ". . . addictions to the Internet are usually in the form of either those addicted to chat rooms or those addicted to fantasy role playing games. . . In this author's view, both chat rooms and fantasy games allow an anonymous individual user to take on other social identities since there is no face-to-face interaction." Likewise, Kandell [Brown 1996] says, ". . . there's a danger that people will substitute these activities for real activities, get involved in chat rooms and lose their skills in dealing with people."

From this perspective, interaction through computers is a social problem; it pulls participants away from so-called real social interaction and limits their ability to deal with others because they are accustomed to being able to manipulate situations involving the computer. Further, people are said to be indiscriminate in their choices of what information to believe or what interactions to engage in simply because such information has passed through the computer medium. Traditional critiques of television claimed similar outcomes when they suggested that people are 'tricked into believing' everything they see on television. However, there is an alternative means of understanding what forms of interaction are to be labeled 'real', just as there is an alternate (to addiction) explanation as to why individuals spend time, in some cases a great deal of time, online. This alternative means is through the sociological lens of symbolic interaction.

SYMBOLIC COMMUNITIES

The symbolic interactionist response to critiques of mediated communications (such as loss of personal identity, loss of 'real' community and loss of ability to deal with 'real' relationships and interactions) has generally hinged upon challenging the one-way, stimulus-response model of participants in such forms of communications. According to George Herbert Mead [1934], all meaning, including the meaning of the self, lies within the social act. The meaning of the self is a social process because it requires the individual to take the role of the other in interaction, thus making the self a social object. The meaning of the interaction is a social process because involves both taking the role of the other and interpreting the other's acts in the context of a particular situation.

Theorists of mass communications argue that this two-way process of interaction continues to be the case; the mediation of interaction through electronic technologies does not negate role taking or the construction of meaning as a social process. For example, Franklin Fearing [1964] adapts Mead's concepts of human interaction to mass communication and suggests that if communication is to occur between human beings, both parties must be implicated. That is, the meaning of the text communicated is not inherent in it, but must be constructed or interpreted locally by each participant in that interaction.

Regarding the notion of loss of personal identity, the symbolic interactionist approach has been to suggest that, while C. Wright Mills [1968] may be quite correct in suggesting that people look toward television for confirmation of identity, the manner in which this is done is what is important. That is, as suggested by David Manning White [1971], people may in fact "get partial answers from television to the basic philosophical questions-- who am I, why am I here, what is the meaning of my life." [p. 15] Robert P. Snow [1983] further suggests that, not only do people use mass media as an information source for development of new identities, they also use it as a source of validation for existing identities. The point of distinction between the traditional approach and the symbolic interactionist approach is how one views the participants. In the traditional approach, participants are 'tricked into believing' everything on television; in the interactionist approach, people are highly selective in terms of the formats and contents they choose to pay attention to.

Concerning the critique of mass media as contributing to a loss of community, Lewis Anthony Dexter [1964] suggests two ideas. First, he argues that mass communications have allowed people to achieve consensus on issues with 'strangers' as well as 'neighbors' (what McQuail [1994] calls the social cohesion model). His second and interrelated argument is that, because electronically mediated communications break down traditional barriers of time and place, the distinctions between primary and secondary communications have become blurred; "in specific, actual cases, the difference between secondary and face-to-face communications is hard to work out." [pp. 9-10] Further, McQuail [1994] argues that what are generally thought of as mass media can also be used as social activities:

> There is little doubt that much media use is sociable, contrary to the image in mass society theory of the audience as made up of isolated individuals, in an atomized society. While it is true that the rise of mass media increased the possibility for solitary attention to more channels of public communication (radio, newspapers, cinema, etc.) and reduced the dependency of the individual on other people for human contact, media use is in practice as sociable or as solitary as a person wants it to be. [p. 308]

Today, according to McQuail [1994], the interactionist claims regarding an active audience have the upper hand; participants in mass mediated communications, in general, are no longer seen as the passive victims they were claimed to be. However, despite the acceptance of activity on the part of the audience, the meaning of such activity remains unclear. Critics of mass media, particularly television and the Internet, continue to maintain that, while such activities may have the potential to be social, they continue to be used in solitary ways and, for this reason, *serve to isolate participants from real, face-to-face community.*

However, many, many participants in online activities, as well as academics who study computer-mediated communications, would beg to differ with such an assessment. In fact, much of what constitutes 'the known' regarding the question of meaningful interaction through CMC has its basis in first-hand accounts of the experiences of participants. Often such accounts make the case for the meaningfulness of such interaction implicitly by assuming that it is self-evident that communication mediated through computers is just like face-to-face encounters.

For example, regarding gender-specific spaces on the net, users say "It's an attempt to connect, not to show off" and "I see us struggling with being male in this society, and dealing with pain and emotional hurt". Some participants are extremely committed to the reality of 'virtual relationships' as the following quotes suggest: "On Women's Wire, people speak my language. It's not that men are not present, it's just that they're not central. It makes a world of difference"; "I use it to feed my soul.", and; "I'm fascinated with what women deal with and hooked on a level of emotional involvement and information I've never been able to find anywhere else in my life." [Ness 1994, E1]

In other instances, the comparison between face-to-face encounters and Internet encounters is more explicit. Consider the following examples. Yvete Colon, a social worker who is launching her second virtual group for online therapy says, "It actually works better that they never see each other. Since they're not busy watching each other, they concentrate more on themselves. The level of self-disclosure and trust is far greater than traditional groups." [Copilevitz 1995, D5]. Lorraine Harrington, middle school student in Colorado involved in a 'kid-space' portion of the Internet comments, "It's a lot easier to communicate on-line. We talk about life. We talk about anything and everything". Another student says "It's easier to talk to girls on the Internet than in school. Sometimes I can't talk well in person. It doesn't come out like I want." Another says, "People treat you more like an adult than they do in person "[McCartney and Rigdon 1994, B1]

David Woolley and Michael Hauben, both contributors to *Computer-Mediated Communications Magazine*, comment on their experiences with a conferencing system named Plato and a UseNet group named nyc.general, respectively. Woolley says that while the Plato system was ". . .designed for computer-based education, its most enduring legacy is the on-line community spawned by its communication features. The Talkomatic portion of the system was an instant hit. There was no way to contact a specific person to let them know you wanted to talk, so it was more like a virtual water cooler than a telephone substitute. People would hang out in a channel and chat or flirt with whoever dropped by." [Woolley 1994, 7] And Hauben [1995] discusses nyc.general, a UseNet newsgroup that "demonstrates a friendliness of a good neighborhood in the midst of an ever growing city. . ." and likens the group to the "Greenwich Village 1963" model of community proposed by Sally Banes in a community study in which she suggested that community is not a static social form that is disappearing, but that new, dynamic and overlapping forms of small-scale networks have arisen. [p. 12]

Elderly people involved with SeniorNet [McCartney and Rigdon 1994] comment, "It's like a group of people sitting around a big table having coffee and kidding each other."; "It is a way for homebound people to get out and see friends."; "Even friendships that remain limited to cyberspace seem as good as the real thing."; and another says, "It doesn't matter. Your disabilities, the color of your skin. It makes no difference to these wonderful people." [p. B1] Two people who met online and then got married explain,

"We are having some difficulty in getting people to understand that we know all about one another." (He popped the question on-line and she immediately responded 'yes'). [*Love On the Line* 1995, A4].

Perhaps the most extensive discussion about meaningful interaction and the Internet as a human community is *The Virtual Community: Homesteading on the Electronic Frontier* [Rheingold, 1993]. In this work, Rheingold, who is widely recognized as an expert on computer culture, describes in detail his experiences as a member of the Whole Earth 'Lectronic Link (WELL) on-line community. While he acknowledges that critics of computer-mediated communication may have some valid concerns regarding the extent to which such interaction is a substitute for face-to-face interaction, he makes the case that there is something very real about on-line community, as the following quote suggests: "There's always another mind there. It's like having the corner bar, complete with old buddies and delightful newcomers. . . and fresh graffiti and letters, except instead of putting on my coat, shutting down the computer and walking down to the corner, I just invoke my telecom program and there they are. It's a place." [p. 24]

Rheingold goes on to suggest that what may be happening now with the Internet is similar to what Tonnies called a transition from *gemeinschaft* to *gesellschaft*, from community to society, noting,

> The mass psychological transition that people made to thinking of ourselves as part of modern society and nation-states is historically recent. Could people make the transition from the close collective social groups, the villages and small towns of premodern and precapitalist Europe, to a new form of social solidarity known as society that transcended and encompassed all previous kinds of human association? [p. 63]

It is interesting to note that Benedict Anderson's *Imagined Communities* [1983] makes a similar case; all communities are imagined and must be commonly imagined in the minds of people if they are to exist at all. With these arguments in mind, one could suggest that the Internet community may be as real as any other.

While the scholarly work available regarding these questions of meaningful interaction and computer-mediated community is still limited, a few studies have been done of CMC participation that make the case for the existence of Internet communities. *Voices from the WELL: The Logic of the Virtual Commons* [Smith 1992] is an ethnographic account of the production of collective goods, and the processes employed to maintain and disrupt that production in the intentional community of the WELL. The author employs the theoretical frameworks of collective action dilemmas and network theory to examine the production of three collective goods, social network capital, knowledge capital, and communion, within the virtual community.

He begins with Erving Goffman's [1959] discussion of the creation of the self and argues that participants in the WELL, though their means are limited, still create personality and identity for themselves using text alone. The fact that WELL interaction is aspatial, asynchronous, acorporal and thus relatively anonymous does not mean that identity is not present. Identity remains because people invest expectations and evaluations in other's user i.d.'s. [Smith 1992] If people wish to maintain their social network and knowledge capitals and the status that derives from those, they will continue to act in-line with their established identity or suffer the consequences. He concludes that "despite the unique qualities of virtual worlds, people do not enter new terrain empty-handed. . . Interaction in virtual space is not fixed, determined or easily controlled or directed. If we are to understand this new terrain of interaction, detailed work should be done which addresses how virtual communities form and mature, and how those relations are similar to and different from social relations in 'real-life'. " [Smith 1992]

In *The Sociology of Culture in Computer-Mediated Communication: An Initial Exploration,* Elizabeth Lane Lawley [1995] makes a similar argument for the community nature of on-line communications. Utilizing Bourdieu's [1984] sociology of culture and his constructs of field, class, habitus and symbolic capital, Lawley argues that computer-mediated communications (CMC) do constitute fields worthy of scholarly analysis. She proposes working definitions of his constructs, as they apply to CMC and suggests that they be tested through empirical observation. She suggests that 'field' can be looked at from a number of different perspectives; CMC in its entirety could constitute a field, or a single bulletin board service (BBS) could constitute the field. Because Bourdieu allows for such overlap in the definition of field, either of these two extremes (or a field somewhere in between) could be appropriate. Likewise, 'class' can be defined through one's expertise with CMC and an affiliation with a particular system of relatively 'high' or 'low' status. Such measures endow CMC participants with a history, and to this history accrues a certain amount of authority within the system. Finally, 'habitus' can be seen as the linguistic conventions unique to CMC and the system of netiquette (each of which is a form of symbolic capital) because they fall within Bourdieu's definition as individually operationalized but collectively effective methods for the regulation of behavior within the field. [Lawley 1995]

In *The Network Nation*, Starr Roxanne Hiltz and Murray Turoff [1993] offer an analysis of CMC ranging from the sociological nature of CMC to the applications and possible impacts of CMC on everyday life. In their analysis of the social processes of CMC, Hiltz and Turoff use data collected from one computer conference to discuss the socialization process from a Goffmanesque perspective. According to the authors, because communication channels are narrowed, participants lose all visual and some audio cues regarding social category or 'type' of other participants, facial expression, eye contact, body language and so forth. Thus beginners in CMC experience the equivalent of culture shock because the known rules for combining data from channels do not apply. For example, they cannot acknowledge and yield turn-taking in conversation without difficulty. However, Hiltz and Turoff do note that new participants begin to learn the new rules of interaction almost immediately and within a short time (30 minutes) report greater facility of use. The authors argue that this narrowing of communication channels does not mean that meaningful interaction is not taking place. In much the same way Smith argues that WELL participants learn to construct identities, Hiltz and Turoff's participants learn to construct new means of communication. In fact, according to Goffman [1959], such cue-searching inadequacy is present in any medium of interaction. All that is required is that new participants are socialized to the new rules.

Finally, and very recently, a body of scholarly work has begun to emerge which challenges the virtual/real argument inherent in most, if not all, critiques of online interaction.

According to Baym [1995]:

> Too much of the work on CMC assumes that the computer itself is the sole influence on communicative outcomes. This is sometimes called the 'cues filtered out' approach because, in this perspective, the computer is assumed to have low social presence and, therefore, to deprive interactants of salient social cues. . . .The presumed lack of contextual cues and feedback is seen as producing several interrelated communicative outcomes. Interactants gain greater anonymity. . . participation is said to become more evenly distributed across group members. . . .The anonymity and lack of socioemotional information is taken to erase norms for interaction. . .people become less socially inhibited and more likely to be rude. . . [pp. 139-140]

Baym then goes on to describe her research on a UseNet newsgroup dedicated to the discussion of soap operas. She suggests that there are at least five sources of influence on CMC which are overlooked by many scholars of communication: external contexts of the participants; the temporal structure of the computer medium being used; the particular computer system infrastructure; the purposes of the group being studied; and the characteristics of the individual participants in CMC. The author concludes by arguing that "The creation of forms of expressive communication, identity, relationships, and norms through communicative practice in computer-mediated groups is pivotal to this process of creating community. Social realities are created through interaction as participants draw on language and the resources available to make messages that serve their purposes." [p. 161]

Similarly, in their analysis of UseNet codes of conduct, McLaughlin, Osborne and Smith [1995] "assume analogic (to 'real life') processes and structures in CMC...discourse processes generate social structures, which in turn affect discourse processes", where discourse processes include the development of distinctive language, truncated speech, emoticons, face-saving mechanisms and socioemotional content, and social structures include social and professional roles, sex roles, community boundary indicators, rituals, and commitment to communal goals, rules, norms and community standards. [p. 94]

While the studies cited above indicate that there are aspects of 'real' community and identity in interaction via computers, it is by going directly to the source—to the online social spaces themselves—that one gains the fullest understanding of just how 'real' these online communities are. This is the task that this author set out to accomplish in *NetLife. Internet Citizens and Their Communities*. While there is much debate within the field of community sociology about exactly what social forms constitute communities, my criteria, based upon generally accepted sociological principles, were as follows: 1) social institution(s), either formal or informal, which maintain(s) social order, including a generally accepted system of values and beliefs; an established set of norms of interaction which, when violated, result in either formal and informal sanctions; a means of socializing new members and exerting social control over deviant behavior; and a means for resolving ambiguity and establishing accountability among actors for their actions; and 2) social institution(s), either formal or informal, which aid in establishing and maintaining personal identity, including the achievement of commitment/reciprocation between and among members regarding 'who each person is'; and the achievement of legitimation of communication regarding 'who said what and what it meant'.

My conclusion, as the reader by now has guessed, was that there are countless communities online that are just as 'real' as those created through face-to-face interaction, and whose members develop online identities and relationships that are just as meaningful and as real as those developed through more traditional interaction. What follows is an overview of the evidence I found that supported such a conclusion. It was a conclusion reached after many months and several thousand hours of time online conducting research on a wide variety of groups within Internet Relay Chat, Usenet and Fidonet. And it was research that ultimately revolved around the nature and 'realness' of all community, identity and interaction, online or off.

THE REALITY OF ONLINE COMMUNITIES

Defining 'community' has always been a difficult task. Even for individuals who specialize in the study of community, a clear, meaningful and lasting definition has proved elusive. The term is one which is complex and abstract; research on the subject mainly consists of case studies of particular settings which researchers assume to be communities because the basic question, 'what is a community?' is a question with many possible answers.

One possible definition of community is a people who interact within a limited territory and who share a culture. Or it might be defined as the largest social organization whose patterns make a significant difference to the individual's actions; the social organization within which all other social organizations exist. But exactly what constitutes territory and interaction, and how one can determine which social organization is the largest one which makes a 'significant' difference to the individual? With the advent of the telephone, the television, the computer, the multinational corporation and so forth, is any system of social relations bound by a geographic limit other than a global one? According to Colin Bell and Howard Newby [1974, p. xliii] "...out of community studies, there has never developed a theory of community, nor even a satisfactory definition of what a community is. The concept of community has been the concern of sociologists for more than two hundred years, but even a satisfactory definition of it in sociological terms appears as remote as ever."

This dilemma regarding which social groupings may legitimately be called communities has its roots in the work of Ferdinand Tonnies. Tonnies defined community (*gemeinschaft*) as a type of social organization in which people are bound closely together by kinship and tradition; any social setting in which people form what amounts to a single primary group. He contrasted gemeinschaft with the idea of '*gesellschaft*', meaning 'association'. Associations are types of social organizations in which people typically have weak social ties and a great deal of self-interest. People are motivated by their own needs and desires rather than a desire to advance the well-being of everyone. In this context, modernization is equated with the progressive loss of human community, which provided personal ties, a sense of group membership and loyalty within small communities. The social world of the community was circumscribed in space as well as in its way of life; modernity erodes such possibilities.

Tonnies' definition imbued the study of community with a focus on physical place, moral undertones and a romanticism for the past, by suggesting that gesellschaft is a kind of social life which is cold and impersonal. By contrast, gemeinschaft is warmer and more affectionate. This idea is reflected in the current debate about what a community is; the role of physical space or territory in the development of group cohesion is of paramount importance. While many would agree with Tonnies' focus on bounded locale and the sense of solidarity often presumed to result from such circumstances, others argue that the role of physical territory, as traditionally viewed, is increasingly irrelevant.

Within the field of community sociology, there are definitions of community which attempt to alter the definition of space, and thereby allow for new forms of community; forms that more accurately reflect how people live today. For example, Gerald Suttles [1972] advances the idea of 'community of limited liability'. He argued that, in order to understand community forms today, one must focus on the intentional, voluntary and partial involvement of the members. Communities are no longer defined solely as locality-bound individuals who 'must' work together. Rather, participation in community today consists of voluntary associations of individuals who focus on specialized and often limited issues. Such communities have 'official' identities, meaning they are recognized by both members and non-members as 'real' groups; communities of limited liability have external advocates and/or adversaries. It is this voluntary participation, combined with recognition from 'outsiders', rather than physical space limitations, that constitute community boundaries today.

Similarly, David Minar and Scott Greer [1969] propose that while community used to refer to a physical concentration of individuals in one place, one must now look at community as the social organization among a concentration of individuals. They borrow from George Homans' [1950] concept of the 'human group' and state that the root of all community is organization. Community begins with the interaction and mutual modification of behavior. Such action eventually becomes patterned, and through such mutual modifications emerge shared perspectives and commitments to the 'place' and its group. These shared perspectives represent the group's culture; the agreed upon definitions of what the world is and should be like. They ultimately conclude that what binds a community together is a state of mind on the part of its members. Community is not a place, it is the set of social identifications that emerge from interaction. And out of such interaction, both cooperation and conflict can and do result. Thus, it is inaccurate to suggest that older forms of communities (gemeinschaft) are necessarily circumscribed social spaces which result in cooperation, while modern day associations (gesellschaft) are large, impersonal social spaces that necessarily result in conflict.

Benedict Anderson [1991] takes this notion of community as a state of mind one step further. He suggests that all communities are imagined communities, and that they must be imagined, because ". . .the members of even the smallest. . .will never know most of their fellow-members, meet them, or even hear of them, yet in the minds of each lives the image of their communion. Thus, communities are to be distinguished, not by their falsity/genuineness, but by the style in which they are imagined." [p. 6]

These later conceptions of community, which attempt to redefine space in order to take into consideration the rise of a global order, reflect the symbolic interactionist perspective on community. In essence, this perspective suggests that:

". . .the world in which the self exists is no less a fiction than is the self: both are created from symbolic stuff. . . for the human animal, space is cultural--it has to be conceived within the cerebral cortex, and not be merely 'out there'. The boundaries of the space that we live in do not have to be in our immediate experience; in fact, they may never be. But we must be able to imagine them, so that our world has compass points. . . .The self, in order to exist, has to 'be' in relation to something else. The individual has to exist in reference to past, present and future places." [Becker, 1962, pp. 53-54]

This symbolic interactionist view of 'space' goes to the very heart of what community means in computer-mediated communications. As Steven Jones aptly summarizes,

"In assessing the history of community studies, one finds that space was understood less as socially produced and more as that which produced social relations. So, for instance...threads running through definitions of community in the sociological study of community include territory, social system and sense of belonging, social interaction based on geographic area, self-sufficiency, common life, consciousness of a kind, and possession of common ends, norms and means. . . On the one hand, it (CMC) appears to foster community, or at least the sense of community, among its users. On the other hand, it embodies the 'impersonal' communication of the computer and of the written word...Traditional life, supposedly, was marked by face-to-face intimate relationships among friends, while modern life is characterized by distant impersonal contact among strangers. Communities are defined as shared, close and intimate, while societies are defined as separate, distanced and anonymous."[1995, pp. 18-23]

In the symbolic interactionist tradition, Jones argues that CMC is *socially produced space*. Communities formed by CMC can be defined as 'incontrovertibly social spaces in which people still meet face-to-face' but under new definitions of both 'meet' and 'face', In that sense, cyberspace hasn't a 'where'. Rather, the space of cyberspace is predicated on knowledge and information, on the common beliefs and practices of a society abstracted from physical space; the community is social interaction or social networks. Ultimately, CMC can be understood to build communities because it renders the idea of physical place irrelevant.

Regardless of how one defines 'community', all human communities, including those formed online, must solve a few basic problems in order to survive. They must establish a system of values and norms of behavior that members live by. They must socialize new members effectively so that they, too, abide by these rules. They must develop a system of sanctions that can be used to hold individuals accountable for their actions. And they must provide the means for individuals to simultaneously develop distinct identities and a sense of group membership.

The primary means by which human communities achieve these goals is through the creation of both formal and informal organizations. Such social groups are generally classified as primary or secondary. According to Cooley [1913] primary groups are those characterized by intimate, face-to-face association and cooperation. They are fundamental in forming the social nature and ideals of the individual. These groups, for example, the "family", are the essential mechanism of socialization and the primary source of social order; they represent a sense of 'we' in that they involve the sort of sympathy and mutual identification for which 'we' is the natural expression.

When such a group makes patterns of interaction explicit through writing down rules, it becomes a secondary group, or formal organization. As a small group increases in size, it reaches an upper limit at which point the group is altered and establishes 'formal' rules and regulations. In the formal organization, relationships are impersonal, everything is written down, and members rely on rules that can be read. However, it is also noted that:

> "...formal organizations inevitably inspire the formation of informal patterns which often become more important than the formal. The way things are supposed to be on paper is balanced by patterns that actors negotiate on their own in face-to-face interaction. Formality aids people when they interact--it makes it relatively easy for new members to know very quickly what to do--but it is usually more important to alter the written patterns and bend them to fit our own situation, since those who wrote them could not possibly know our situation exactly. Indeed, most people in formal organizations seem to understand that written rules are guides which are not usually strictly adhered to." [Charon 1993, 50]

Symbolic interactionists, taking this assessment of social groups one step further, argue that the human group is an organized pattern of interhuman activity; it is not a collection of individuals. ". . .There are two fundamental reasons why the individual should not be considered the fundamental unit of the group. First. . . no group exhausts all possible behaviors of the individual. . .The second reason. . .is that within remarkably wide limits, one individual's activity can be substituted for another's, while the group remains essentially unchanged. The true unit of the group is not the individual, but the activity or performance." [Martindale, 1962, 1966]

Martindale goes on to argue that organizations are strategies of collective life. Defining human groups as concrete patterns of interactions, rather than as collections of individuals, eliminates the need to distinguish between groups that are 'formal' versus 'informal'. What needs to be understood are the various types of interaction and how they are utilized in order to establish and maintain social order and social identities for the individuals involved. There is nothing 'magical' about the presence or absence of face-to-face interaction or written rules when one is attempting to discern the presence or absence of social order. What is important is whether participants in theses groups act *as if* the means of maintaining social control exist and behave accordingly; do they agree to agree.

Similarly, social institutions may be thought of as organized patterns of behavior. Rather than being concrete social structures, they are ultimately problem-solving strategies. Drawing on the work of Cooley [1913], Hertzler suggests that, "Institutions are first and foremost psychic phenomena. The institution has primarily a conceptual and abstract, rather than a perceptual and concrete existence. Their essence is ideas and other concepts, interests, attitudes, traditions. In a very real sense, institutions are only in our heads; they are common and reciprocating attitudes." [p. 35] He notes, however, that institutions are also 'societal structures', secondarily, in the sense that various social groups with norms of behavior and 'physical extensions' utilize these psychic phenomena to create and justify systems of social organization.

Don Martindale [1962, 1966] continues this characterization of the relationship between the institution and the group by arguing that institutions are the relational patterns manifested by groups. Groups are organized sets of interhuman behaviors, and institutions are the relations displayed therein:

> "Groups are systems or patterns of social behavior which arise when pluralities pursue their individual and collective aims in common. . . Groups are not something different from social behavior; they are merely special semi-established regularities of social behavior. Institutions are defined as the standardized solutions to the problems of collective life. . . A group is a strategy of interhuman behavior, that is, a plan of action intended to achieve common objectives. . . .A group is a concrete system of activities; a group institution is the solution to the problems of social life". [pp. 39-46]

For example, "the family" is both a social institution and a group. The concept of 'family' is an institution in the sense that it solves the collective problem of socialization. It is an ideal, a concept, that most community members value. Though its concrete form may change over time, the idea of family remains relatively constant. In a more concrete sense, 'family', one's own family, is an actual social group with regularized patterns of behavior.

What does all of this mean for the existence of IAD? It means that in order to understand why people choose to spend time online, sometimes to the detriment of other social roles, one must set aside unexamined assumptions about the nature of online interaction and personal choice. Rather than assuming that self-labeled Internet addicts are 'victims' of their apparent inability to control whether and when they log on because they are inadvertently 'sucked in' to a non-real social environment, it is instructive to examine just how 'real' such online social groups are and the extent to which they offer companionship that has much in common with face-to-face interaction. For, in the end, what distinguishes online social realness from the realness that is assumed to exist in face-to-face interaction is found not in the fundamental nature of those interactions, but in the social structures imbued with the power to de/legitimate realness. This legitimation is carried out according to those standards of reality that serve the interests of the rule makers.

Online participants construct communities and interpersonal ties that are no less real than those found in face-to-face interaction. They build social institutions and groups, socialize newcomers to group rules, and provide a forum for meaningful interaction and a sustainable sense of self. How do they accomplish this? In a nutshell, they accomplish this in the same manner as do people in face-to-face communities; through language, through talk.

As discussed in Chapter Three, research for this book was guided by the conceptual framework of symbolic interaction; the study of the making of meaningful behavior. To review, symbolic interaction theory states that human beings have the capacity for thought; this capacity is shaped by social interaction, in which people learn meanings and symbols that allow them to develop that capacity. Further, these meanings and symbols allow people to carry on action and interaction, and people can modify or alter meanings and symbols on the basis of their interpretation, or definition, of the situation. People can make these modifications because they have selves. That is, they can interact with themselves, examine courses of action and the advantages and disadvantages of each, and then choose one course of action over another. These intertwined patterns of action and interaction are what constitute groups and societies.

"From the standpoint of its individual members, a society is a thing with an existence independent of themselves, even though its continued being depends very much on them and their behavior. A society, in short, is an object toward which its members act, and to a great extent the fact of social order is simply the fact that people act toward, and so constitute, this object in a stable, orderly fashion." [Hewitt 1984, 188] Thus, any social relationships that individuals act toward constitute real relationships and involve real identities, regardless of whether they are online or off. As one can see from the descriptions that follow, participants in the online relationships this author examined have gone to great lengths to develop and maintain their online communities. Further, they are involved in these communities of their own volition, and not because of some addictive quality of life online.

The Internet Relay Chat Community

Internet Relay Chat (IRC) is a very complex system of online communication and contains several parallel networks and countless individual chat room communities. EFNet was the first IRC network and was developed in 1988. By 1990, however, political differences among key people in the IRC hierarchy resulted in the formation of a number of other real time chat networks which have since, for the most part, withered away. It was not until late 1992 that the Undernet, the other key network within IRC, began to take shape:

> "In October, 1992, people had already started feeling the effects of user overload on EFNet, not to mention many other factors. In an effort to strike out new territory in cyberspace, many 'groups' of individuals had relentlessly attempted to sustain the onslaught of the forbidding isolation, and start up a server of their own. Many failed in their ventures, many just got bored with it and many just got shut down forcibly by paranoid system administrators (sysadmins). Through the scattered outposts emerged two groups. . .one in the U.S. and the other in Europe-Canada. . . . In the last week of December, 1992, the two nets merged. Ever since, a wide variety of servers have appeared and disappeared from the face of the Undernet, but the ones that have held on have always carried forth the spirit. In the face of all odds, against an almost non-existent userbase, they have clung to one another, each operator giving encouragement to the other, trying to lighten up those gloomy days when there were hardly any users. . .the Undernet lives on…"[Mirashi, p. 3]

The significance of statements such as those above, which represent the official history of the Undernet, cannot be overemphasized. The individuals who have worked to establish the Undernet pride themselves on their historic split from what they consider to be a largely 'overrated' EFNet system, and much of the cultural identity of Undernet springs from this split. That is, Undernet, as a culture, defines itself in relation to EFNet and vivid descriptions such as the one above serve to reflect this pride in identity.

What little written history is available regarding Undernet tends to revolve around exploding the myths that 'EFNetters' have supposedly created about the Undernet in order to discredit its worthiness as a system. For example, according to the *Undernet IRC FAQ*, the top six derogatory myths that EFNetters attempt to perpetuate regarding the Undernet are: 1) the Undernet is lame; 2) the Undernet has no users, or, the Undernet has more servers than users; 3) the Undernet was formed by people who couldn't get to be IRC operators (ops) on EFNet; 4) the Undernet servers are run on-the-sly, with no approval from system administrators; 5) Undernet solutions to [computer) protocol work only on a small net--they do not work on large nets; and 6) the Undernet operators are clueless and know nothing about routing.

Against such accusations, 'Undernetters' attempt to redefine themselves and their culture in a positive light:

> "The Undernet consists of some very highly motivated and dedicated people, enthusiastic to make a success of their venture. EFNet is becoming more and more politicized. . .With the various EFNet administrators forming groups against one another, the amount of cooperation between them has become almost nil. The time which they could spend in serving you, the user, is instead spent in endless bickering. Undernet is a net where the operators are friendly, easy going folks, and are always happy to help the user. Abusing users is highly frowned upon, and Undernetters follow a certain Undernetiquette. The goal of the Undernet is to provide a better environment for its users, with protection against malicious users who try to work against IRC principles" [*Undernet IRC FAQ*]

Thus, members of the Undernet have created, from a sociological perspective, a 'we' and a 'they' which they then utilize in order to legitimate their own social institutions and identities. The Undernetter argument is that their community way-of-life revolves around two basic values. First, they pride themselves on the friendly atmosphere they have worked to create. And second, they are dedicated to a more 'fair and efficient' communications system. To those ends, members have developed: 1) rules of netiquette (net etiquette); 2) an IRC-specific lingo; 3) a system of emoticons and action commands to convey body language; and 4) computer protocol enhancements that lessen the likelihood of both netsplit and lag--two communications problems that have the potential to severely disrupt the ability of participants to maintain personal identity and group cohesion.

The basic IRC rules of netiquette, or norms of behavior, are as follows: 1) do not 'flood' the channel with text; 2) do not use beeps in messages; 3) do not use profanity in public messages; 4) do not harass other users with unwanted messages or comments; and 5) do not engage in 'destructive' behavior which reduces the functioning of IRC (running clonebots, floodbots and nick colliders).[21] In general, these rules serve to create a 'level playing field' socially. Rules two, three and four represent the philosophy that all users have the right to participate in the conversation free from harassment and offensive behavior; they serve to maintain the light-hearted and easy going atmosphere.

Rules one and five are intended to enhance social equality by simulating technical equality. It is understood by IRC system administrators that users represent a wide range of technical abilities, and that the technical limitations of users can result from both individual knowledge of computers and physical limitations of the systems being used. So, for example, there is a rule against 'flooding' a channel with text because this can easily cause users with slow modems to experience lag and/or netsplit. In addition, there are rules against running clonebots and floodbots for the same reasons; not only can slow users be forced off the system, but unsuspecting 'newbies' (new users) can be lured into running such bot programs without fully understanding the technical implications. When this occurs, the likelihood of channel disruption is very high. Finally, programs known as 'nick colliders' are prohibited because they, in essence, take over an individual's identity by assuming his or her nickname (nick). Because nicks cannot be registered and because they are the first form of identification to other users, 'jacking' someone else's nick, especially through use of a nick collider, is a serious offense.

Members of IRC have also developed a lingo which is simultaneously designed for maintaining both communication efficiency and the identity of the individual as a member of a given channel. For example, 're' is a 'repeat

---

[21] 'Bot' is short for robot. There are many types of bots on IRC, some of which are necessary and helpful to channel operators. However, clonebots and floodbots serve only to harass others and clog IRC channels, often resulting in 'lag' and 'netsplit', which are two serious problems among IRC users; lag and netsplit prevent the easy, ongoing and lighthearted conversation which is the raison d'etre of IRC.

hi' and is used when one leaves a channel momentarily and then rejoins. The use of 're' saves time and space because users are not required to go through the elaborate welcomes that usually occur when a 'regular' has joined a channel for the first time that day. In addition, the use of 're' is an acknowledgment on the part of others that they are aware that the user was in the channel only moments ago; it is easy, when one lacks a visual presence to others, to be forgotten in the conversation relatively quickly after one has left the room. 'Re' acknowledges that the group recalled the user's presence even during his or her absence, and such acknowledgment is a very reassuring thing indeed.

Similarly, 'brb', 'bbl' and 'bbiaf', which stand for 'be right back', 'be back later' and 'be back in a few', respectively, are used when an individual plans to leave the channel for only a short time. Users, particularly channel regulars, utilize these statements to both announce their intentions to leave the group and to emphasize that they will not be gone long. Such statements are commonly used to maintain group or conversation cohesion in a technically uncertain atmosphere. That is, IRC users are aware that technical problems are a constant threat, and that, at any time, any individual may have to exit the channel to correct such a system problem. Brb, bbl and bbiaf are efficient means of communicating to others in the group that one must leave, often immediately, through no fault of one's own, and that one intends to rejoin the conversation as soon as possible. Basically, this allows others involved in the conversation to maintain a sense of identity and cohesion; their selves have not been simply dismissed by the other.

There are many additional examples of IRC lingo, such as 'lol' and 'rotfl' which stand for laugh out loud and rolling on the floor laughing. Such statements are very commonly used, and reflect the 'just fun' atmosphere of IRC. Other examples of efficiency-oriented lingo are: 'u' for you; 'y' for why; '2' for to or too; 'b' for be; 'r' for are; and 'c' for see. Sometimes, these shorthands are combined, for example in 'oic' which stands for the exclamation, 'oh, I see!'.

IRC participants have also developed and are constantly experimenting with emoticons, a system of symbols which, when combined yield pictures intended to convey body language and facial expressions. This symbol system is so extensive that emoticon dictionaries have been published in order to guide newbies through this new language. The most basic emoticon is the 'smiley', which commonly appears as :) or :-). There are endless variations on smileys now, but some of the most commonly used are :(or :-(to represent sadness; :0 to represent shock or surprise; ;), the winking smiley, which represents sarcasm or an inside joke; :-> to suggest a devious smile; 8-) which is a smiley with glasses; the list is endless.

Beyond smileys, keyboard symbols are also combined to produce other representations of physical appearance or physical activity. For example, (@)(@) may be used to represent breasts; ( )*( ) may indicate that one has been 'mooned'; @>-,--'-- indicates that one has been offered a rose; and {{{{{{nick}}}}}} indicates that one has been hugged. As this communication system evolves, individuals are experimenting with altering the standard computer keyboard in order to allow for the development of new shapes and symbols to convey additional meanings.

In addition to the use of keyboard symbols, IRC participants may also use the "/action" command to simulate physical activity or indirect thought. In order to do this, the user types "/me stares at Fred" for example. To the other channel members, this statement appears on the screen as "Mary stares at Fred". Another possible use of the /action command is to simulate an indirect question or statement. This is done when one wants to make a point or raise an issue without violating the easy going feeling of IRC channels. So, for example, instead of asking "Fred, why did you say that?", which is in a threatening format that violates the friendliness norm, the statement would appear as "Mary wonders what Fred meant by that." In this way, one user may point out a potential problem to another without any sort of direct confrontation.

In general, emoticons and /action commands are developed and utilized in order to account for the most common emotional and physical requirements of a text-based identity. They allow for the efficient creation of a rich social context, in which users are able to convey socioemotional and physical cues. Such cues, in turn, allow for meaningful communication, the development of a sense of self, and a sense of group membership in an environment that might otherwise be devoid of meaning.

Finally, Undernet community members have enhanced the protocol of the server-server system to retard the occurrence of both lag and netsplit. The term 'lag' refers to the delay in messages reaching their destination. For example, if user number one does not receive any messages from user number two for several minutes, and then receives messages from user two all bunched together, user two is lagged. Or, if user one sees no messages from any user, and is then flooded with messages from everyone, user one is lagged. This can occur when users are not connected to servers that are closest to them or when a particular server is overloaded with users.

Netsplit, in a sense, is the ultimate form of lag. That is, when a server is severely overloaded, it can no longer accommodate all users and some users are 'split' from the 'real' channel off into what amounts to a parallel universe. They are separated from the real channel and cannot communicate with the members of that channel, even though the computer they are using tells them they are in that channel. Users must then sign off of IRC and sign back on in what they hope is the 'real' channel. However, this process can often take several minutes and as a result can be very frustrating.

It is easy to understand, given that IRC is a system of real-time chat, that both lag and netsplit effectively remove the affected individuals from the ongoing group conversation. The group conversation continues, and the affected individuals, for technical reasons, are prevented from engaging in it; one 'misses out' on what the group is doing until one can get back to the channel. Even when one returns successfully, that portion of the conversation that was missed is often gone forever, thus leaving the lagged or split individuals with holes in their understandings of the conversations. Particularly for the newbie, the experience of lag and netsplit can be frustrating because, not only does one not know how exactly to go about correcting the situation, one's attempts at 'fitting in' and becoming a member of the group are interrupted midstream.

Recognizing these issues as important in the development of stable channels, one of the primary goals of the individuals who split from EFNet to form the Undernet was to create server-server systems that minimized these possibilities. To that end, users have developed a protocol that disallows netsplit 'op riders'. If netsplit occurs in EFNet, it is difficult to maintain the notion that only one of the channels is the 'real' one. This is because people may intentionally induce a netsplit and then 'ride the split' into a channel and take over the status of channel operator, with all of its accompanying powers. Once in power, the new operators may do as they please, and the first thing they usually do is take the operator status away from the real channel operators. It is self-evident that such behavior, particularly when it is a constant possibility, makes the task of creating a sense of group cohesion and identity extremely difficult. Undernet protocol does not allow for such activities and, as a consequence, the stability of channel and participant identity is ensured. Even if some channel members are periodically lagged or split, there is the understanding that there is only one 'real' channel, the integrity of which cannot be violated. These basic rules of netiquette, and systems of language, emoticons and action commands, combined with the technical improvements and the philosophy of those who started the Undernet, are what give the Undernet its feeling as a culture, as a place. And the feeling, or ambience, is that of Ray Oldenburg's [1991] 'third place'.

According to Oldenburg, the third place is "inclusively sociable, offering both the basis of community and the celebration of it. . . they (third places) host the regular, voluntary, informal and happily anticipated gatherings of individuals beyond the realms of home and work." [p. 16] He goes on to describe the eight basic characteristics of third places as follows: 1) they are established on 'neutral ground'; 2) they are social status levelers; 3) conversation is the main activity; 4) they are accessible and accommodating in terms of time and location; 5) they are given character by 'the regulars'; 6) they keep a 'low profile'; 7) the mood is a playful one; and 8) the environment is congenial--a home away from home.

As any Undernet channel regulars will attest, IRC is a prime example of a third place. IRC channels are neutral ground; participants can come and go as they please, and no one has to be the host (though everyone feels at home). Channels are also status levelers for participants. That is, they are accessible to the general public, do not set formal criteria of membership or exclusion, expand the types of people one can get to know, and put the emphasis on personal qualities not confined to status distinctions. While this does not necessarily mean that everyone is perfectly equal in the Undernet, what it does mean is that "the charm and flavor of one's personality is what counts. . .Those who, on the outside, command deference and attention by sheer weight of their position find themselves in the third place enjoined, embraced, accepted and enjoyed where conventional status counts for little." [Oldenburg, p. 24]

Furthermore, it is self-evident that conversation is the main activity of the Undernet; conversation is all there is. But IRC's quality as a third place goes deeper than this. Not only is conversation the main activity, it is the type of conversation that is important. It is lively, scintillating, colorful and engaging. IRC dialogue conforms to the 'simple rules of good conversation': people share the talking time relatively equally; they are attentive while others are talking; they are careful not to hurt others' feelings while still managing to say what they think; they avoid topics not of general interest; they say little about themselves personally (at least during public chat room conversations); they avoid trying to instruct others (instead making suggestions about possible issues); and they speak in 'as low a voice' that will allow others to 'hear'. All people contribute about the right amount of time, and most everyone participates to some degree, even the newbies.

Undernet channels are 'open' 24 hours a day, and one may go alone at almost any time of the day or night and see people one knows. And, while there exist groups of regulars at various points during the day, there is fluidity in the timing of meetings--people come and go at somewhat similar hours, but not exactly the same, and sometimes days are missed by some regulars. Of course, these days missed are duly noted and commented upon by the regulars who do drop by; people are questioned as to the whereabouts of someone who is missing. Activity is unplanned, unscheduled and unstructured, and that is what lends the group character.

And what of the regulars? Oldenburg suggests that it is the regulars that gives the third place its conviviality: "Third places are dominated by their regulars, but not necessarily in a numerical sense. It is the regulars whose mood and manner provide the infectious and contagious style of interaction and whose acceptance of new faces is crucial." [p. 34] In IRC, just as in other third places, one becomes 'a regular' through a certain process. Acceptance into the circle is not difficult, but it is not automatic, either. A newbie must establish trust between him- or herself and the regulars; one continues to reappear and tries not to be obnoxious. No 'serious' conversation is allowed; personal problems and moodiness must be set aside. Conversation is lively, and consciousness of time and circumstances slips away. Ultimately, "every topic and speaker is a potential trapeze for the exercise and display of wit. The unmistakable mark of acceptance into the company of third place regulars is not that of being taken seriously, but that of being included in the play forms of their association." [p. 38]

Third places are said to have a low profile physically; often they were originally designed to serve a different purpose, and haphazardly evolved into places for sociability. Clearly, IRC channels represent the lowest 'physical' profile possible, as they are socially created places. For its members, IRC is a 'home away from home'. It roots people in time and place as people tend to go at around the same time everyday and see familiar faces. It allows for a sense of control over one's environment as regulars are accorded special privileges not granted to others. After visiting one's channel, one feels socially regenerated and restored. Thinking back to much of the anecdotal critique of CMC, it tends to revolve around the idea that such forms of communication are an 'escape from reality'. Oldenburg argues that, while third places are an escape, they are not *just* an escape. To view such places in this manner emphasizes the *outside* world and neglects the examination of what happens *inside* third places.

The Usenet Community

While no one would argue that Usenet is a third place, it still displays all of the basic attributes of a community. Usenet most definitely has its own system of language, as well as a clearly defined set of beliefs, values and norms. The difference is ultimately one of style.

According to Tom Seidenberg, the best way to describe Usenet culture is through the 'room analogy':

> "You've got this enormous building with thousands of rooms. Each room has a sign outside describing what is being discussed inside. . .Some rooms are very organized. These rooms have a large audience and a few selected speakers, and a spokesman or two. . .Some rooms do not have any spokesmen, but are still very well organized. Every now and then some people go over to a corner and have a quiet conversation, but nothing terribly loud. Other rooms are like big social gatherings with many smaller groups talking (or yelling) among themselves. There are many people in these rooms, most of them just walking around and listening in on the various conversations. . .There are also play rooms, some with very few people, but they make a terrible racket! Often, these play rooms have a king of the mountain, a demi-god, or even a bully..."[1995, pp. 3 & 4]

This is an excellent explanation of Usenet culture because it simultaneously expresses the idea that each individual Usenet newsgroup has its own particular atmosphere, while at the same time all newsgroups share certain basic values about how Usenet life should be conducted.

There are two seemingly contradictory beliefs that participants in Usenet hold about their community, both of which are claimed to stem from consensus of personal experience. The first generally held belief is that Usenet is anarchy. The second belief is that Usenet behavior is fairly predictable. For example, according to Henry Hardy:

> "Usenet is unusual among computer networks or communications systems in that it has no formal rules, no formal enforcement mechanism. . . .The combination of public, nonprofit and commercial networks over which Usenet is transmitted makes for a complex and controversial situation with regards to liability, free speech, obscenity, appropriate use, commercial use

and other issues. The lack of a central regulatory or governing body makes the Usenet a study in functional anarchy. . .The current decision making structure of usenet might best be described as 'cooperative anarchy'. Usenet operates more like a culture than a formal system. The rules of conduct are implicit and are only explicitly stated in the news.* hierarchy groups and in some FAQs. The FAQs and the memories of the 'ancient ones' represent the collective wisdom of the net" [1993, pp. 2, 4, & 7]

Such descriptions of 'Usenet as anarchy' are fairly common in much of the written documentation on the history and culture of this community. The basic premise is that, because there is no single central governing body, Usenet is an anarchic system. However, the cultural beliefs outlined below regarding the predictability of Usenet social life belie the proposition that Usenet is anarchy. In fact, a lack of central, formalized controls have lead to the development of sophisticated, if informal, means of social organizing; means that are 'formal enough' to accomplish the tasks at hand.

Regardless of the fact that the Usenet community enjoys and perpetuates the myth of anarchy, 'true' members of the Usenet community believe that they are capable of predicting Usenet social life. This belief is so strong that it has been formulated into a set of laws and concepts which are generally understood by the core Usenet population.

Among the most important laws and concepts are: 1) Aahz's Law--the best way to get information on Usenet is not to ask a question, but to post the wrong information; 2) Boigy's Law--the theory that there are certain topics in every newsgroup that are discussed cyclically. Often, the period of the cycle and the length of the resulting discussion, can be accurately estimated by those who have been around long enough; 3) Sturgeon's Law--ninety percent of everything on Usenet is crud. What that ninety percent is depends on who you are. This does not imply that the remaining ten percent is not crud; 4) Religious Issues--questions which seemingly cannot be raised without touching off Holy Wars. Almost every group has a Religious Issue of some kind, and they are guaranteed to start a long running, tiresome, bandwidth-wasting flame war; 5) September--the time when college students return and start to post stupid questions, break rules of netiquette and just generally make life on Usenet more difficult. However, with the growing popular media discussion of the 'information superhighway', it now seems like September lasts year round; 6) Signal to Noise Ratio--a subjective quantity describing someone's idea of just how much content a group has, relative to the junk the group has. Each person has their own threshold and if a group falls below that threshold, a member will unsubscribe; and 7) The

Imminent Death of Usenet--a cyclical prediction which shows up in the popular press and references the assumption that Usenet is anarchy; the latest upheaval, technological or social, is more than likely to bring about the demise of the Usenet system. This particular term is now a myth-become-joke among core Usenet members. [*alt.culture.usenet FAQ* 1995, 5- 6]

Beyond typifying laws of behavior, Usenet participants also classify some personality types within their community. For example, there is the Kook--a weirdo who randomly appears in random groups and who causes no end of trouble. Often placed in kill files[22], the kook usually only disappears after everyone finally stops responding to their ridiculous or improperly posted articles. Then there is the Lurker--one who reads a newsgroup but posts no articles. The Lurker has reached such mythical proportions as to provoke estimates that 90 percent of people who use Usenet are lurkers.

And finally, there is the Net.God, which is a concept best understood through use of a specific example. According to the *Net.Legends FAQ* [1995], Kibo is a genuine net.god. "Perhaps the single defining hallmark of genius is to do something that no one else has ever done before, or even thought of doing, and making it look blindingly obvious afterwards. James 'Kibo' Parry, confronted with the vast reality of Usenet, decided to 'grep' his entire newsfeed for posts containing "kibo" in order to look them over and see if they were worth replying to. He has now become a Usenet term: grepping your newsfeed is "kibozing", and one who does so is a "kibozer". He also has his own newsgroup: alt.religion.kibology, which is also his own religion. If you receive email from him, you are given a kibo.number."

This typification of social phenomena and personalities in Usenet has become extensive enough to warrant a document (cited above) known as the *Net.Legends FAQ*. The *Net.Legends FAQ* is described as ". . .a collection of descriptions of net.phenomena one hears about in passing and wishes one had more information about. Not all are completely factual entries: in some cases the true facts are known only to one person, or lost in the mists of time, while in others the facts pale in relation to the mythology. In any case, the actual facts included, sparse though they may be, are true as far as I know. Since these are net.legends, not much of a real attempt to verify this

---

[22] A 'kill-file' is a program that users can install in their newsreaders that will automatically delete unwanted postings from the selected individual. This way, the user is not required to sift through what he or she considers to be waste-of-time postings.

information has been made." Despite the description, within the Usenet community this document represents 'the truth' with relation to social history. This is the case with all FAQ documents; they establish Usenet as a community. And, while they may not be 'formal' means of social control, when referenced they carry a great deal of weight in making a case for or against certain actions or behaviors.

One can see that, sociologically, there is a "we" in Usenet and this "we" has a history together. Further, "we" refer to ourselves as being present in physical places--rooms. We share beliefs about ourselves and our social system and we also believe that we know ourselves, each other and our relation to the 'outside world' well enough to predict the behavior of those around us. In the face of evidence to the contrary and self-identification as a community, Usenet members continue the myth of anarchy. It is a myth that allows for the development of group identity relative to the outside world; a world which is, to a large extent, complicit in perpetuating the myth of anarchy. This belief allows members to feel a sense of solidarity and of participation in the development of a new form of social organization; something which has never been done before. Of course, this myth of anarchy is predicated on the assumption that anarchy is the opposite of order. As Robert Bierstedt [1970] points out, however, the opposite of culture or order is not conflict or anarchy or disorder. The opposite of order is non-involvement.

Like IRC, the basic values in Usenet are efficiency (relative to time and bandwidth), and quality communication. Accordingly, participants in Usenet have developed a system of netiquette and an interrelated, Usenet-specific language-form (the troll), which are intended as informal means of maintaining these core values. There are several documents that lay out Usenet rules of behavior. Some of them are designed for users, and some of them are designed for system operators (sysops). However, they all emphasize two main points: conservation of scarce resources, and being generally 'polite' to others, thus creating a positive self image.

For example, according to Chuq von Rospach's *A Primer on How to Work With the Usenet Community*, users are encouraged to: 1) never forget that the person on the other side is human; 2) be careful what you say about others; 3) be brief; 4) remember your postings reflect upon you-be proud of them; 5) think about your audience; 6) be careful with humor and sarcasm; 7) only post a message once; 8) rotate (encrypt) material with questionable content, answers or spoilers; 9) summarize what you are following up; 10) use email-don't post a follow-up; 11) read all follow-ups and don't repeat what has already been said; 12) double-check follow-up newsgroups and distributions; 13) be careful about copyrights and licenses; 14) cite appropriate references; 15) do not ignite a spelling flame war; 16) don't overdo signatures; 17) do not use Usenet as a resource for homework assignments; 18) do not use Usenet as an advertising medium; and 19) avoid posting to multiple newsgroups. Clearly, two key issues are concern for other users' feelings and impressions of you and concern for the conservation of scarce Usenet resources.

Of course, in order to have a full appreciation of Usenet etiquette, the role it plays in establishing social order and the degree of seriousness community members attach to those rules, one must read them through the satirical framework that gets to the heart of the 'feeling' of Usenet; one must read Brad Templeton's *Dear Emily Postnews*. Consider, for example, netiquette rule number four--'your postings reflect upon you, so be proud of them'. Within the Emily Postnews format, this issue is addressed as follows:

Question:
"Dear Emily Postnews,
I can't spell worth a dam. I hope your going to tell me what to do?
Answer:
Don't worry about how your articles look. Remember it's the message that counts, not the way it's presented. Ignore the fact that sloppy spelling in a purely written format sends out the same silent messages that soiled clothing would when addressing an audience."

Or, consider netiquette rule number ten--use email, don't post a follow-up:

Question:
"Dear Emily Postnews,
I read an article that said, 'reply by mail, I'll summarize'. What should I do?
Answer:
Post your response to the whole net. That request applies only to dumb people who don't have something interesting to say. Your postings are much more worthwhile than other people's, so it would be a waste to reply by mail."

Ultimately, in the Usenet community, a user's postings *are* his or her identity. And a critical point in defining oneself as a good community member is recognizing that one's time and thoughts are no more (or less) valuable than those of other users. Usenet is not intended as a one-way broadcast medium. It is for people to carry on discussions about specific topics in which they are already interested. Using Usenet in a means that violates this rule, commonly called net-abuse, is a serious offense.

Besides using rules of netiquette as a means of maintaining values and conveying meaning, Usenetters utilize both the language of the emoticon (as did IRC members) and Usenet specific language forms designed for the control of 'deviant' behavior. There has been a great deal of confusion about two Usenet language forms; the flame and the troll. Briefly, to flame in Usenet means "to post a message intended to insult or provoke; to speak incessantly and/or rabidly on some relatively uninteresting subject or with a patently ridiculous attitude; either of these two, directed with hostility at a particular person or persons, for example, posting an article on how to run over dogs in rec.pets.dogs." [*alt.culture.usenet FAQ* 1995, 5] A troll, on the other hand, is a posting that is designed specifically to generate follow-ups about something trivial, but not in the sense of a flame, or a post designed to instruct readers to ignore obvious drivel by making those who reply feel utterly stupid. Such things as misspellings, incorrect facts or concepts can be used as trolls. After the follow-ups have died down, the troller will usually inform the victims of their status as guinea pigs and then move on to another group.

Now, the reason that it is critical to bring up this particular 'deviant' behavior here is that the argument against Usenet as 'real' community rests in large part on the notion that interaction in Usenet is 'uncivilized'. It is claimed that in Usenet, it is too easy to flame people and discussions often break down into name-calling that would not be tolerated in a real-life meeting or social setting. This claim demonstrates a lack of understanding of Usenet culture. First, one must consider the context of the flame. While it can be, and often is used as described above, simply to 'irk' people, it is also used in boundary work. That is, as one experienced Usenetter says, "we especially like to flame people who even hint at newbieness." Thus, flames have multiple purposes, one of which is to make the social distinction between the 'lowly' newbie and the 'true' Usenetter; being flamed as a newbie is a rite of passage.

Second, when the flame does consist of a 'patently ridiculous attitude', its use is controlled by community members, sometimes through use of the troll:

"The purpose of trolling is not to deliberately start a flame war. Deliberately starting a flame war is flame-baiting, and it requires absolutely no intelligence to post something obscene that'll get people mad. Trolling is more subtle. It's a tactic to discourage flaming, by posting intelligently and cleverly crafted (but marked) inaccuracies; someone attempting to flame a posted troll finds that he has acted too rashly and has succeeded only in making a fool of himself. It reinforces netiquette; flamebaiting encourages the breakdown of netiquette. A good troll is an impressive thing." [alt.culture.usenet FAQ 1995, 8]

Though it is markedly different from IRC, Usenet may easily be viewed as a community with its own distinct culture. It displays norms, customs and traditions different from the external cultures in which it is embedded. Enforcement of these norms begins with the individual community members, and consensual interpretation by the Usenet public becomes the 'law'.

The Fidonet Community

> Fidonet is no longer just a piece of software;
> it has become a complex organism.
>   Tom Jennings, Fidonet founder

The easiest way to get a general sense of Fidonet culture is to draw some comparisons between it and Usenet culture; both are asynchronous messaging systems which are similar enough in technical structure and purpose that the main concerns of Usenet (conservation of bandwidth, efficiency and proper presentation of self) are also the main concerns of Fidonet. However, where Usenetters see their community as "anarchy" (even though behavior is considered predictable), the basic belief system within Fidonet is that volunteerism and cooperation combine to create an orderly (enough) community.

The primary difference between Fidonet and Usenet is one of funding. While Usenet is funded largely through universities and commercial sponsors, Fidonet is a completely voluntary system. Further, while Usenet was designed with 'serious' concerns in mind (e.g. transmission of data among universities), Fidonet's purpose, ". . .very simply, is as a hobby; a non-commercial network of computer hobbyists ('hackers' in the older, original meaning) who want to play with, and find uses for, packet-switch networking. It is not a commercial venture in any way; Fidonet is totally supported by its users and sysops (system operators), and in many ways is similar to ham radio, in that other than a few 'stiff' rules, each sysop runs their system in any way they please, for any reason they want." [Jennings 1985, 3]

Fidonet was created, by accident, in June, 1984 and had only two nodes. By August of that year, it had 30 nodes. This pattern of growth quickly became the justification for a new system of message routing. While this routing system required additional people to assist with the network, it remained a cooperative voluntary system; it did not immediately become a bureaucracy. According to Jennings, "Well, at first, everyone knew each other; we were in more or less constant contact. However, when the node number got into the twenties, there were people bringing up FidoNodes who none of us knew. This was good, but it meant that we were not in close contact anymore. The Net started to deteriorate; every single week without fail there was at least one wrong number, usually two. Fidonet is just too large today to run as an informal club". [1985, p. 2] This process of routing messages in a low cost manner to all nodes was how the zone/region/net/node/point hierarchy explained in Chapter 2 came about; the original intent was to "decentralize Fidonet" and maintain messaging efficiency.

However, Randy Bush was correct in his assessment that, because Fidonet has been operated by end-users and hobbyists, rather than 'computer professionals', it has experienced social and political issues more rapidly and more seriously than have other network cultures:

> "In 1986, a well-intentioned but naive group formed the International Fidonet Association, intending to promulgate the technology and coordinate publication of the newsletter (FidoNews) and other writings about the network. Unfortunately, as Fidonet operators were far more socially oriented than their more technical brethren in the other networks, the formal organization of IFNA tended to draw considerable political interest and attracted the less constructive political elements of the Fidonet culture. The issue came to a head in 1989 with an attempt to load the IFNA board of directors and pass a motion which explicitly put IFNA in complete control of the network. The motion was cleverly forced into a netwide referendum (Fidonet's only global vote to date) which required a majority of the network assent to IFNA rule. The referendum did not pass, and IFNA was subsequently dissolved." [1993, p. 7]

In 1987, what is known as *Policy4* came into existence. The first policy document of Fidonet, *Policy1*, was written in 1985 and adopted by informal consent. "It was mainly a record of currently accepted policies. It worked for a long time and only became obsolete as we grew in complexity. It was good. This original policy grew and grew, and somehow culminated into the monstrosity of Policy4, which is not a policy, but an attempt at law, related to Policy1 only in name. It stinks." [Jennings 1992, vol. 9-34, 1]

Policy4, written by Regional Coordinators, has 'a large amount of social and political content enshrining a hierarchy of coordinators', all of whom are either elected or appointed by those Regional Coordinators. Beyond that, and perhaps even more importantly, the *Policy4* document also has a 'tone' to it that violates Fidonetters' commitment to voluntary cooperation. The tone violates basic cultural beliefs by assuming that Fidonet community sysops, to whom it is directed, need some sort of official document that will tell them, in detail, every responsibility and obligation they have in Fidonet life; that without such dictates, "Fidonet is large enough that it would quickly fall apart of its own weight unless some sort of structure and control were imposed on it." [p. 1] It is a legally stylized document in its numbering system, and many sentences begin with 'You are responsible for...', 'It is your responsibility to...', 'You must...', or 'You should...'. One Fidonet member, to point out the offensiveness of such a tone and the ridiculousness of the formal hierarchy, wrote a satire of *Policy4* which culminated in, "These levels act to put everybody under the thumb of whoever takes charge; this is considered desirable because the author of this document is in charge." [Priven 1988, vol. 5-06, 10]

There have been other political upheavals in Fidonet, for example the Zone 2 War during 1992. Such problems have caused enough concern within the Fidonet community that the 'Fidonet History Project' was begun in 1994. The Fidonet History Project is an attempt to chronicle the first ten years of Fidonet's growth. It was begun because there was concern that,

> ". . .with all of the changes that have occurred in just the last year or two, Fidonet is in very real danger of losing its roots. We have a noble heritage being the first grassroots communications network, literally by the people and for the people. It would be a shame to lose that. Fidonet is a rather unique entity that tends to defy description. . . it has burgeoned into an indescribably loud and boisterous while at the same time quiet and thoughtful communications network comprising sysops and users from all walks of life. I greatly fear that no writer. . .can do justice to Fidonet, its culture and tradition. Yet I feel it's important that Fidonet's roots be preserved for future generations of cybernauts." [Robbins 1995]

The main point to be gleaned from this brief overview is that Fidonet has a history and tradition that its members are proud of. As with both Undernet and Usenet, one definitely gets the sense from this description that Fidonetters have a sense of community. Not only do they get into heated political debates about where they are going as a group, they have set up an organization to preserve their cultural heritage. And, as with the other CMC communities previously discussed, they talk about themselves as being co-present in physical places, and they design norms of behavior, systems of language, and formats for communication (specifically, *FidoNews*) to endow those physical places with meaning. Consider the following description of Fidonet by founder, Tom Jennings [1985]:

> "In the dark ages of modems (pre-1982), there were so few bulletin boards and users that there basically wasn't a problem. You somehow managed to get a modem . . . and started dialing. You got nervous and made a mess of the message base, and if you were real unlucky, crashed the board. Everyone knew you were 'new', and so were tolerant while you learned how to get around. Crashers and trashers weren't really a problem. . . .Now, however, it frequently becomes a situation like a traveler to a foreign country who is totally unfamiliar with local customs. Visitors embarrass themselves by saying the wrong thing, or insult the locals with totally inappropriate reactions. . .In face-to-face encounters with people that you don't know well, there are thousands of unwritten rules that just about everyone follows. A big problem with modeming is that you miss all non-verbal communication details. You have to make up for this in other ways. Get an idea of what kind of people are there. Bulletin boards are no different than a local bar or whatever. . . .This is no different than joining a conversation at a party or cafe; you just can't jump in and blaze away with your wit. . . .Keep in mind that some things that are wonderful person to person can be absolute disasters in print." [pp. 2,3]

Bearing in mind this sense of place, combined with the need for efficient, low-cost communications, Fidonetters have developed two simple rules of netiquette (which parallel the rules of IRC and Usenet): 1) thou shalt not excessively annoy others; and 2) thou shalt not be too easily annoyed. In order to avoid 'excessively annoying others', one should: 1) remember that each conference in the bbs has a subject--don't get too far off of it; 2) be cautious about starting a new topic if one has newbie status; 3) in responding to a message, mention enough of the previous message so that other readers can tell what you are replying to; 4) remember the delay involved in Fidonet messaging; many may be replying to a piece of mail at once, and you may get repeats or a flood of similar responses all at once; 5) keep messages short; and 6) avoid flaming; it is bad form to spend more time in the reply discussing personalities than the real issues.

In order to avoid 'becoming excessively annoyed', one should: 1) remember that people may call in everyday, once a week or maybe never again; be patient when waiting for a reply. After a while, one gets an idea of who calls in how often; 2) remember that, in the user-sysop relationship, "There is a human out there somewhere. Sysops are saints and assholes like everyone else, and they have the responsibility of keeping the system up and running. Getting angry at the sysop for not answering a request as quickly or as thoroughly as you want is definitely not the way to get in good graces on that board." [Jennings 1985, vol. 2-30, 4]

Given the previous discussion of emoticons and their ability to enhance meaningful communications, it is unnecessary to discuss this again for the Fidonet system. Suffice it to say that Fidonetters use emoticons in the same way Usenetters do, and like Usenetters, they do not have as extensive an array of emoticons as do Undernetters. Like Usenetters, they tend to use emoticons relatively infrequently, and to use only the more basic styles of smileys. However, Fidonet does employ one additional communication format that is critical to the establishment and maintenance of community; the weekly newsletter, *FidoNews*.

Like the FAQ system in Usenet, the *FidoNews* newsletter brings together what might otherwise be isolated and individualized bulletin board systems (BBSs). Like Usenet newsgroups, each Fidonet BBS has a somewhat different 'feel' to it. Some are centered around playing games, while others may be family-oriented. But, as the FAQ documents in Usenet provide all newsgroups with a sense of belonging to something larger, so does *FidoNews* for BBSs. This fact is readily acknowledged by Fidonet founder, Tom Jennings, and by others in the Fidonet community. "The newsletter, *FidoNews*, was and still is an integral part of the process of Fidonet. *FidoNews* is the only thing that unites all Fidonet sysops consistently." [Jennings 1985, 8]

FidoNews provides a sense of being a community of people with common interests; it provides, what Benedict Anderson calls the imagined community:

> "We know that particular morning and evening editions will overwhelmingly be consumed between this hour and that, only on this day, not that. . .this mass ceremony is performed in silent privacy, in the lair of

the skull. Yet each communicant is well aware that the ceremony he performs is being replicated simultaneously by thousands of others of whose existence he is confident, yet of whose identity he has not the slightest notion. . . .What more vivid figure for the secular, historically clocked, imagined community can be envisioned?" [1991, p. 35]

While *FidoNews* is not necessarily read simultaneously by all sysops, it is a regular, weekly ceremony, performed in privacy, through which individuals develop the sense that they know other Fidonetters and belong to that community. As founder Tom Jennings points out:

"There are quite a lot of us here. About a thousand sysops, and at least ten times that many users. Many of us have gotten to know each other quite well. This is quite amazing, especially when you consider that few of us have ever met. We know each other by the words we type. We see each other as little dots of light forming text on our screens." [1986, vol. 3-23, 2]

Chapter 6

AN INTERACTIONIST VIEW
OF INTERNET ADDICTION DISORDER:
CONCLUDING REMARKS

"Although descriptions of madness and its subtypes have been around since the ancient Greeks, until the last half of the 20th century a handful of unofficial, broad categories appeared to be sufficient for the task. By the 1990s, however, the count had grown to about three hundred and appears to be rising rapidly. Moreover, categories of disorders are all now carefully encrusted in a nationally approved classification system. How, in brief, did this evolve?" [Kirk and Kutchins, 1992]

Answering this question has been the ultimate objective of this work. But while my focus here has been on the social construction of computer-mediated communications as a behavioral disorder, this project, in the end, is but one contribution to a long campaign against the idea that human behaviors and choices are medical disorders. This work, in many respects, follows the framework of Davies [1997].

In his *Myth of Addiction*, Davies argues that "...most people who use drugs do so for their own reasons, on purpose, because they like it, and because they find no adequate reason for not doing so; rather than because they fall prey to some addictive illness which removes their capacity for voluntary behavior." He also offers reasons why this "second type of explanation is nonetheless more popular and is generally preferred, and why scientists and practitioners frequently seek out evidence relevant to that view rather than to any other and subsequently impose it on their clientele for reasons that have noting to do with scientific knowledge." Finally, he suggests that, "a different context or 'system' is required within which an alternative view of drug use can thrive; a view which stresses volition and control deriving from the ability to make and implement personal decisions." [p. xi]

I have attempted here to make the same case regarding Internet Addiction Disorder. This new-found disorder, which has coincided with exponential growth in the number of linkage points, host computers, connected networks and individual users plugged in to the Internet, is largely the result of apprehension about the nature of the Net's impact on our collective psychological well-being—apprehension that has always been felt about any new technology. Though many regular Internet participants have scoffed at such an idea, and have created satirical Web sites, IRC chat rooms and Usenet newsgroups to make their point, a growing number of professionals in the field of psychology have been captivated by this apparently new disorder. They have argued that Internet participation is addictive, and that in many ways, its symptoms, diagnosis and treatment parallel those of other addictions, such as compulsive gambling, shopping and even drug and alcohol abuse.

What are we to make of this new disorder? What, precisely, does 'addiction' mean, and does the social label of 'addict' provide a satisfactory explanation of the human behavior patterns to which it is commonly attached? Can individuals really become addicted to the Internet? Is there an alternative explanation as to why people choose to spend time, in some cases very large amounts of time, online? These are the questions I asked at the outset of this book. And, through the sociological lens of symbolic interaction, I have tried to answer them. By bringing together analyses of the evolution of addiction and the historical apprehension of new technologies, I have attempted to demonstrate that the 'discovery' of Internet Addiction Disorder (IAD) should come as no surprise. On the contrary, the birth of Internet Addiction Disorder has followed, in logical procession, the social construction of a complete lineage of other sorts of behavioral disorders. Its discovery was by no means instantaneous or accidental. Behind the creation of IAD lay nearly 150 years of research into, theorizing about, and labeling of so-called addictive behaviors.

Addiction, the last of three generations of disease, evolved from the 'germ theory' of disease. This theory, first applied to physical ailments, or what Peele [1989] refers to as the first generation, was based on the notion that one could, in a laboratory setting, isolate specific agents in the external biological environment that caused physical ailments. This discovery ushered in the era of modern medicine as we know it, and paved the way for the two generations of disease that were to follow, as human behaviors, rather than physical ailments, became medicalized. Medicalization of behavior, rooted in this germ theory, ultimately resulted in the application of scientific medicine to human behavior patterns. This scientific medicine, in which the body is viewed as a machine, focuses on the internal environment (the physical body) and ignores the external *social* environment. As this doctrine has, over time, been applied not only to physical ailments, but to mental, emotional, and behavioral issues as well, the focus has shifted to the medicalization of deviant behaviors specifically. Thus, in short, medicalization is the defining and labeling of deviant behavior as a medical problem, usually an illness, and the mandating of the medical profession to provide some type of treatment for it. This process has two steps; the social construction of an illness, and the social construction of deviance as a special type of illness.

Consider first the social construction of illness in general. At its core, illness is nothing more and nothing less than a negative human social judgment of existing conditions in the natural world. When such negative social judgments, based as they are on the germ theory of disease, are applied to human behavior, the end result is a redefinition of devalued behaviors as illnesses (step two). In contrast to deviant behaviors defined as crimes (of which there are relatively few today), behaviors defined as illnesses "locate the source of deviant behavior within the individual, postulating a physiological, constitutional, organic, or occasionally, psychogenic agent or condition that is assumed to cause the behavioral deviance . . . usually mandating intervention by medical personnel with medical means. . ." [Conrad 1980, 25] Thus, while willful deviance is equated with crime and dealt with by agents of social control such as the police and court system, 'unwillful' deviance is equated with illness, and the appropriate agent of social control is medicine.

In the second generation of diseases, the scientific medical model was applied to mental illnesses and emotional disorders. However, unlike the first generation diseases, which are apparent to the observer because he or she can measure them in the body and observe the physical damage that results, second generation diseases "...are apparent to us. . . because of the feelings, thoughts and behaviors that they produce in people, *which we can only know from what the sufferers say and do.*" [Peele 1989, emphasis mine] It is this reliance on the say-so of the sufferer that renders a diagnosis of mental illness that is qualitatively different from a diagnosis of physical illness.

Regardless, the model was generally accepted by the medical community, despite serious questions about its validity.

This framework was then applied to the concept of addiction, the third generation of illness. In this generation, the logical connection between biological cause and measurable physiological effect that was the hallmark of the original disease model continued to disintegrate, though the reliance on and assumed relevance of that model itself did not. Whereas mental disorders become apparent through the feelings, thoughts and behaviors they produce, either as described by the sufferer or interpreted by the observer, *addictions are nothing more and nothing less than the behaviors they describe*: "How do we know a given individual is addicted? No biological indicators can give us this information. We decide the person is addicted when he *acts* addicted. . . . we believe a person is addicted *when he says that he is*." [Peele 1985, 18 emphasis mine] That is, addiction cannot be said to exist in the absence of the ongoing behavior that the specific addiction label describes; behaviors themselves, an ever-expanding list of behaviors, are the disease. Thus, over time, the concept of 'drunkenness as an uncontrollable disease' fused with the germ theory of disease to yield and idea that has simultaneously become increasingly formalized and increasingly generalized. This combination has allowed the term to be used, not only by professionals, but by members of the general public, as an explanation of an ever-broadening range of human behaviors.

This view, which defined addiction as a disease (as opposed to a 'sin' or 'maladaptive behavior pattern'), has allowed the social role of "addict" to become, over time, a defining and legitimating identity within the American cultural framework. Equally important as the transformation of the 'causes' of addiction is what such redefinition has accomplished for the role attributes and responsibilities of "the addict", his significant others, and society. In the sin framework, which was historically the first means people used to explain excessive use of drugs or alcohol, the individual in question was defined as refusing to abide by the common moral code. In this way, drug or alcohol abuse was seen as a freely chosen behavior; individuals have free will. Accordingly, the only appropriate 'treatment' for problems caused by excessive substance use was punishment, and no further discussion of the issue was required.

With the rise in social status of the medical profession in the late 1800s came the creation of the disease model of addiction. Within this framework, addiction is viewed as the result of an 'underlying disease process', usually brought about by early childhood psychological damage, genetic predisposition, or a combination of both. Such factors render the individual susceptible to addiction. This susceptibility, in combination with environmental stress and exposure to drugs and alcohol, leads first to addiction and ultimately to the problems commonly associated with such a state – criminal behavior, family breakdown, depression, aggression, and so forth. In other words, a core disease within the individual *causes* the compulsive act of drinking or drugging excessively, rather than vice versa. This disease renders the abuser helpless; his or her actions are not freely chosen. As a result, the individual requires treatment, specifically medical treatment, rather than punishment.

Subscribing to this disease model of addiction requires the acceptance of five core concepts which have traditionally represented the model: addiction as a primary disease; loss of control; addiction as a progressive disease; addiction as a chronic disease; and denial. Further, acceptance of these five core concepts requires one to concede that addiction cannot be said to exist in the absence of the ongoing behavior that the specific addiction label describes. Behaviors themselves, an ever-expanding list of behaviors, are the diseases. In this co-dependent world view [Rice 1996], anything, any activity, may become addicting. Revolving around the presumption that human beings have 'relationships', not only with other people, but with food, work, shopping malls, books, playing cards, exercise machines, televisions, and, most recently, computers, the co-dependent world view asserts that all of those relationships, including those we have with other people, are to be evaluated and labeled according to how well they measure up to a predefined, ideal-type relationship.

However, as Peele [1989] points out, there are any number of problems with medicalizing behavior in general and with defining addiction as a disease in particular:

"(Medicalizing behavior is) bad science...Biology is not behavior, even when drugs or alcohol are used. Alcoholism involves a host of personal and environmental considerations aside from physical effects...Disease categorizations fail at the central goal said to justify them–they cannot be treated by medical therapy. Treated patients fare no better than untreated people with same problems in the case of alcoholism, drugs, and smoking, and especially with pms, love addiction, etc... Sanctioned by medicine...people are persuaded they have a disease through group pressure techniques–ordinary people are branded and brand themselves as sick and debilitated...denial is sign of sickness... Disease notions actually increase the incidence of the behaviors of concern because they legitimize, reinforce and excuse the behaviors in question, convincing people, contrary to all the evidence, that their behavior is not their own. Disease conceptions now dominate major parts of ordinary experience, incorporating common problems associated with growing up or conducting ordinary relationships." (pp. 26-28)

And as Davies [1997] goes on to add:

"With drugs...the single-level mechanistic account is based on the pharmacology of drug action. Once it has been established that a drug has a measurable pharmacological effect on someone, it is a short but supremely illogical step to assume that 'therefore' the person has no further decision making capacity. It is simply assumed that drug pharmacology has wiped out and replaced the pharmacology of choice behavior. From here, we can easily arrive at an absurd conceptualization of addiction by implying that a person can engage in a coherent and carefully-planned sequence of actions such as getting out of bed, phoning a taxi, going into town, stealing a coat from a shop, selling the coat, and finally keeping a rendezvous with an acquaintance who has spare heroin to sell, because he/she *has to*; while all the time he/she is desperately trying not to do any of these things. The pharmacology of drug action is assumed to compel the behavior irrespective of, or against, the person's 'will'.

"The word 'addiction' is taken to signify a state. The state is different from the state of being normal though, as in the case of hypnotism, and components of the state remain a mystery. Individuals from different disciplines will, however, have quite different ideas about what the underlying basis of this state is likely to be.

"The most salient feature of the supposed state is that it interferes with, or in the extreme case removes, the capacity for voluntary behavior with respect to a substance or drug. The process which is thought to be responsible for this can range from the 19th century idea of a 'disease of the will' through to more modern conceptions based on biochemistry or pharmacology. Whatever the case, a metaphysical or physical mechanism is proposed which in the extreme case, so it is believed, makes a person unable not to take their drug of preference. This inability to make certain types of choice differentiates them from other 'normal' people.

"...some would probably claim that use of the word 'addiction' does not have to imply a state, but may be used to specify a group of people showing a particular behavior to an extreme degree. In other words, it is merely quantitative. However, while this may be true in other instances, it is argued here that psychologically the word is categorical in function, and that sooner or later its categorical nature imposes itself on our thinking. 'Addicted' is the opposite of 'not-addicted' rather than 'less addicted', and with the sureness of inevitability the categorical nature of the word leads to the search for differences between those who are 'addicted' and those who are 'not addicted'; and subsequently to cures or treatments for those who have 'got it' as opposed to those who 'haven't got it'.

"Although it is possible to argue that words like 'addicted' and 'dependent' refer to continuous variables, the postulation of concepts like 'slightly addicted' or 'somewhat dependent' removes from the central concepts most of the denotative or diagnostic value they might otherwise have; and like the oxymoron 'fairly unique', they confuse rather than clarify the issue. The concept of addiction as an 'it' cannot be salvaged by towing it to safety with linguistic qualifiers, like some broken-down vehicle.

"The second argument suggests that ultimately there is no difference between 'scientific' explanations and explanations in terms of will-power, decision-making, intentions, and so forth. The latter, it can be argued, are terms of convenience pitched at the level of phenomenology, simply because they refer to events with which no current pharmacology or physiology can deal, but which in principle are explicable ultimately at that level. Consequently, there are not really several competing types of explanation, but only one. People use the 'disease' model despite overwhelming logical flaws and evidence to the contrary because it is functional for them to do so. [pp. 30-32, 45-47]

Regardless of all of the problems inherent in labeling human behaviors and choices as 'disorders', professionals in the field of mental health continue to do so with regularity. This trend is best illustrated by the explosive growth of the 'bible' of mental disorders--the Diagnostic and Statistical Manual of Mental Disorders (DSM). First published by the American Psychiatric Association in 1952 and subsequently revised four times by 1994, the DSM has expanded from 132 to 886 pages. And during that time, 'addiction' shifted from a 'personality disturbance or disorder' encompassing alcoholism and drug abuse to 'substance-related' and 'impulse control' disorders, encompassing eleven categories of drug or alcohol substances as well as behavioral patterns such as pathological gambling, stealing (kleptomania), and so forth.

These often radical, never-ending changes that have occurred with regard to the definition and diagnosis of mental disorders, and of substance-related and impulse control disorders in particular, were not the result of significant improvements in objective, scientific knowledge and diagnostic technologies. Rather, they were the result of a continuing effort on the part of moral entrepreneurs, in the face of evidence to the contrary, to define mental disorder and addiction as 'real' social problems. Individuals in the field of mental health used changing social values to their advantage to create socially functional truths, despite the research that consistently refuted this 'common sense' disease model of addiction. In large part, these changes took place as a defense against a more sociological perspective on the rise of mental disorders and addictions as diseases.

Any discipline that claims to be a science has two concerns; reliability and validity. With regard to psychiatry, reliability is the extent to which clinical practitioners can agree on the diagnosis of individual patients. Validity, on the other hand, has two meanings. On a superficial level, validity is the extent to which a model actually measures what it purports to measure. On a deeper level, however, validity is the extent to which the mental constructs underlying that measurement are accurate. Throughout the 1960s and 1970s, symbolic interactionists within the field of sociology challenged the validity of mental illness at this deeper level. They challenged the very nature of this constructed reality, arguing that the nosology (classification system of diseases) presented in DSM I and II were based entirely on 'symptomology', and not on a biologically-based etiology. As such, there was no logical basis for the distinction the mental health field had attempted to create between mental disorder as a medical problem and simple social deviance. The interactionists argued, in essence, that mental illness itself was merely a label for deviant behaviors that had been placed within a medical frame for the purpose of classifying individuals as either 'normal' or 'sick'.

According to the interactionists, society *is* symbolic interaction. [Blumer 1969] That is, all human interaction is mediated by the use and interpretation of symbols. And, in order for such interaction to occur and be meaningful, each participant in that interaction must be able to take the role of the other through the use of the sign system, or technology, of language. An important consequence of this use of language to bring meaning to the self and the world is that there is no ultimately 'real' world; the world and the self are 'real' insofar as they are known through language. [E. Becker 1962] But what has symbolic interaction to do with whether or not individuals suffer from some sort of mental disorder, addiction in particular? It is through this process of talking that individuals simultaneously construct 'the normal' and 'the deviant'. And, as we have seen, mental illness and addiction are merely behaviors that have been collectively defined as deviant. In general, deviance refers to violations of social norms. Norms are behavioral codes, or prescriptions, that guide people into actions and self-presentations that conform to social acceptability. All social groups make such rules and attempt, at some times and under some circumstances, to enforce them. Social rules define situations and the kinds of behavior appropriate to them, specifying some actions as 'right' and forbidding others as 'wrong'.

However, whether an act is deviant, whether it violates social norms, depends on how other people react to it; it is the response of the 'other' that is problematic. Variations in response to particular actions occur over time, and depend as well on who commits the act and who feels he has been harmed by it; rules are applied more to some persons than to others. Thus, deviance is not a quality that lies in behavior itself, but in the interaction between the person who commits an act and those who respond to it. Because human action is normative, human values determine what is to be considered a 'problem'. Seen in this way, mental disorder is precisely that; a form of social deviance, of *dis-order*, that violates social rules, norms and expectations. In fact, as Kirk and Kutchins [1992] point out, it was precisely this symbolic interactionist argument that threatened the underlying theoretical construct of 'mental disorder' (as discussed in Chapter Two) and ultimately lead to the creation of DSM III in 1980, as the discipline of psychiatry attempted to defend its historically and empirically weak ties to medicine through application of the disease model to human social behaviors:

"... sociologists viewed mental illness as they would any other label for deviant behavior. Mental illness, they suggested, told us not so much about internal, individual pathology, as about the social processes through which certain behaviors became defined by people in authority as instances of insanity. Mental illness was viewed as an arbitrary social label, conveying more about the structure of authority in a particular social situation than about pathology. This view spawned an active sociological literature on the conditions and processes by which some people were labeled as mentally ill and the consequences of such labeling for self-attitudes and the reactions of others. . . (arguing that) behaviors that are labeled mental illness are simply behaviors for which other explanations were unconvincing. Mental illness is merely a residual category of behavior, an explanation of last resort. . . mental disorder is viewed as a label behind which psychiatrists and the public hide their ignorance. . (and) the act of labeling 'residual deviants' played an important part in encouraging the individual to meet the role expectations of someone who is 'insane'." [p. 21]

The process of labeling 'residual deviants' is most powerful, of course, when the 'residuals' themselves do the defining. This is exactly what transpired with the rise of the process addiction movement. Merging liberation psychotherapy's cultural critique with the disease model of addiction lead to a revolutionary change in the conceptual framework underpinning the alcoholism movement. The disease model (which emphasized the biological nature of addiction) fused with the adaptation model (which emphasized environmental factors) and yielded a logic in which culture (and environment) causes a disease (addiction) and consequently, all problems in living (in adapting to said culture) are addictions. It is in this way that the co-dependency movement, which arose from the co-alcoholism (Adult Children of Alcoholics) movement of the mid-1980s, utilized the then newly official conceptualizations of behavior as disease found in DSM III-R to bring to the general public an entirely new way of thinking about addictions. In this new framework, all addictions are 'process addictions'.

Like any social movement, the process addiction movement requires members; those who are willing to adopt the ideology of the cause, and to reconfigure their identities in accordance with that cause and with the rules of the group. "Becoming co-dependent demands that they acquire and cultivate the ability to conceptualize and talk about themselves in the requisite ways, and acquiring that ability rests, in the first instance, upon deciding that that is the course of action they want to pursue." [Rice 1996, 142] Typically, this decision is made when newcomers are able to identify with the experiences of other group members; drawing connections between the comments of regulars and their own situations is the first step in the process. The newcomer must be able to 'relate' to what is being said: "The co-dependent, the process addict, is a social role, defined by a set of obligations and privileges. . . The first set of obligations is biographical. Falling under the twelve-step rubric of 'getting out of denial', the biographical obligations entail admitting powerlessness over an addiction and the unmanageability of one's life. At one level, this means acknowledging that one is sick; at another, it entails fitting one's life story with the discourse's symbolic system." [p. 144].

In this way, people undergo "conversion". An important factor in doing so is to adopt a new "universe of discourse" through a three step process. First, one must engage in a biographical reconstruction in which one retrofits one's life story within the new symbolic system. Second, one must adopt a master attribution scheme through which one may frame all life troubles in terms of the co-dependent model. Finally, one must suspend analogical reasoning and believe the model literally, rather than merely metaphorically. But the co-dependency movement is not the only arena in which such fragile arguments are constructed or in which such pains are taken to assure that people take the creation of a new 'addiction' seriously. If co-dependency was the disease of the 1980s, then Internet Addiction Disorder is the disease of the 1990s. For it is during the 1990s that computer-mediated communications and interactive computer technologies such as the World Wide Web, Usenet, Internet Relay Chat, and Multi-User Dungeons became increasingly sophisticated and popularized. And it is during the 1990s that such technology became the victim of its own success; symbolic specialists, utilizing the same unexamined framework and methodologies as had been used to create other forms of addiction, worked to create a new 'illness' known as Internet Addiction Disorder. Let us examine in greater detail a few of the Internet Addiction Support Group (IASG) posts from Chapter Four in order to understand how, exactly, this conversion, this re-construction of reality, was accomplished.

Consider first two posts from self-labeled Internet addicts who are also researchers in the field of mental health. The first post is by Kim Young, who the reader by now recognizes as a major proponent of IAD. The second is by Storm King, a researcher and mental health professional in training:

From: "Kimberly S. Young"
Subject: Clarification

While I do study Internet addiction, I have tried not to offer my opinions as an authority but I share my views as a fellow participant. As many of you know, I struggled with my *own* addiction to the Internet. Especially when I began to study this phenomenon, I had a difficult time pulling myself away from chat rooms and found that on-line relationships filled a void in my life. Therefore, I personally find this group helpful.

I first thought about studying Internet addiction when my friend called me whose marriage almost ended due to her husband's obsession with chatting. However, it was my own experience along with those I began to interview early on which motivated me to devote my field of study to on-line behavior. As I spoke with more people, it quickly became clear to me how serious compulsive Internet use was as their lives had become completely unmanageable (lost jobs, divorce, parents worried for their children, students failing school, financial debt). In also speaking with family members, I saw how cyber affairs broke up marriages and the pain for the entire family this caused.

Many complained that little information on the topic was available which inspired me to write "Caught in the Net" and build my web site. But even as I caution in the book, these things are only a first step for further discovery with more research and clinical study needed. And I am glad to see that continued work is being done.

And:

From: "Storm A. King"
     Subject: intro

Hi. My name is Storm (that's my real name :-)and I am a net addict.
I was actually one of the very first members of this list when it was created in 1994.
I, like Kimberly, am also a researcher of net stuff. I have done a lot of, and am doing my dissertation on that topic.
Part of what I want to share is how I partially recovered from my net addiction. I know that I had it bad, in late 96 early 96, cause my wife was fit to be tied and very very upset with my online behavior, and, I could not change it. It took some time for me to realize that I was ruining my marriage. What finally happened is we took a vacation. It turned out, in my case, if I was not around my computer, I really didn't experience much of an urge to go online. So, when I got back after a week, I was able to unsubscribe from a bunch of emails lists, and started to pay attention to my wife when she needed me to - not just when I felt like it.

There are three key points in these two posts; instances which point to the circular, non-scientific fashion through which IAD has been constructed. The first point is that the authors of both posts are mental health professionals. As professionals, they have utilized their understanding of human behavior, a clinicalized, medicalized understanding, to define their own behaviors as problematic. Each individual found that s/he spent a great deal of time online. However, rather than sorting through alternative accounts that might 'explain' such decisions, they chose the one most familiar to them—the medical account. Then, asserting that such an account was 'the real reason' for their behavior, rather than acknowledging it for what it is (a socially functional, constructed account), they brought their experiences and assertions of reality into an online, self-help format. So, while they assert that they are just 'regular group members' coping with addiction issues, this is not in fact the case. The very fact of their assertions about the realness of IAD serves to strengthen that account in the minds of other group members.

The second, and interrelated, point is that Young asserts, from a professional standpoint, that IAD victims' lives are, in fact, unmanageable. However, as Rice [1997] points out, the notion of unmanageability presumes a benevolent model of human intentionality:

"They (addicts) did not intend to harm others and only did so because they have a disease, an addiction. Drawing upon that overlap in the causal logic between conventional addiction discourse and liberation psychotherapy but still faithful to the ethic of self-actualization, co-dependency conceptualizes the psychological condition that is caused by cultural repression of the self as an addiction. Thus, such problems as incest, the various forms of abuse, and criminality are all instances of 'unmanageable' behavior resulting from people's 'powerlessness' over their own actions. . . (they) cannot be intentional acts because, 'the basic nature of the human being, when functioning freely, is constructive and trustworthy'. Therefore, those who engage in such acts cannot be functioning freely." [p. 103]

Not only is this an assumption that cannot be proved scientifically, in a realm that is somehow more objective than the statements, or accounts, of those engaged in the behavior in question, it violates one's common sense understandings of human behavior. However, it is precisely these sorts of assertions that are repeated continuously in the self-help framework of the IASG. With the help of mental health professionals and group regulars, these claims continue to gain strength, particularly in the eyes of newcomers and significant others who are searching for the most plausible, functional explanation of interest in online interaction. We will return to this point momentarily.

The third, and perhaps most interesting, point is that made by King: "...if I was not around my computer, I really didn't experience much of an urge to go online." This sort of statement points precisely to the fact of personal choice, rather than to the illusion of 'loss of control' in matters related to online interaction. Contrary to the assumption that people are 'lured' into online interaction against their will, such comments point to the fact that people get interested in online interaction, engage in it for as long as and to the extent that it remains interesting, and then move on to something else. Because 'addiction' is a description of behavior that occurs with regularity, it can be said to 'exist' only in the continued presence of that behavioral regularity. These are hardly appropriate criteria for classification of a medical disease.

As noted in Chapter Four, many IAD 'victims' and the significant others of such victims have sought therapy for the net addiction problem. Through such therapy, these individuals learn to apply a clinical, disease framework to their experience and to bring such a framework into the online group setting. They become accomplished in the art of what Rice [1997] calls 'selecting' co-dependency (also read addiction) as the 'real' explanation for their choices and identities. As the following thread (series of related posts) relates, victims and significant others work in concert in the environment of the IASG to accomplish this selection and the accompanying, socially legitimated roles of addict and co-dependent:

From: Tina Bolli
Subject: Re: Depression and Internet Usage

A lot of this applies to me. First of all, I suffer from depression. It wasn't caused by the internet, however, since it's been going on since I was a kid. But I guess I fit the stereotype of someone who can easily become addicted to the net.
Second, I recognize myself in your description of your husband. It's causing many problems with my boyfriend. I feel like he's smothering me when all he wants is a normal relationship. And I'm very insensitive to his needs. I also wish he had an "off" switch.
Thanks for your observations. It's helpful to see what a net addict looks like from a non-addict's point of view.
--T

From: Cydlyne
Subject: Re: Depression and Internet Usage

Hi--

My husband also has some history of depression, although he wasn't obviously depressed when he started online (now I wonder if he may be manic). He is extroverted, but doesn't have friends now, as he had in the past (he lost friends when he got divorced about 7 years ago, and hasn't really made new ones).
I suppose there are a lot of aspects of our culture which are very alienating, and leave us at a loss for community. That recent article suggests that the Internet is a very poor substitute, however.

My husband is also a trauma survivor--I don't know how much that has to do with it. The part that seems relevant for him is the sense of emotional safety, which is compromised for him. And the control he experiences, where he has had severe experiences being helpless, in the past. The rough part for me is that he has lots of control now, and isn't helpless in his current life, but I know these experiences are sustained over time. So that may make him more susceptible--I'm not sure. He is also a creative person, and perhaps fantasy-prone (although prior to this, he seemed to like to be pretty grounded in most respects). He used to be very into television to help him mellow out; and he also used to like video games a fair amount, especially the ones where you build a community or mini-culture.

Well, I have to say, I am kind of obsessing about him. So maybe he has become my addiction! Co-dependents (myself for example) need to develop our own lives more, so that we're not dominated by our family member's emotional absence/addiction, etc. So it's a similar need, to develop a fuller life...

From: Mwzoeplace
Subject: Re: Depression and Internet Usage

I think you make a good point (re: depression, introversion, and closeness).However, it probably varies--with my husband, we were very close (I thought)before he got online, and he distanced as soon as he got into the Internet(and couldn't tolerate real closeness). So--I suppose it can be a matter of controlling the intimacy (which could make intimacy more workable, although probably not as healthy--I guess it's not true intimacy, more of a facsimile, like plastic intimacy, surrogate love, etc.--given the article that recently came out about people being more lonely and depressed as the use the Internet more).

I hope that as we discuss the variations, we'll keep seeing patterns.

Incidentally, how old was your mother when this started? And how soon after getting the computer did she get addicted? For us, my husband was 50, but it was very shortly after we got the computer (within 5 -6 weeks of getting online). He also became anxious and had trouble sleeping a few weeks after he got online, and I don't know whether that's a coincidence that made him more susceptible, or whether the online activity stimulated his anxiety.

Hi--the idea of predisposition is a good one--it would be interesting to know what triggers it. Someone I know said she went to a conference where they discussed Internet addiction, and she heard that people who are bipolar feel soothed by the kind of light the computer emits.

I guess that in purely behaviorist terms, there must be high reinforcement value to the computer--something about pushing buttons and getting whatever you want, pretty much right when you want it. It obviates the need for delayed gratification.

In this thread, there are several points of interest. Together, they construct a story that goes like this: There exists a correct, accurate stereotype of persons who easily become addicted to the Internet; those who are 'predisposed' to such uncontrollable behavior. I understand and identify with the parameters of that social role. Further, there exist 'real' and 'normal' interpersonal relationships and communities. While I cannot define the specific components of these real, normal interactions, I know them when I "see" them (read, when an authority figure or, at a minimum, peers, define them, as such, for me). Computer-mediated interactions do not meet these criteria. They are not 'real'. They are not 'normal', and they don't conform to the 'true definition' of what a community is or does. I know this either because I am the significant other of a person who is, at the moment at least, more interested in such interactions than in interactions with me, or because I myself have such an interest, much to the chagrin of my significant other. Finally, if I talk with others who are of like mind (that is, people who also subscribe to the disease framework of addiction as an adequate explanation of human behavior), I will eventually be able to "see patterns" of behavior. These patterns will make it self evident that all of the core assumptions of the addiction framework are, in fact, true. Thus, I will be correct in my assessment that my inability to control my behavior, or the behavior of those around me, is not my fault.

The dilemma in this story, however, is that it pretends to be more than it is. It pretends, as do many stories told from the 'scientific' framework, to be the only plausible, logical explanation for an event. It pretends to be 'the truth'. It ignores completely the fact that all truth, all 'reality' is constructed through the use of language in social interaction. It is the process of talking, of sharing and interpreting experience that creates meaning and patterns.

Quite simply, patterns cannot be said to exist in the absence of their interpretation as such. Thus, in order to understand why such an explanation is the preferred one, one must examine not the 'objective truth' of it, but the social function of it. This preference for such 'lack of control' types of accounts serves functions which are social, rather than scientific:

> "Let us be quite blunt. Describing a behavior as compelled merely on the basis of observations that it happens with great regularity is an act of superstition, and has nothing whatsoever in common with normal processes of scientific deduction. Furthermore the switch from a volitional view of behavior to a mechanistic one is philosophically absurd ...mechanism and volition cannot be used simultaneously within the same explanation. We cannot imply that some people work according to volitional principles while others are operating according to the laws of mechanism, and one cannot hop between these modes of explanation according to preference or convenience, in order to serve the needs of the moment. They are alternative modes of explanation for the same thing. Yet for some reason we seem to prefer mechanistic explanations in certain circumstances. With respect to addiction, we want to know that addicts operate according to a set of principles that do not apply to the rest of us, and the primary purpose of the 'addiction' label is to provide for that need." [Davies 1997, pp. 31-32]

While significant others often work with the victims of IAD in this construction of the real explanation, often times in self help group environment, it is the victims themselves who are most active in this performance. Given only the bare essentials of the disorder's symptoms, causes and consequences, the regulars in this group are quite capable of retrospective interpretation, of aligning their past behaviors with self-selected labels and role criteria. This ability stems largely from personal experience within the clinical framework. That is, it is immediately apparent to the casual observer of interaction in this online group that the regulars are schooled in the addiction model. They have had experiences in self-help groups for other 'problems', they have been involved in one-on-one therapy, and they are very aware of all of the current academic research and phraseology that offers legitimated explanations of their problems in living.

However, in order to sustain such selected identities as legitimate ones, regulars (in both the IASG and in the world of addiction in general) must continually seek out companionship. Not only can one not be 'an addict' in the absence of the behavior in question, one cannot be an addict without the presence of others to legitimate the role. After all, the meaning of the self is found in the responses of others to it. In the spirit of liberation psychotherapy and the co-dependency movement, one of the best ways to ensure the self as addict is to continue to bring new members into the self-help group setting. The more continuously recovering addicts one can construct, the more real the disorder. As a result, interactions in online support groups often take on the flavor of marketing seminars. Potential recruits enter the group, offer up their personal experiences for public consumption, and await a group response that would indicate that they have come to the right place—that their experiences can be explained and their problems solved, if only they select the identity of addict. It is quite clear in the posts that follow, some of which are stand-alone and some of which are related to one another, that newcomers are in search of an identity. They are in search of an explanation, the real reason, which they can offer up to others in their personal lives:

From: "Linda Clayborn"
Subject: Hello all my name is linda

Hello to everyone who is reading this my name is Linda and I am a 17 year old female, who has become very addicted to the internet. I am on it all the time, it has took place of my regular life, instead of going out with my friends to meet people I get online to meet people. I have several people online who think that there are in love with me and this makes me fill good, but I know its not normal I should be meeting guys in real life. I have several home pages that I work on hours on end, and I go crazy when the server goes down and I can not get online. My family asks me why I spend so much time on the net and I have no real reason to explain this. When I am not around my computer I think about all the things happening online that I am missing. It seems like I have quite doing everything I used to like, like going out, watching t.v., listening to music, talking on the phone, etc. just to be online all the time.

In the post above, it is abundantly clear that this potential new recruit is searching for 'the real reason' to explain why she spends a great deal of time online. Significant others, in an attempt to control her behavior, have asked her repeatedly to offer up some sort of linguistic account that would legitimate her choice of activities. Having none that are acceptable, she seeks out alternative explanations in this online support group. The idea that she is 'addicted' to the Internet is a socially useful one for her; it allows her to offer up an account of her behavior that will satisfy significant others, one which 'proves' that she has no choice in the matter. Interestingly enough, she claims that she 'knows' this activity is not normal, and that she should be spending more time doing normal things. For her, these normal activities largely include using other forms of mediated communications—television, stereos, telephones, and the like. These are precisely those forms of mediated communications that were deemed 'not normal' when they first became available. Now, apparently, they are acceptable.

Now consider another post by a new group member. Its author has, again, quite clearly gone online searching for an acceptable definition of his behavior. During the course of his online activities, he came across a survey on Internet addiction. Having taken the survey, he has now adopted a ready-made social role of Internet addict. While one cannot be certain whether the author actively sought out such a survey, its results did serve a social function for him. It offered him a legitimated opportunity to reinterpret his history of online activity in a light that better suits his needs now. He can now claim that 'the potential for Internet Addiction was always there'. This is functional because it allows him, as it did for the author of the post above, to offer up a 'scientific' account of his behavior to significant others. While neither he nor his significant others took the idea of online addiction 'seriously' in the past, this online survey has offered definitive 'proof' of what his problem has been all along.

Two additional points about this post should be made. First is the fact that this individual, though willing to accept the label 'Internet addict', is unwilling to accept what he quite obviously considers to be a far worse label—sexual deviant. He makes it clear that, while he may have his own problems, something as perverted as addiction to cybersex is not one of them. This points quite clearly to the self-selection aspect of the addiction label; people choose labels that will serve a purpose for them, and discard the others. The second, interrelated point is that he is interested in (addicted to) the social aspect of online interaction. It is statements such as this, and similar ones in the posts that follow, that point to the difficulty people have, in the abstract, in separating 'real' from 'non-real' relationships. It is also these sorts of statements that point to the absurdity of IAD. In order to believe that IAD is a medical disorder, an addiction, one must also believe, in addition to other things, that human beings acquire their human qualities in some way other than through interaction. However, as professionals in the fields of psychology and sociology have asserted for some time, it is only through contact with other humans, through socialization, that we acquire that which makes us human. One is forced to question the validity of a disorder that, at its foundation, implies that people are addicted to the basic necessities of human life:

From: "Christopher J. Caraballo"
Subject: Hi.. I'd like to introduce myself.

Hi Everyone

My Name is Chris Caraballo I'm 19, and a freshman at Penn State.
I realized that I am addicted to the Internet a few weeks ago when I took a survey at the Online Addiction Clinic (some think like that anyway). The results of the survey showed that not only am I addicted but it is affecting my life in a negative way.
...this has LONG been a problem for me. It really began when America Online released their unlimited usage plan. For me, the potential for Internet Addiction was always there... because as soon as they made the plan public, I was practically the first person in line to SIGN UP! That was when it began to interfere with my life. From that day on the phone line at home (I was then still living with my parents) was almost always busy. My parents complained, my nuclear family complained. Once or twice there where emergencies and no one could reach up because I was online chatting on AOL. I would get in trouble with my parents constantly because I was online too much. Though no one ever took it seriously, and neither did I. My mother has been telling me for over a year now that I'm addicted to the Internet, though the thought of Online addiction was not really serious. Though I have begun realizing that it's not the actual act of being addict that's the problem but not doing what I should be that is.
I'm not into cyber sex or anything like that so I don't believe it's the sexual aspect of IA that I have a problem with.. I believe it's the social aspect.

From: "Olivia H"
Subject: Introduction

Hi,

I would like to introduce myself to the members of this support group. My name is Olivia. I am 31 years old, married, and have 4 children ages 14, 12, and 6 yr. old twins. I work full time outside of my home.

I am, without a doubt, addicted to the internet. I fancy the social scene in particular. I spend an average of 7 hours per day online using programs such as IRC, Mplayer, ICQ, Powwow, etc. On any given day, I can be found staying online until the early hours of the morning. I have been so sleep-deprived, that I have fallen asleep while at work, or worse, while driving home. Needless to say, my marriage is falling apart as I am disinterested in my relationship with my husband; I would much rather communicate with one of my cyber friends which, by the way, are all male. I have also neglected many areas of my household; chores, bill-paying, etc. I don't spend the time with my children that I should and if they interrupt me I usually don't hear them or become very agitated that they have taken my attention away from the screen.

I thought about ending all of my online relationships cold-turkey, but that would be seemingly harsh on me as well as my cyber friends. These people make me feel good, and I in turn do that same for them. Maybe that's what I'm looking for, I'm not sure.

My hope is to relate with people who have the same problem, and to maybe shed some light on why I am doing this. My family needs me.

From: "Gaebryl Firuz-Zamrl"
Subject: Re: Introduction

This is in response to Olivia

Hi!

Hey, great to hear from you. It's always gratifying to find out I'm not alone with my addiction. I was on the IRC for a number of years myself, then abstained for a few years due to IRC-related factors in RL, then rejoined via another client, MUDs. I have a great number of friends and 'allies' on MUDs, good people I wish were my friends in RL, and vivid almost-real experiences shared with these people of on-line interactions. I hate going cold turkey, I don't believe in going cold turkey, but I find I have to just to save my relationship with my RL fiancee. But it's more than that, as well. I have friends in RL who I have conflicts with now due to constantly comparing them with my MUD buddies, and it's not fair on them. They can't compete with people who largely exist in my own head. People who in RL I might have less in common with than my good, loving RL friends. This is from my own personal experience. I still check e-mail, I still do company work on-line, but for leisure, I find myself doing weird things like reading a book, or calling up my fiance and actually talking to her instead of just nodding off at everything she says and then logging on for a few hours afterwards. And I find when I'm 'clean' from MUDs, I can actually talk to my friends with less judgement, and am actually open to what they say and find myself enjoying their company...3 days 'clean' today, my head feels kind of groggy like I'm really withdrawing from the intense MUDding... but I also feel good about myself. I really really loved smelling the air outside on the way to the office today, and I have been reading this great book which had been lying beside my home PC for the past three months. Today was a good day... :o)

-gaebryl

In the two related posts above, Olivia and Gaebryl discuss their experiences with Internet addiction. Olivia points out that she is, without a doubt, addicted to the Internet. She indicates that she 'fancies the social scene in particular', but that this new interest has caused some consternation among her significant others. Further, she comments that her cyber friends make her feel good, and that she does not wish to give up either her online friends or her family. Finally, she adds that she would like to "shed some light on why I am doing this." Quite clearly, Olivia is another example of an individual who has developed a new interest in online interaction. This interest has caused problems with her offline commitments, primarily because her offline significant others have defined her new interest as a problem for them. Since she has become interested in developing a life online, they have not received whatever sorts of commitments from her that they feel entitled to. As such, they have attempted to control her behavior by putting pressure on her to end those online commitments. For Olivia, the social role of addict is ideal. It affords for her the possibility of maintaining her relationships both online and off. She can remain involved in online activities because 'she has no choice', and her offline significant others are inclined to accept such a definition of reality because it allows them to believe that she is not choosing other activities over them—she just cannot help herself. It also holds out hope that, in time, she will 'recover' from her affliction.

Gaebryl's role is to empathize with Olivia; to explain to her that she is not alone in her addiction and to share with her his 'almost-real' online experiences. It is through such interaction that group members solidify their identities as addicts caught in the grips of something more powerful than their own will. Gaebryl suggests precise parallels between IAD and drug addiction, claiming that he is feeling 'withdrawal' symptoms because he has not been involved in MUDs for three days. He is 'clean'. Again, the belief in some underlying, if vague, distinctions between 'real' and –non-real' relationships and communities are vital to the continued legitimacy of IAD. For, if life online is just as real as life offline, the entire foundation upon which addiction to human interaction has been built begins to crumble. As the following post makes clear, Gaebryl is ideally suited to this role of empathizer and legitimator. He has a great deal of experience within the addiction framework, and is capable of using all of the appropriate jargon:

From: "Gaebryl Firuz-Zamri"
Subject: welcome all newbies,

i used to go to an actual 12-step program dealing with internet addiction on 12th street in New York, which was rather cool, `cept we had more of a coke-binging, acid-trippin' corporate IT programmers assemble there. `course, there was also a nintendo-addicted 15 year old reformed crack dealer (no kidding), but other than him and me, there was little interest or acknowledgment on the subject of internet abuse. When i moved back home to Malaysia a year ago (i sorta emigrated to the States to stay with this girl i met on the irc), i just went around the 12-steps circuit, doing Narcotics Anonymous, Alcoholics Anonymous, Marijuana Anonymous, and even Alanon meets. i don't talk much about my net addiction there, and don't really plan to. i mean, how do you rate when someone has a 'relapse' or 'slip' with our ailment? However, when my fiancé threatened to break off the engagement and i started taking sick leave from work due to marathon runs d/l stuff off the net or goofing off on MUDs (or even just preparing spreadsheets and powerpoint presentations for the next session) then i sorta figured out i musta have had something akin to a 'relapse'. i still miss my old group though...
It kinds of get lonely thinking you're unique in your addiction.

In this final sample post, the idea of marketing the addiction framework for online interaction is most clear. Here, Piet is responding to an earlier post by Driven Zen. In that post, Driven Zen suggested that using the term 'addiction' for online interaction was inappropriate because it was 'overkill'. Piet agrees with this assessment but argues that, nevertheless, the IASG should continue to use the term addiction for precisely that reason. The social role of addict is firmly entrenched in the American cultural framework, and is a label that people can and do freely apply to themselves. By contrast, labels such as 'pathological' are 'too heavy' and 'might scare people away'. Internet Addict, then, is clearly a label easily constructed by mental health professionals and readily adopted by individuals desiring to select that role, and its accompanying explanations for their behaviors. One wonders how long it might take for group members to develop some sort of branding slogans and logos to further enhance loyalty to the commodity (social identity) of Internet Addict:

> *From: "Piet Slaghekke"*
> *Subject: Built on the Ashes of a Joke*

> *driven Zen wrote:*

> *As I keep reminding people, this listserv was originally a joke by Ivan Goldberg. As are his "proposed" criteria for the disorder. I agree that it is a support group. But, it is built on the ashes of a joke. So, a new name might be good. The authors of "Alcoholics Anonymous," the first major self-help book for addictions (also applicable to impulse control disorders) was written with meticulous attention to the meaning of each word. "Using the term "addiction" for every form of impulse control problem, compulsive behavior, or actual addiction, eventually renders the word useless. Sort of like overusing an antibiotic. When you really need to be able to use it specifically it may have lost its power."*

> *Piet Replies:*

> *My experience with Jokes is that many times there is a serious truth lying within them.*
> *So all IASG mailing list members do we vote on a new name?? Lets come up with a few? Here is one: Compulsive-Obsessive Internet users support Group*

But (as driven zen stated earlier) the term addiction is so embedded in our pop culture that if we change the name of the list now, people may not be able to find the list. The term "Pathological Computer Users Support Group" sounds very heavy to me. I would not describe myself as "Pathological" I would much more easily describe my self as "addicted", in a pop culture kind of way. The idea is that as many people who need this list should be able to find it. "Addicted" is most probably what people will label themselves and will therefore search using this term. Also I think the term "Pathological" would scare many people away.

Until there is a better name, that has also become a popular name, I think we should keep the name of this list as it is. This list has gained a momentum. A change to the name would most certainly disrupt that momentum.

Where do we stand? Can people become addicted to the Internet in the same way as they evidently can to alcohol and drugs? Or, is excessive Internet use closer to the family of impulse control disorders such as pathological gambling and kleptomania? Or, as psychologist Ivan Goldberg stated, is it "...all bullshit. . .There is no such thing as Internet addiction."? And if there really is no such thing, then how, Dr. Young queries, can we explain all of those people out there who feel addicted, who claim they are addicted, and who spend inordinate amounts of time online, often to the detriment of their other relationships and life goals? Those are the questions I set out to explore for this research. And they are precisely the questions that Young [1996, 1997], Egger [1996], Brenner [1997], Griffiths [1997] and Scherer [1997] set out to explore as well. To that end, these mental health professionals used the DSM IV criteria for pathological gambling to develop and administer online surveys regarding the existence and extent of Internet Addiction Disorder. They asked questions about the amount of time spent online, peoples' feelings about their online time, any problems it may have caused them in their personal lives, and so forth.

While all of these studies cite differing requirements for 'addicted' versus 'normal' levels of usage and differing degrees of external negative consequences of that usage, they are all based upon three interrelated underlying assumptions. First, they assume that mental disorders, specifically the disorder of addiction, exist and that they can be understood, diagnosed and treated through the disease (or medical) model outlined at the outset of this chapter. Second, they assume that, within this medical framework, people may theoretically become addicted to a process or behavior in the same way that they presumably become addicted to a substance. Third, they assume that, given the diagnostic categories and criteria made available in official manuals and casebooks, they can construct objective, scientific surveys that will accurately assess the extent and specific etiology of another, newly discovered disorder.

However, the insight received from such surveys was in no way gathered through direct observation. And, as Davies [1997, p.26] has noted, "...the further we move from the situation of direct observations, the less any given explanation is derived in the manner of the naive scientist, on the basis of what is perceived; and the more the explanation derives from things that the explainer brings to the situation at the outset, in the form of longer-term social cognitions. [Davies 1997, 26] At a minimum, from the list of researchers above, Young has readily admitted to bringing preconceived explanations and social cognitions to the table in her exploration of online interaction. As a consequence, it hardly comes as a surprise that her research yielded precisely the results it was designed to yield; the existence of a new disorder. Nor does it come as a surprise that other researchers' results, based as they are on the 'truth' of Young's research, yield the same conclusions. The question within those projects was not so much 'does IAD exist', but to what degree, and how much time online does it take to make a person an addict.

Research such as this misses the point about the social construction of reality. Not only is reality socially constructed, it is constructed in such a manner that the results are functional for those doing the defining:

"When asked questions by members of the research establishment, it is functional for drug users to report that they are addicted, forced into theft, harassed by stressful life events, and driven into drug use by forces beyond their capacity to control. ...such self reports have their own internal functional logic which is independent of reality ...and other research methods and forms of analysis would consequently produce a different picture. Furthermore, the fact that the explanations people provide for their behavior make some reference to their own motives and intentions is hardly new; it is a central feature of social interaction, and not specific to drug users." [Davies 1997, p. x]

The same case may be made with regard to any other activity currently defined as an addiction. The underlying assumptions of the addiction framework, including tolerance, withdrawal, craving, loss of control, and so forth, are merely functional linguistic accounts developed by those people from whom an explanation of their choices was demanded. When forced to offer accounts that both separate them from 'normal' people and explain 'why' they do not fit in to the dominant sociocultural framework, 'addicts' offer up such linguistic causalities to rationalize their chosen courses of action in the minds of those who have chosen otherwise. They have 'explained themselves'. However, there is no scientific truth to any of these explanations. Tolerance, withdrawal, craving, and so forth are nothing more and nothing less than ideas that people offer up when asked appropriate questions by a treatment specialist. As Davies [1997] notes:

"In its starkest form, the process involves the psychologist asking someone to provide ratings in terms of some semantic label, on the customary five- or seven point scale, the labels coming in the first instance from the psychologist. The fact that the subject complies is carelessly taken as proof that the word (craving) must refer to something real, an entity; otherwise how could he/she produce systematic ratings? In fact, however, the subject's acquiescence, and subsequent performance, can more parsimoniously be described in terms of the demand characteristics of the interview, and any systematic variation in terms of strategy and response bias, or 'making sense of the task'.

"... it is regularly observed by clinicians that clients with drug problems report feelings of loss-of-control and lack of volition. It is statements such as these that tend to become enshrined in the work on drug action; and in consequence the pharmacological quest becomes a search for 'scientific proof' to back up the verbal reports. However, there is a basic misconception about the nature of statements from drug users who so regularly assert that they 'cannot stop'. The statements themselves are not 'scientific' in the first place, but functional. The earnestness with which the statements are made attest to their functional necessity, rather than their literal truth.

"If we observe that, with great regularity, we over-indulge in some activity to the detriment of health, family, friends and economic functioning, we require a linguistic formula that enables us to explain these circumstances in an acceptable fashion. The statement that 'I cannot stop' is not a statement of fact, but an inference based on the self-observation that I reliably fail to do so (emphasis mine). The statement 'I cannot stop' is thus primarily a metaphor; and no other linguistic device adequately captures the moral and behavioral dilemma in which the 'addict' finds him/herself." [50, 61-62]

Where do we stand? We stand precisely where we have so many times before. We continue, without any scientific evidence of the underlying theoretical assumptions, to define addiction as 'real', with 'real' being anything that we can medicalize and popularize sufficiently. We alter and bend the scientific method as we wish, picking and choosing among its attributes those we wish to adhere to, in order to construct the definition that suits our needs. We assert that this social construction is science, when, in reality, the scientific truth is but one of any number of truths we could come up with. The only difference between the scientific story of reality and any other is that science pretends to be the *only* story, to the exclusion of all others. Thus, we wind up with the strange notion that there are subjective realities (those which 'other people' make up), and the one true scientific reality. And we assert that if we pretend to adhere to the politics of scientific construction, the reality we end up with is in some way truer than any other.

In the end, all realities are nothing more and nothing less than our accounts of them. It is the fact that some claims to the truth are more functional, and thus more popular, that yields the appearance of official-ness. This is true for all mental constructs, including addiction. In the end, "the idea that an 'addict' is nothing more or less than a person who has become accustomed to explaining that he or she is one, deserves serious contemplation."[Davies 1997, 71]

SOURCES CONSULTED

Alexander, Bruce K. "The Disease and Adaptive Models of Addiction: A Framework Evaluation." In *Visions of Addiction: Major Contemporary Perspectives on Addiction and Alcoholism*, ed. Stanton Peele, 45-66. Lexington, MA: Lexington Books, 1988.

alt.culture.usenot faq, electronically available at www.cis.ohio-state.edu/hypertext/faq/usenet/usenet/culture-faq/faq.html 1995 (maintained by Tom Seidenberg)

Aluve, Warren. *UnderNet User's Committee--Guidelines.* electronically available at http://aslan.pr.mala.bc.ca/~warren/usercom_guidelines.html

American Psychiatric Association Committee on Nomenclature and Statistics. *Diagnostic and Statistical Manual of Mental Disorders.* Washington, DC: American Psychiatric Association, 1952.

_____. *DSM-II Diagnostic and Statistical Manual of Mental Disorders.* 2d ed. Washington, DC: American Psychiatric Association, 1968.

_____. *DSM-III Diagnostic and Statistical Manual of Mental Disorders.* 3d ed. Washington, DC: American Psychiatric Association, 1980.

_____. *DSM-III-R Diagnostic and Statistical Manual of Mental Disorders.* 3d ed. revised. Washington, DC: American Psychiatric Association, 1987.

_____. *DSM-IV Diagnostic and Statistical Manual of Mental Disorders.* 4th ed. Washington, DC: American Psychiatric Association, 1994.

Anderson, Benedict. *Imagined Communities: Reflections on the Origin and Spread of Nationalism.* New York: Verso, 1991.

Anderson, J.A. and T. P. *Meyer. Mediated Communication: A Social Action Perspective.* Newbury Park, CA: Sage Publications, 1988.

Baym, Nancy K. "The Emergence of Community in Computer Mediated Communication." In *Cybersociety: Computer-Mediated Communication* and *Community*, ed. Steven G. Jones, 138-163. Thousand Oaks, CA: Sage Publications, 1995.

Becker, Howard S. *Outsiders: Studies in the Sociology of Deviance*. New York, NY: The Free Press, 1963.

Bell, Colin and Howard Newby, eds. *The Sociology of Community: A Selection of Readings*. London: Frank Cass & Co, Ltd., 1974.

Belluck, Pam. "The Symptoms of Internet Addiction." *The New York Times*. December 1, 1996 Section 4, 1.

Bendtsen, Bo. *The FidoNet Homepage*. electronically available at: http://www.gpl.net/terminate/fidonet/

Bierstedt, Robert. *Power and Progress: Essays on Sociological Theory*, chapter 13, "An Analysis of Social Power." New York: McGraw-Hill, 1974.

Bierstedt, Robert. *The Social Order*. New York: McGraw-Hill, 1970.

Blumer, Herbert. *Symbolic Interactionism*. Englewood Cliffs, NJ: Prentice-Hall, 1969.

Boehm, Alyssa. *Addicted to the Net*. electronically available at: http://www.tripod.com/tmp/.computers_internet,boehm,970813.html,89 7340559.22611.nfhtml

Brenner, Viktor. "Psychology of Computer Use: XLVII. Parameters of Internet Use, Abuse and Addiction: The First 90 Days of the Internet Usage Survey." *Psychological Reports*. 80, 1997, 879-882.

Bricking, Tanya. "Internet Blamed for Neglect: Police Say Mother Addicted to Web." *Cincinnati Enquirer*. June 16, 1997. electronically available at: http://enquirer.com/editions/1997/06/16/loc_hacker.html

Brissett, Dennis and C. Edgley, eds. *Life as Theater: A Dramaturgical Sourcebook*. Chicago, IL: Aldine Publishing, 1975.

Bruckman, Amy. *Identity Workshops: Emergent Social and Psychological Phenomena in Text-Based Virtual Reality*. Master's thesis, MIT Media Laboratory, 1992.

Brown, Janelle. "BS Detector: 'Internet Addiction' Meme Gets Media High." *Wired News Online*. electronically available at: http://www.wired.com/news/story/844.html

Bush, Randy. *FidoNet: Technology, Use, Tools, and History*. electronically available at gopher://rain.psg.com:70/00/networks/fidonet/inet92.paper 1993.

Caplan, Paula J. *They Say You're Crazy: How the World's Most Powerful Psychiatrists Decide Who's Normal*. Menlo Park, CA: Addison-Wesley Publishing Company, 1995

Charon, Joel M. *The Meaning of Sociology*. Englewood Cliffs, NJ: Prentice Hall, 1993.

Chesebro, James W. and Donald G. Bonsall. *Computer-Mediated Communication: Human Relationships in a Computerized World*. Tuscaloosa, AL: University of Alabama Press, 1989.

Cohen, Anthony. *The Symbolic Construction of Community*. New York: Tavistock Publications, 1985.

Conrad, Peter and Joseph W. Schneider. *Deviance and Medicalization: From Badness to Sickness*. St. Louis, MO: C. V. Mosby Company, 1980.

Cooley, Charles Horton. *Social Organization: A Study of the Larger Mind*. New York: Charles Scribner's Sons, 1913.

Copilevitz, Todd "Troubled Gather To Sort Out Their Problems On-Line." *The Arizona Republic*, 4 January, 1995, D5

Davies, John Booth. *The Myth of Addiction*. 2d ed. Amsterdam, The Netherlands: Harwood Academic Publishers, 1997

_____. *Drugspeak: The Analysis of Drug Discourse*. Amsterdam, The Netherlands: Harwood Academic Publishers, 1997.

Denzin, Norman K. *The Alcoholic Society: Addiction and Recovery of the Self*. New Brunswick, NJ: Transaction Publishers, 1993.

Dern, Daniel. "Just One More Click." *Computerworld*. July 8, 1996, 93.

Dexter, Lewis A. "Introduction." In *People, Society and Mass Communications*. eds. L.A. Dexter and David M. White, 3-28. Glencoe, CA: Free Press, 1964.

Elias, Norbert. "Forward." In *The Sociology of Community*. eds. Colin Bell and Howard Newby, iv-ix. London: Frank Cass & Co, Ltd., 1974.

Egger, O., Rauterberg, M., "Internet Behavior and Addiction." Swiss Federal Institute of Technology, Zurich. electronically available at http://www.ifap.bepr.ethz.ch/~egger/ibq/abstract.htm

Elias, Marilyn. "Net Overuse Called 'True Addiction'." USA Today Online. August, 28, 1997. electronically available at: http://www.usatoday.com /life/cyber/tech/ct5073.htm

Ellul, Jacques, "Preconceived Ideas About Mediated Information." In *Taking Sides: Clashing Views on Controversial Issues in Mass Media and Society*, eds. J. Hanson and A. Alexander, 344-54. Guilford, CN: Dushkin Publishing Group, 1991.

Fearing, Franklin. "Human Communication." In *People, Society and Mass Communications*. eds. L.A. Dexter and D.M. White, 37-68. Glencoe, CA: Free Press, 1964.

Fearing, James. "Computer Addiction: Hooked on the Net." National Counseling Intervention Services, Inc. electronically available at: http://nationalcounseling.com/cmpadict.html

Festa, Paul. "Net Addiction a Campus Problem?" *Cnet News Online*. January 21, 1998. electronically available at: http://www.news.com/News/Item/0,4,18340,00.html

FidoNet Policy4 Document, version 4.06 May 6, 1989. electronically available at: gopher://rain.psg.com:70/00/networks/fidonet/policy4.doc

Garfinkel, Harold. "Conditions of Successful Degradation Ceremonies." *American Journal of Sociology* 61 (March 1956): 420-24.

Goffman, Erving. *Presentation of Self in Everyday Life*. New York: Doubleday, 1959.

_____. *Behavior in Public Places*. New York: Free Press, 1963.

_____. *Stigma: Notes on the Management of Spoiled Identity*. New York: Simon and Schuster, Inc., 1963.

_____. *Interaction Ritual: Essays on Face-to-Face Behavior*. Garden City, NY: Doubleday & Company, 1967.

Gold, Steve. *Court Acquits Teenage Hacker*. electronically available at: http://www.eff.org/pub/Net_culture/Hackers/uk_court_acquits_teenage_hacker. article.

Goldberg, Ivan. *Are You Suffering from Internet Addiction Disorder?* electronically available at: http://www.iucf.indiana.edu/~brown/hyplan/addict.html.

Goodwin, D. W., Schulsinger, F., Hermansen, L., Guze, S. B., and Winokur, G. "Alcohol Problems in Adoptees Raised Apart from Alcoholic Biological Parents." *Archives of General Psychiatry* 28 (1973): 238-243.

Gravino, Patrice. "Heavy Use May Be Creating Cyberjunkies, Researchers Say." *The Arizona Republic*, 2 January 1995, E1.

Great Renaming FAQ. electronically available at http://media2.jmu.edu/users/ leebumgarner/gr.html 1994

Griffiths, Mark. "Psychology of Computer Use: XLIII. Some Comments On 'Addictive Use of the Internet' by Young." *Psychological Reports*, 80, 1997, 81-82.

Grohol, John. "What's Normal? How Much is Too Much When Spending Time Online?" at Psych Central: Mental Health Page. electronically available at http://www.grohol.com/archives/n100397.htm

Gusfield, Joseph R. "Moral Passage: The Symbolic Process in Public Designation of Deviance." In *The Collective Definition of Deviance*, ed.

F. James Davis and Richard Stivers, 85-98. New York, NY: The Free Press, 1975.

Halloran, S. Michael. "Comment on the Civility Debate." *Computer Mediated Communication Magazine*, 1 July 1995. electronically available at: http://sunsite.unc.edu/cmc/mag/1995/jul/last.html

Hamilton, K. and Kalb, C. "They Log On, But They Can't Log Off." *Newsweek*. December 18, 1995, 60.

Hardy, Henry Edward. *The Usenet System*. electronically available at: gopher://english.hss.cmu.edu/of-2%3a2355%3ahardy-the%20usenet%20system.

Hauben, Michael. "Exploring New York City's Online Community: A Snapshot of NYC.GENERAL." *Computer Mediated Communication Magazine*, 1 May 1995. electronically available at: http://sunsite.unc.edu/cmc/mag/ 1995/may/haubel.html.

Heather, N., and Robertson, I. *Controlled Drinking*. London: Methuen, 1981.

Heim, Michael. "The Nerd in the Noosphere." *Computer Mediated Communication Magazine*, 1 January 1995. electronically available at: http://sunsite.unc.edu/cmc/mag/1995/jan/heim.html.

Henderson, Diedtra. "Is the Internet Addicting?" *Seattle Times Online*. March 1, 1996. Electronically available at: http://www.seattletimes.com /todaysnews/browse/html/addi_030196.html

Hendrick, Bill. "Internet Addiction Starting to Wreck Lives." *Computer News Daily Online*. August 18, 1997. electronically available at: http://computernewsdaily.com/230_081897_112212_31262.html

Hewitt, John P. *Self and Society: A Symbolic Interactionist Social Psychology*. Boston: Allyn and Bacon, Inc. 1984.

Hiltz, Starr R. and Murray Turoff. *The Network Nation: Human Communication via Computer*. Cambridge, MA: MIT Press, 1993.

Hints on Writing Style for UseNet. electronically available at: http://www.smartpages.com/faqs/usenet/writing-style/part1/faq.html.

"Internet Addiction Growing On College Campuses New Cyberpsychology Journal Reports." Mary Ann Liebert, Inc. Publishers, electronically available at: http://www.liebertpub.com/new/whatnew/cyberpsych.htm

IRC for the Newcomer. electronically available at: http://irc.ucdavis.edu/undernet/underfaq/underfaq.1.html 1995.

IRC Related Resources on the Internet. electronically available at: http://urth.ascu.buffalo.edu/irc/WWW/ircdocs.html#hyper.

Jellinek, E. M. "Phases in the Drinking History of Alcoholics: Analysis of a Survey Conducted by the Official Organ of Alcoholics Anonymous." *Quarterly Journal of Studies on Alcohol* 7 (1946): 1-88

Jennings, Tom. *FidoNet History and Operation*. electronically available at: gopher://rain.psg.com:70/00/networks/fidonet/fidonethist 1985.

_____. "BBS Etiquette." *FidoNews*, 9 September 1985, 1-4.

_____. "Editorial: Faceless Community." *FidoNews* 16 June 1986, 2..

_____. "Editorial: The War Years." *FidoNews* 24 August 1992, 1-4.

Jones, Steven G., ed. *CyberSociety: Computer-Mediated Communication and Community*. Thousand Oaks, CA: Sage Publications, Inc., 1995.

Kaij, L. *Alcoholism in Twins: Studies on the Etiology and Sequels of Abuse of Alcohol*. Stockholm: Almquist & Wiksell, 1960.

Kerr, Elaine B. and Starr Roxanne Hiltz. *Computer-Mediated Communication Systems: Status and Evaluation*. San Francisco, CA: Academic Press, 1982.

Kiesler, Sara, Jane Siegal and Timothy W. McGuire. "Social Psychological Aspects of Computer Mediated Communication." In *Computerization and Controversy: Value Conflicts and Social Choices*. eds. Charles Dunlop and Rob Kling, 330-49. San Diego, CA: Academic Press, Inc., 1991.

Kirk, Stuart A. and Herb Kutchins. *The Selling of DSM: The Rhetoric of Science in Psychiatry*. New York, NY: Aldine De Gruyter, 1992.

_____. *Making Us Crazy DSM: The Psychiatric Bible and the Creation of Mental Disorders*. New York, NY: The Free Press, 1997.

Lawley, Elizabeth Lane. *The Sociology of Culture in Computer-Mediated Communication*. electronically available at: http://www.well.com/user /hlr/vircom/index.html 1994.

Lea, Martin, Tim O'Shea, et. al. "'Flaming' in Computer-Mediated Communication." In *Contexts and Computer-Mediated Communication*, ed. Martin Lea, 89-112. New York: Harvester Wheatsheaf, 1992

Legislating Against Computer Misuse—R. v Bedworth and the "Addiction Defence electronically available at: http://www.hull.ac.uk/Hull /Law_Web/complaw/compart/compbedw.html

Levy, Steven. "Breathing Is Also Addictive." *Newsweek*. December 30, 1996, 52.

Lindesmith, Alfred R. and Anselm L. Strauss. *Social Psychology*. 2d ed. New York, NY: The Dryden Press, 1956.

"Love on the LIne: Pair Meet on Internet, Wed." *The Arizona Republic*. 3 January 1995, A4.

Loftus, Geoffrey R., and Elizabeth F. *Mind at Play: The Psychology of Video Games*. New York, NY: Basic Books, 1983.

MacAndrew, Craig. "On the Possibility of an Addiction-Free Mode of Being." In *Visions of Addiction: Major Contemporary Perspectives on Addiction and Alcoholism*, ed. Stanton Peele, 163-181. Lexington, MA: Lexington Books, 1988.

MacDonald, Dwight. "A Theory of Mass Culture." In *Mass Media and Mass Man*, ed. Alan Casty, 12-23. New York: Holt, Rinehart & Winston, Inc., 1968.

Martindale, Don. *Social Life and Cultural Change*. New York: D. Van Nostrand Company, 1962.

Martindale, Don. *Institutions, Organizations and Mass Society*. Boston, MA: Houghton Mifflin Company, 1966.

Maxwell, Bill. "Internet Addiction." February 18, 1998. electronically available at: http://www.techserver.com/newsroom/ntn/info/021898/info3_90 40_noframes.htm

McLaughlin, Margaret L., Kerry Osborne and Christine B. Smith. "Standards of Conduct on UseNet." In *Cybersociety: Computer-Mediated Communication and* Community, ed. Steven G. Jones, 90-111. Thousand Oaks, CA: Sage Publications, 1995.

McQuail, Denis. *Mass Communication Theory: An Introduction*. Thousand Oaks, CA: Sage Publications, 1994.

Mead, George Herbert. *Mind Self and Society*. Chicago: University of Chicago Press, 1934.

Mendelsohn, Harold. "Sociological Perspectives on the Study of Mass Communications." In *People, Society and Mass Communications*, eds. L.A. Dexter and D.M. White, 29-36. Free Press of Glencoe, 1964.

Meyer, John W. "Self and Life Course: Institutionalization and Its Effects." In *Institutional Structure: Constituting State, Society and the Individual*, George M. Thomas, et. al., 242-260. Beverley Hills, CA: Sage Publications, 1987.

Miller, Norman S. *Addiction Psychiatry: Current Diagnosis and Treatment*. New York, NY: John Wiley & Sons, 1995.

Mills, C. Wright. "Some Effects of Mass Media." In *Mass Media and Mass Man*, ed. Alan Casty, 32-4. New York: Holt Rinehart and Winston, Inc., 1968.

Minar, David W. and Scott Greer, eds. *The Concept of Community*. Chicago: Aldine Publishing Company, 1969.

Mirashi, Mandar. *The History of the UnderNet*. electronically available at: http://sunsite.unc.edu/pub/academic/communications/irc/undernet/

Moraes, Mark. *Hints on Writing Style for UseNet*. electronically available at: http://www.smartpages.com/faqs/usenet/writing-style/part1/faq.html

Moraes, Mark. *Rules for Posting to UseNet*. electronically available at: http://www.smartpages.com/faqs/usenet/posting-rules/part1/faq.html

Mossberg, Walter S. "Accountability Is Key to Democracy In the On-Line World." *The Wall Street Journal*. 26 January 1995, B1.

Murray, Bridget. "Computer Addictions Entangle Students." American Psychological Association Monitor. electronically available at: http://www.apa.org/monitorjun96/onlinea.html

Najarian, Jeff. *Caught in the Web: Free Internet Access Makes Students Candidates for the Newly Recognized Internet Addiction Disorder*. electronically available at http://www.cavalierdaily.com/.Archives /1997/April/16/lfiad.html

National Institute on Alcohol Abuse and Alcoholism. *Alcohol and Health: Sixth Special Report to the U.S. Congress*. DHHS Publication No. ADM 87-1519. Washington, DC: U.S. Government Printing Office, 1986

Net.Legends FAQ. electronically available at: http://www.shadow.net /~proub/ net.legends/index.html#kibo

Oldenburg, Ray. *The Great Good Place: Cafes, Coffee Shops, Community Centers, Beauty Parlors, General Stores, Bars, Hangouts, and How They Get You Through the Day*. New York: Paragon House, 1991.

O'Neill, Molly. "The Lure and Addiction of Life on Line." *The New York Times*. Wednesday, March 8, 1995, C1.

Orzack, Maressa Hecht. *Computer Addiction Services*. electronically available at: http://www.computeraddiction.com/

_____. *Q&A with Dr. Orzack*. electronically available at:http://www.computeraddiction.com/peter.htm

Papai, Jonathan. The AFU and Urban Legend Archive. electronically available at: http://www.urbanlegends.com/misc/addicted_to_ computers.html

Peele, Stanton. *The Meaning of Addiction: Compulsive Experience and Its Interpretation*. Lexington, MA: Lexington Books, 1985

_____. *Diseasing of America: Addiction Treatment Out of Control*. Lexington, MA: Lexington Books, 1989.

Pfuhl, Erdwin H., and Stuart Henry. *The Deviance Process*. 3d ed. New York, NY: Aldine De Gruyter, 1993.

Pope, Justin. "Computers Make Our Lives Easier—and Pull Us Further Apart." *Stanford Today Online*. electronically available at: http://www.stanford.edu/dept/news/stanfordtoday/ed/9709/9709ncf01.shtml

Priven, Aaron. "NaughtNet: Another New Network." *FidoNews* 8 February 1988, 6-10.

Quittner, Joshua. "Kevin Mitnick's Digital Obsession." Time Domestic. February, 27, 1997. 145. 9.

Rath, Tiare "Internet an Addiction?" *Cnet News Online*. August 15, 1997. electronically available at: http.//www.news.com/News/Item/0,4,134 36,00.html?st.ne.ni.rel

Reid, Elisabeth. *Electropolis: Communications and Community on Internet Relay Chat*. electronically available at: http://www.well.com/user/hlr/vircom/index.html 1991.

Rheingold, Howard. *The Virtual Community: Homesteading on the Electronic Frontier*. New York: HarperCollins, 1993.

Rice, John Steadman. *A Disease of One's Own: Psychotherapy, Addiction, and the Emergence of Co-Dependency*. New Brunswick, NJ: Transaction Publishers, 1996

Richard's Web Central—Interneter's Anonymous. electronically available at http://www.itw.com/~rscott/ia.html

Robbins, Marge. *FidoNet History Project*. electronically available at: ftp://ftp.netins.net/showcase/fidonet/.web/.index.html

Rosecrance, John D. *The Degenerates of Lake Tahoe: A Study of Persistence in the Social World of Horse Race Gambling*. New York, NY: Peter Lang Publishing, 1985.

Schaef, Anne Wilson. *Escape from Intimacy: The Pseudo-Relationship Addictions*. San Francisco, CA: Harper & Row Publishers, 1989

Scott, Marvin B. and Stanford Lyman. "Accounts." In *Life as Theater: A Dramaturgical Sourcebook*, eds. Dennis Brissett and Charles Edgley, 171-91. Chicago, IL: Aldine Publishing Company, 1975.

Shotton, Margaret A. *Computer Addiction? A Study of Computer Dependency*. New York, NY: Taylor and Francis, 1989

"Shrink Speaks: The Net Is Addictive." *Wired News Online*. electronically available at: http://www.wired.com/news/news/culture/story/6101.html

Shriver, Art. "Webaholic: Compulsive Computing on the Rise." *Computer Currents Magazine Online*. May 1996. Electronically available at: http://www.currents.net/magazine/texas/605/hmcp605.html

Smith, Marc. "Voices from the WELL: The Logic of the Virtual Commons." Master's Thesis, Department of Sociology, UCLA, 1992.

Snow, Robert P. *Creating Media Culture*. Beverly Hills. CA: Sage Publications, 1983.

Springer, Tom. "Web Junkies: When Does Interest Cross the Line Into Addiction?" The Middlesex News. November 9, 1997. electronically available at: http://www.jernbergeap.com/web_docs/webjunkies.html

Stansel, Ed. "Internet Addiction: Local Support Group Forming to Help Those with Web Obsessions." *Jacksonville News Online*. January 31, 1998. Electronically available at: http://www.jacksonville.com/tu-online/
stories/020198/Netaholi.html

Stephens, Richard C. *The Street Addict Role: A Theory of Heroin Addiction*. New York, NY: State University of New York Press, 1991

Sterling, Bruce. "A Short History of the Internet." *Magazine of Fantasy and Science Fiction*. February 1993, electronically available at: http://www.well.com/user/hlr/vircom/index.html.

Stone, Allucquere Roseanne. "Will the Real Body Please Stand Up? Boundary Stories about Virtual Cultures." In *Cyberspace: First Steps*, ed. Michael Benedikt, 81-118. Cambridge, MA: MIT Press, 1991.

Templeton, Brad. *Dear Emily Postnews*. electronically available at: http://www.clari.net/brad/emily.html

Tonnies, Ferdinand. *Community and Society*. New York: Harper & Row Publishers, 1957.

Thombs, Dennis L. *Introduction to Addictive Behaviors*. New York, NY: The Guilford Press, 1994

UnderNet IRC FAQ. electronically available at: http://irc.ucdavis.edu/undernet/underfaq/underfaq.1.html

Valenza, Joyce Kasman. "Lonely and Bored Children May Use Computer As Escape." *TechLife Online*. electronically available at:http://www.philly
news.com/tech.life/92597/SKUL25.htm

van der Haag, Ernest. "Of Happiness and of Despair We Have No Measure." In *Mass Media and Mass Man*, ed. Alan Casty, 5-11. New York: Holt, Rinehart & Winston, Inc., 1968.

Von Rospach, Chuq. *A Primer on How to Work With the Usenet Community.* electronically available at: http://www.cis.ohio-state.edu/hypertext/faq/usenet-primer/part1/faq.html

Webaholics Testimonials. Seattle Times Online, March 1, 1996. Excerpted from Webaholics Web Site. electronically available at: http://www.seattletimes.com/extra/browse/html/neta_030196.html

What is Usenet. electronically available at: http://www.smartpages.com/faqs/usenet/what-is/part1/faq.html 1995.

What is Usenet, A Second Opinion. electronically available at: http://www.smartpages.com/faqs/usenet/what-is/part2/faq.html

White, David Manning. "Mass Culture Revisited II." In *Mass Culture Revisited,* eds. B. Rosenberg and D.M. White, 13-24. New York: Van Nostrand Reinhold, Co., 1971.

Woolley, David R. "PLATO: The Emergence of On-LIne Community." *Computer Mediated Communication Magazine.* 1 July 1994, 5-16. electronically available at: http://sunsite.unc.edu/cmc/mag/1994/july/plato.html

Young, Kimberly. *Center for Online Addiction FAQ.* electronically available at: http://netaddiction.com/resources/faq.html.

_____. *Internet Addiction: The Emergence of a New Clinical Disorder.* paper presented at the 104th annual meeting of the American Psychological Association, Toronto, Canada. August 15, 1996.

_____. *Internet Addiction: Symptoms, Evaluation and Treatment.* electronically available at http://www.netaddiction.com/articles/symptoms.html

_____. *What Makes the Internet Addictive: Potential Explanations for Pathological Internet Use.* paper presented at the 105th annual conference of the American Psychological Association, Chicago, IL. August 15, 1997.

_____. "Psychology of Computer Use: XL. Addictive Use of the Internet: A Case That Breaks the Stereotype." *Psychological Reports.* 79, 1996 899-902.

Ziegler, Bart and Jared Sandberg. "On-Line Snits Fomenting Public Storms." *The Wall Street Journal.* 22 December 1994, B1.

INDEX

E

D

F

T

U

V

W